THE NEW JUDICIARY

To M

The New Judiciary
The effects of expansion and activism

KATE MALLESON
London School of Economics

with a Foreword by
LORD JUSTICE SEDLEY

Ashgate

DARTMOUTH

Aldershot • Brookfield USA • Singapore • Sydney

© Kate Malleson 1999

Published by
Dartmouth Publishing Company Ltd
Gower House
Croft Road
Aldershot
Hants GU11 3HR
England

Ashgate Publishing Company
Old Post Road
Brookfield
Vermont 05036
USA

British Library Cataloguing in Publication Data
Malleson, Kate
    Thr new judiciary : the effects of expansion and activism
    1.Courts - England 2.Courts - Wales 3.Judges - England
    4.Judges - Wales
    I.Title
    347.4'2'01

Library of Congress Cataloging-in-Publication Data
Malleson, Kate
        The new judiciary : the effects of expansion and activism / Kate
    Malleson
        p.   cm.
        Includes bibliographical references and index.
        ISBN 1-84014-077-1 (hb)
        1. Judges--Great Britain. 2. Political questions and judicial
    power--Great Britain. 3. Judicial power--Great Britain. I. Title
    KD7285.M35   1998   98-37427
    347.41'014--dc21   CIP

ISBN 1 84014 077 1

Printed in Great Britain by Galliards, Great Yarmouth

Contents

Acknowledgements

I am very grateful to the Institute of Advanced Legal Studies, the London School of Economics and the Lord Chancellor's Department for providing funding for the research which generated the material for much of this work. In addition to providing financial assistance, the Lord Chancellor's Department was very generous in providing me with various materials which I requested, as were the staff at the Judicial Studies Board.

I am particularly grateful to Hugh Collins, John Griffith, Carol Harlow, David Schiff and Michael Zander at the London School of Economics for reading drafts and providing helpful comments. Further from home, I owe a debt of gratitude to Peter Russell at Toronto University who shared his ideas on the judicial system so openly. He will find much that is familiar in this work. Lastly, I would like to thank Peter Susman QC who, in his capacity as a Recorder, invited me to sit with him and observe the work of a judge from the perspective of the bench. The experience brought home to me the responsibility which judges bear on a day to day basis and the high degree of care and attention which is required to perform the job of judging well.

Foreword

Activism is not a neutral word. In its origin (in Weimar Germany, where *Aktivismus* was coined to describe the involvement of intellectuals in politics) and in much modern usage, it connotes – politely – the crossing of accepted boundaries or – less politely – some form of politically correct hyperactivity. If the readiness of modern British judges to intervene is rightly described as activism, with the implication that standing by when injustice occurs is a neutral activity, then this book concerns an activist judiciary. The sense in which Kate Malleson explores it, however, is closer to that which as developed in the United States, where judicial activism has been used to denote the deployment of principle and policy to enhance or defeat enacted legislation where no literal application of the constitution is possible. The consequent debate between (among others) activists and originalists is replicated in one shape or another throughout the common law world. It is suffused, however, by a largely unspoken parallel dispute not about inputs or methods but about outcomes. Put crudely, it is doubtful whether the originalist arguments which have featured prominently in public debates about new appointments to the Supreme Court would be anything like as strident if the Supreme Court had spent the postwar years deciding that the poor had no right to counsel, that racial segregation in schools was constitutional and that since the Constitution said nothing about abortion, restrictive state laws were permissible.

In the United Kingdom, no such drastic powers are possessed or claimed by the courts. But in the new human rights regime judges will have the obligation to act comformably with the Convention, to ensure that public administration does likewise, and to read in Convention rights where legislation permits, together with the fallback power to tell Parliament that legislation is in breach of the Convention. To do this they will be called on to gauge interferences with primary rights by criteria which include what is acceptable in a democratic society – a conscious Parliamentary enlargement of the judicial role. Kate Malleson suggests – and I agree – that this is not a revolutionary step but the continuation of a long postwar trend, not confined to this country of growing judicial concern with the just exercise of public power. Although it is repeatedly remarked on as a form of usurpation (in particular by journalists with an agitated editor and a deadline), what is more remarkable is the long sleep which judicial review of government fell into at the time of the First World war (I am not sure that it is rightly backdated to the 1880s) and did not begin to wake from until the 1950s. This seems to me to have been a period – with honourable and less honourable exceptions – of abdication of a major part of the judicial function. Both periods, the passive and the active, as well as the earlier mid-Victorian period of strong judicial interventionism have a history which has still to be written.

But, as this book goes on to argue, a judiciary which accepts a role that places it increasingly in the mainstream of public controversies has to expect to be surveyed with a critical eye. This does not render acceptable some of the crass and abusive comments which have come from parts of the press in recent years. Nor is the seemingly indelible image of the judge as a dyspeptic old fool particularly useful, even when it carries the imprimatur of Ted Hughes, whose judge:

> Clowning, half imbecile,
> A Nero of the unalterable...
>
> ...squats listening
> To his digestion and the solar silence.[1]

But doing a job well, albeit in one's own way, rather than badly is something in which people have a legitimate interest, whether the incumbent is a plumber or judge. And judging is a lonely occupation. Many judges would welcome a reasoned appraisal from time to time of how they are coping – not simply in terms of appellate outcomes but in terms of the experience and satisfaction of court users. The received view that anything of the kind would be an invasion of judicial independence is giving way, I think, to a realisation that the daily round of trial and adjudication - judgery, you could call it - can be sometimes improved. More controversial no doubt, is the training of judges in questions of substantive law; but training does not have to mean dictation or coercion, and many of us think that any increment in our stock of knowledge and ideas is worth having so long as we do not forfeit the thing which makes us judges, our judgment.

Kate Malleson's thoughtful and useful study picks out the changes which are starting to reshape perceptions of the judicial role. These have, as she recognises, to accommodate the principle, fundamental to the rule of law in a democracy, that judges must function independently of the state which appoints and pays them, and which now helps also to train them. There are too many places in the world where judicial autonomy is constrained or disregarded for us to be able to take it indefinitely for granted. But if the symbiotic relationship between the Parliamentary and judicial severeignties continues to function in the 21st century as it has done, with ups and down, since the end of the 17th, the best hope for justice is that an active rather than an activist judiciary (in the American sense) should continue to populate the bench.

Stephen Sedley

[1] Ted Hughes, 'The Judge', from *Cave Birds,* (Viking, 1978) © Faber and Faber.

1 Introduction

The English judiciary is not generally regarded as an institution that welcomes radical change. Yet despite its reputation for conservatism, it is currently undergoing a process of transformation in its structure and style which has long-term implications for its future role. The origins of this development are the growth in size of the judiciary and the expansion of its policy-making role. In 1970 there were 288 judges. By 1998, this figure had increased to just under 3,000.[1] As the number of judges has grown, so too has the scope of their powers. The development of judicial review since the 1960s has meant that judges' decisions have come to impact on more areas of public life than ever before. The incorporation of the European Convention on Human Rights in the Human Rights Act 1998 will take this activism a stage further by giving judges the power to determine whether legislation and the policy-making decisions of public bodies conform to the provisions of the Convention. The combined effect of these quantitative and qualitative changes has been to turn judging into a 'growth industry' (Stevens, 1993a, p. 12).

This book examines the impact of the expansion in the size and role of the judiciary on the way judges are appointed, trained and scrutinised. It highlights the growing formalisation and professionalisation of those processes and the increasing pressure for greater accountability and openness. In some areas the changes are already substantial, in others they are only just beginning. In 1973, Sir Robert Megarry, a High Court judge, described the main features of the English judiciary in the following way: 'Machinery for discipline? Nil. Training? Nil'.[2] It is unlikely that Sir Robert would have predicted (or indeed approved of) the central and expanding role which judicial training now occupies in the judicial system. The disciplinary machinery, in contrast, remains virtually non-existent, but is very unlikely to do so for much longer. Here the pressure for the creation of formal complaints and disciplinary systems is building up, and significant reforms now seem inevitable. Similarly, the traditionally closed and relatively informal appointments system is in the process of being overhauled. The recent introduction of public advertisements, interview panels, appointment criteria and job descriptions would have been almost unthinkable thirty years ago. The proposal for establishing a judicial appointments commission, which now commands widespread support, was no more than a fringe idea in 1970.

An important underlying factor in these developments has been the increase in public attention which the judiciary attracts. Until relatively recently judges were widely considered to be above criticism and were not required to explain or justify the way they worked. Today, they are regularly subjected to media scrutiny and are, in turn, increasingly willing to engage in public debate about the judicial system. As the judiciary loses its fear of publicity, the senior judges are beginning to develop a more professional approach to the media and to appreciate the need actively to promote the public support which once they took for granted.

These developments are not unique to England and Wales. The creation of more formalised, professionalised and accountable processes are evident in many judiciaries around the world. The forces of globalisation which have affected all areas of political and economic life have been particularly striking in the judiciary because of the stark contrast with earlier times. The inward-looking culture which was so characteristic of the old judiciary is gradually being abandoned as judges come to see themselves as members of a global legal community where knowledge and ideas are exchanged across jurisdictional boundaries. The emergence of the new judiciary must therefore be understood as part of a global process of change. The details and timing differ in different countries but the general trends are strikingly similar throughout liberal democracies. The ways in which other judiciaries have adapted in response to these general forces of change provide a pool of experience for the judiciary to draw on. In the past, the judges of other countries, particularly those of the Commonwealth, looked to England and Wales for guidance when shaping their judicial processes. Increasingly, those who once modelled themselves on the English judiciary now provide the models for England and Wales.

Despite the international scope of these developments, they have, to date, attracted relatively little attention outside legal circles. One reason being that the judges' continuing attachment to displays of tradition in matters of ritual and form has had the effect of reinforcing the popular image of the judiciary as being committed to archaic practices. In 1992, Lord Taylor, on his appointment as Lord Chief Justice, proposed that the judges should dispense with their wigs. His suggestion, which attracted considerable media attention, was ultimately defeated by the opposition of other senior members of the judiciary. In November 1997, Lord Irvine, shortly after his appointment as Lord Chancellor, announced that he would be dispensing with his wig and regalia for daily use, though with no plans to require other judges to follow his lead. Thus far, few have shown any enthusiasm for doing so.

Such examples of the strong role of continuity and tradition which underpins the culture of the judiciary have served to obscure the extent of the changes which are occurring. They have also reinforced the image of the judiciary as an exclusively legal institution which lies outside the mainstream political structure. Changes to its size, structure and processes are therefore generally viewed as being of relevance to lawyers but of limited concern to society at large. However, the new role which the Human Rights Act creates for the judges will do much more than the incremental expansion of judicial review to raise public awareness of the increase in judicial power. On the day that the Government published the White Paper on incorporating the European Convention on Human Rights, one newspaper ran the headline: 'Judges given more power'. While it is generally recognised that the Act involves a redistribution of political power, there is surprisingly little comment about the fact that we are about to transfer power to a body about which we know very little other than that its members are demographically unrepresentative.

As awareness of the implications of the increasing policy-making function of the judges grows, the debate on the role and function of the judiciary is very likely to attract the interest of a wider audience. To date, what little debate there has been about the expanding role of judges has generally focused on the broad political and social consequences of incorporating the European Convention on Human Rights. Will the change provide better protection for minority rights? Will it undermine the democratic process? Will the judiciary intrude upon areas which are rightly the remit of the executive or Parliament? Less attention has been paid to the implications of increasing judicial power for the judiciary itself. As the power of the judges grows, it will become increasingly obvious that the way in which judges are appointed, trained and scrutinised is of relevance not just to the judiciary but to the wider political process.

The claim that the judiciary is part of the political landscape is not a new one. The myth that judges operated outside politics was finally laid to rest in 1977 with the publication of John Griffith's *The Politics of the*

Judiciary. His central thesis today reads almost as a statement of the obvious: 'Judges are part of the machinery of authority within the State and as such cannot avoid the making of political decisions' (1977, p. 190). However, at the time, his arguments were highly controversial and attracted strong criticism from commentators both on and off the bench (see, for example, Devlin, 1978; Lee, 1988). But even his critics would acknowledge that the fact that judges can and do make political decisions has never again been seriously questioned as a result of his work (Drewry, 1992, p. 10; Jacob et al., 1996, p. 11).

In one respect Griffith's thesis has grown stronger as judicial activism has increased. In 1978 Lord Devlin, in a review of Griffith's work, argued that it was extravagant to talk of the politics of the judiciary as one of the 'major issues of British politics' (1978, p. 510). This criticism was far more persuasive in the 1970s than it is in the 1990s. Very few judges today would argue that the judiciary plays no political role; the point of debate arises over the question of how extensive this aspect of their work is. Despite being a radical and groundbreaking work, Griffith's analysis of judicial politics in fact understated the extent of the politics of the judiciary since it focused on one aspect of that politics; the high-level policy-making of the top judges in the High Court and above in such fields as industrial relations, police powers, immigration, housing and public order.[3] Quantitatively, such cases are rare. The senior judges make up less than ten per cent of the judiciary and moreover spend much of their time in decision-making which has little or no policy-making content. But this small policy-making area does not define the limits of judicial politics. Political action is not confined to the work of those institutions traditionally regarded as composing the political machinery, but encompasses all decision-making which involves an authoritative allocation of values.[4]

The strength of this wider perspective on politics is that it emphasises the distinction between politics and partisanship. One reason why judges have been keen to stress the apolitical nature of their work is that political activity has traditionally been associated with the partisan support for the policies of political parties. If politics is broadened beyond this narrow definition, then the political activity of the judges can be distinguished from the party system and understood in more general terms as the exercise of power by those in authority. Although judges still shun the word politics, they are increasingly willing to acknowledge that they exercise power both over individuals and the process of government:

Judges exercise power. They take decisions which affect the lives and interests of people. They make judgments on matters that affect the way in which we are governed (Lord Steyn, 1997, p. 84).

In a small number of high level cases, judges reach policy decisions which directly affect society as a whole. More commonly, on a day to day level they authoritatively allocate value, whether that value takes the form of privilege, status, advantage or money (Jacob et al., 1996, p. 8). The job of the judges, even at the lowest ranks where they perform a social service function by resolving day to day disputes with no direct influence on public policy, is inherently political in the sense of being the exercise of: 'human influence over inter-personal relations' (Bell, 1985, p. 54).

This wider definition of judicial politics has, to date, had only a limited impact on the analysis of the judiciary. Nevertheless, it represents an important change of approach because if the judiciary is reconceptualised as an inherently political institution then the way in which judges are appointed, trained and scrutinised needs to be rethought. The background of the judges, the mechanisms and criteria used for selecting them, the skills which they need to acquire, the way in which their performance is reviewed and improved - all these issues will influence the exercise of judicial power in its broadest sense. One effect of such a redefinition of judicial politics is to draw the judiciary out of its specialist legal niche. While it continues to be believed that 90 per cent of the time of 90 per cent of judges is spent in non-political activity then the structure and processes of the judiciary as a whole need not be the subject of general public interest. However, if all judges are viewed as engaged in political activity as decision-makers who authoritatively allocate value, then the way in which they are appointed, trained and scrutinised should be a matter of general public interest and the subject of wider debate.

This revision of the judicial function also has an effect on the role of accountability. If judging is per se a political activity, then the public are entitled to demand that the judges are socially and politically accountable. Traditionally the judges have resisted this pressure on the grounds that increasing accountability would undermine judicial independence. As the role of the judiciary has expanded, the freedom from accountability which the judiciary traditionally enjoyed has become increasingly untenable. The pressure for greater accountability is a recurring force behind many of the changes reviewed in this study and it is this conflict between the requirements of judicial independence and accountability which lies at the heart of the current transformation of the judiciary.

Notes

[1] The ranks of the judiciary are Law Lords, Lords Justices, High Court Judges, Circuit Judges, Recorders, Assistant Recorders, District Judges and Deputy District Judges. Charting the expansion of the judges is difficult due to the lack of accurate statistical information. Before 1984, the judicial statistics were not collated in any systematic form. The Lord Chancellor's Department's figures are, by its own admission, rather unreliable before that time. Although the workload of the courts began to grow in the post-war period it was not until the 1970s that the significant expansion in numbers of judges occurred. The creation of the Crown Court in 1971 led to an unexpected increase in the caseload which required a significant expansion in the size of the judiciary and, in particular, the increased use of part-time judges. Speaking in 1973 at an international symposium on the judicial system, Sir Robert Megarry commented on the small size of the English bench in comparison to that of Canada. He stated that although the effect of the Courts Act would be significant, he did not expect that it would alter the size and make-up of the bench (Megarry, 1973, p. 105 [?]See also JUSTICE, 1992, p. 6)

[2] Quoted in Morton, Law politics and the judicial process p.100.

[3] The number of senior judges had grown from approximately 30 to approximately 140 as the size of the judiciary expanded by the time of the 1997 edition.

[4] This approach has a long pedigree. See, for example, Easton, 1953.

2 Activism

The development of judicial review over the last 30 to 40 years has transformed a small element of the courts' work into an extensive field of law. Successive areas of public life have been brought within the scrutiny of the courts to the point where no field of government activity is off-limits. The publication of a guide to civil servants in 1987 and updated in 1995 entitled *The Judge over your shoulder* illustrates the extent to which the judges have come to oversee the work of government in its broadest sense. This process of increasing judicial activism is about to enter a new phase with the passing of the Human Rights Act incorporating the European Convention on Human Rights into domestic law. The exact effects of the change are still very much open to debate, but few doubt that one result, in the short term at least, will be to fuel the growth of judicial activism.

This expansion of judicial power is redefining the role of the judges in ways which are only just starting to emerge. As well as raising implications for the political system at a general level, the changes have particular consequences for the structure of the judiciary and the processes by which it operates. Some indication of the likely direction of these trends can be gleaned by reviewing the experience of the judiciaries of other countries since the developments in judicial activism in England and Wales are mirrored by strikingly similar changes world-wide. The process of judicialisation whereby the courts have edged their way into the political arena, is an experience common to all liberal democracies to a greater or lesser extent. The different historical and legal contexts may have resulted in differences of emphasis and style but the trends of expansion are replicated across many different jurisdictions, both common law and civil law, federal and unitary.

What follows is an overview of the emerging expansion of judicial power through the growth of judicial review and the incorporation of the European Convention on Human Rights which places this development in a global context and explores the implications for the judiciary in England and Wales. The growth of judicial activism underpins the changes in judicial training, the appointments process and systems of scrutiny examined in later chapters. It is also is a key factor in the increasing tension between the requirements of accountability and independence which is a recurring theme in the developments in these areas.

The development of judicial review

Judicial restraint

The eighty year period from the 1880s to the 1960s can be seen as an aberration in terms of the long-term history of the judiciary. Throughout that time the power of the judges was unusually limited. Having once played an active role in the development of public policy, judicial power waned in the twentieth century as the expansion of the civil service and the state reduced the role of the courts (Abel-Smith and Stevens, 1967, p. 289). In the immediate period after the Second World War the judges effectively removed themselves from sensitive areas by rejecting any role in determining the legality of administrative actions. Before the 1960s the courts held that actions of administrators could be classed either as administrative or judicial and that the former were not reviewable except under on the basis of illegality.[1] This restrained approach which effectively excluded large areas of government from the scrutiny of the courts, was strongly linked to the doctrine that the judges should be upholders of the law rather than its makers. The rationale for this principle was summarised by Lord Greene in 1944:

> The function of the legislature is to make the law, the function of the administration is to administer the law and the function of the judiciary is to interpret and enforce the law. The judiciary is not concerned with policy. It is not for the judiciary to decide what is in the public interest. These are the tasks of the legislature, which is put there for the purpose, and it is not right that it should shirk its responsibilities.[2]

This perspective had a long a sound pedigree. For Montesquieu writing in the eighteenth century judges were: 'only the mouth that pronounces the words of the law, inanimate beings who can moderate neither its force nor its rigour'.[3]

Paradoxically, it was during this period of judicial passivity that the status of the judges was particularly high: 'As their power and financial status eroded, their prestige flourished' (Stevens, 1993, p. 163). By withdrawing themselves from areas of political activity the judges were insulated from scrutiny and, as a result, widely respected. Brian Abel-Smith and Robert Stevens argue that during this period the judiciary came to see itself as immune from criticism, leading to a collective feeling amongst the judges of 'complacent superiority' (Abel-Smith and Stevens, 1967).

By distancing itself from areas of political controversy the judiciary managed effectively to establish its image as an apolitical body, and this status remained unchallenged for many years. When in 1977 John Griffith first pointed out in *The Politics of the Judiciary* that an underlying commitment to the status quo is in itself a political position his thesis was regarded as highly controversial. The reaction to his work was, in itself, an indication of how de-politicised the judiciary had by then become in the public mind. But although by the late 1970s the association of the judges with politics still amounted to a novel, almost shocking, claim, the isolationism of the judges had already significantly eroded. As the scope of government action which was deemed reviewable had begun steadily to expand, their insulation from controversial political areas was gradually removed.

The expansion of the judges' political role

The origins of the judges' willingness to review areas previously deemed to be off-limits can be dated from the mid 1950s when the period of judicial restraint began to draw to a close. The appointment of Lord Kilmuir as Lord Chancellor in 1954 started a process of reasserting the role of the judges in developing the modern law (Abel-Smith and Stevens, 1967, p. 294). The acknowledgement that judges made, as well as interpreted, the law was a critical step in the development of the judges' political role. Before they could actively participate in law-making which might have public policy implications the judges had first to acknowledge that they were involved in law-making at all. What is surprising about this change of approach to the role of the judiciary is how swift and absolute it was. The claim that the judges' were solely legal interpreters and mere mouthpieces of Parliament which had been the defining feature of the judicial function for nearly a century was swept away in the course of a few years. A defining moment occurred in 1966 when the House of Lords effectively acknowledged its law-making role through the development of the common law by holding that it was no longer bound by its earlier decisions. In 1972, Lord Reid published his classic rebuttal of the collective fiction that judges did not make law:

> There was a time when it was thought almost indecent to suggest that judges make law - they only declare it. Those with the taste for fairy tales seem to have thought that in some Aladdin's Cave there is hidden the common law in all its splendour and that on a judge's appointment there descends on him knowledge of the magic words 'Open Sesame'...We do not believe in fairy tales any more (Lord Reid, 1972, p. 22).

In the period since Lord Reid wrote this piece it has become normal for judges to acknowledge, at a minimum, that they carry out a law-making role in filling the gaps left by Parliament (see for example, Lord Steyn, 1997, p. 86). The open recognition that judges make law has come about in parallel with the expansion of both the type of executive power and the areas of government activity which have been held to be reviewable by the courts (Griffith, 1997). In 1967, Crown Privilege was brought within the remit of judicial review through the judgment that a government decision not to disclose material in litigation was reviewable.[4] In 1984 the Divisional Court held that decisions carried out under Crown Prerogative were also reviewable when it recognised its power to review the Prime Minister's decision to ban employees of the Government Communications headquarters (GCHQ) from membership of a union.[5]

By the 1980s the effect of this change of approach has begun to be acknowledged by the judges. In 1985 Lord Roskill commented that:

> ...since about 1950...there has been a dramatic and indeed a radical change...that change has been described - by no means critically - as an upsurge of judicial activism.[6]

In 1994 Lord Griffiths highlighted the breadth of the judges' role in scrutinising and checking administrative action:

> The judiciary accepts a responsibility for the maintenance of the rule of law that embraces a willingness to oversee executive action and to refuse

to countenance behaviour that threatens either basic human rights or the rule of law.[7]

The factual account of the expansion of judicial review outlined above is relatively uncontroversial. More problematic is the question of what substantive effect this development has had. In a number of procedural areas some important changes undoubtedly have been brought about such as the rights of prisoners to legal representation and due process in prison disciplinary proceedings. However, as the judges themselves are keen to point out when accused of excessive intervention: 'The vast majority of public law decisions go in favour of the executive, a relatively small percentage go against it' (Lord Steyn, 1997, p. 86). Whether the results of judicial review are judged to have represented an overall move to greater conservatism or liberalism depends largely on the political standpoint of the observer. But what the decisions have unquestionably done is to close a long chapter of judicial restraint and in so doing to raise fundamental questions about the role of the judges vis-à-vis Parliament and the executive.

Parliament and the judges

It is worthwhile remembering that the fairy tale exposed by Lord Reid existed for a reason. Despite the absence of a strict constitutional separation of powers between the legislature, executive and judiciary the judges have always been aware of the dangers of seeming to disturb the balance of the constitution by usurping the law-making role of Parliament. For this reason, senior judges who defend the expansion of judicial review have often done so on the basis that the courts are not impinging on the sovereignty of Parliament, but rather the opposite, ensuring that its will is fulfilled.[8] Lord Lloyd argued in 1995 that:

> In granting such a relief the court is not acting in opposition to the legislature, or treading on its toes. On the contrary, it is ensuring that the powers conferred by Parliament are exercised within the limits, and for the purposes, which Parliament intended.[9]

Even those commentators who oppose the further extension of judicial activism do not necessarily regard the current activities of the judiciary as a threat to parliamentary sovereignty:

There is nothing wrong with a judge who knows his or her place. That place is, in a democracy, exactly the position occupied by the judiciary in Britain today. Namely, the judge's primary task is an interpreter of the words deployed by the people (through their representatives in Parliament) to express their will (Gearty, 1996, p. 1).

Conor Gearty's point is that by recognising the clear distinction between the executive and Parliament and ensuring that the enactments of the latter are not thwarted by unlawful or irrational actions by the former, the judiciary can play a role which is an essential one in a democracy: 'There is a type of judicial creativity of which every democrat can approve' (1996, p. 3).

Despite Lord Reid's exposure of the fairy-tale that judges do not make law, there is clearly still scope for disagreement as to the extent of their law-making function. In more clear-cut cases where precedent is strong or the statute relatively unambiguous it is easier to claim that the judges are playing a more limited role of enforcing and upholding the law in a way which sits easily with Lord Lloyd's description. They may even be able to fill gaps or clarify legislation in a way which is still clearly within the scope of Parliament's broad statutory intentions. But at the boundaries, a place where senior judges are increasingly called upon and willing to work, much of their decision-making is effectively law-making since it involves the court in the exercise of choice between conflicting value judgments. It is often said that such choices must be made every time the judges have to decide a point where there is room for argument on both sides (Zander, 1997, p. 84). This description fits most cases which reach the Court of Appeal or the House of Lords, where, almost by definition, there is an arguable case on both sides. Because public bodies rarely act in ways which are blatantly illegal much of the work of the court in the field of judicial review is therefore in grey areas which leave scope for judicial creativity (Griffith, 1997).

An important distinction which needs to be highlighted in reviewing the political role of the judiciary is between law-making and policy-making. In many cases where it would be generally accepted that judges make law the effect of the court's decision cannot be said to have any policy-making implications. In others, the decision has long term ramifications for society in general. In cases where judges have themselves, whether explicitly articulated or not, made an assessment of what consequences will flow from the alternative decisions and which are the most desirable, they have undertaken a cost-benefit analysis of different outcomes which amounts to a policy-making decision (Lee, 1988, p. 11).

This then raises questions about the legitimacy of such decision-making. Some commentators argue that that although the judges do not necessarily have the expertise to undertake these decisions the fact that these areas involve highly controversial subjects means that, realistically, Parliament is unlikely to tackle them, with the result that the courts must be left to undertake the task (Lee, 1988). Others claim that in this 'grey area' of law-making the judges are often not filling a vacuum left by Parliament so much as re-writing policy which has been intentionally and legitimately formulated by the legislature and the executive (Griffith, 1997).

Lord Lloyd's description of the judges' work as giving expression to the will of Parliament is therefore accurate but partial. If it is used to suggest that the role of the judges is confined to a narrow interpretative function limited to reviewing the technical legality of government action it amounts to a latter-day version of the 'fairy-tale' debunked by Lord Reid. The fact that judges exercise choice in such law-making and policy-making cases is one which is increasingly acknowledged by senior judges:

> Between principle and outcome ... there is a sometimes substantial margin of appreciation - in places wide enough to enable the judge to elect between outcomes. In such cases, which are commonly high profile and pathbreaking cases, it is not necessarily healthy to pretend that the conclusion has been inexorably determined by prior principle (Sedley, J 1997, p. 318).

In some respects this new activist approach resurrects the activism of the 17th century judiciary (Sir Stephen Sedley, 1997, p. 313). But the current restructuring of the relationship between the judges and the other branches of government is an ongoing one which moves beyond traditional constitutional arrangements. As a dynamic process it is also one which has the potential to bring increasing conflict between the judiciary and the executive. In the 1990s this potential was realised when tensions between the government and the judges over the expansion of judicial power surfaced. The catalyst for this conflict was a series of extra-judicial statements made by senior judges. In particular, Lord Woolf and Sir John Laws who argued in different degrees and ways, that the judges had a fundamental duty to uphold basic rights which did not derive from Parliament but from more general principles based on the rule of law. With echoes of Lord Reid, Lord Woolf rejected as a fairy-tale the suggestion that the source of the principles of fairness and reasonableness on which judicial review are based could be found in statute:

> My approach...does involve dispensing with fairy tales once and for all. But I would suggest that this is healthy...I see the courts and Parliament as being partners both engaged in a common enterprise involving the upholding of the rule of law (Lord Woolf, 1997, p. 68-69).

Sir John similarly expressed the view that the principles on which judicial review were founded were categorically creations of the judges: 'they have nothing to do with the intentions of Parliament, save as a fig-leaf to cover their true origins. We do not need the fig-leaf anymore' (1995, p. 79) This fig-leaf or fairy-tale, therefore, represents a third variation of the fiction disguising the true extent of the political role of the judges. The first being that the judges do not make law, the second that they do not affect public policy-making and, the third that they have not created the principles upon which judicial review is based.

Up to this point in their arguments, neither Lord Woolf nor Sir John Laws did more than Lord Reid in making explicit what was widely accepted but unspoken. However, they both went further than this by speculating on the hypothetical limits of judicial power. They argued that the principles of the rule of law on which the judges' development of judicial review was based might, theoretically, allow the judiciary to rule an act of Parliament invalid where it conflicted with the rule of law. Lord Woolf suggested that the total removal of all the courts' judicial review powers would amount to such an invalid act: 'ultimately there are even limits on the supremacy of Parliament which it is the courts' inalienable responsibility to identify and uphold' (Woolf, 1995, p. 69). Similarly, Sir John argued that parliamentary sovereignty did not allow for the abolition of fundamental rights since the source of these rights formed a 'higher law' than statute, which, if necessary, the courts would apply above a statute (Laws, 1995).

The decision of senior judges to embark upon this analysis of the boundaries of judicial power in the mid-1990s was not a purely academic exercise nor was the timing incidental but was rooted in the increasing conflict between the Conservative administration and the judiciary. Much of the legislation on sentencing and the legal system introduced in the 1980s was passed without the support of the senior judges. From the late 1980s the judges had begun to argue that their independence was under threat as the Government failed to consult over such reforms or ignored its opinions when it did. The introduction of new minimum sentences and mandatory life sentences against the wishes of the judiciary in 1996 was the peak of this conflict.[10] The extent of this constitutional crisis was noted by the UN Special Rapporteur responsible for monitoring alleged violations of judicial independence. In March 1996 he noted with 'grave concern' the reported attacks by the executive over the activism of the judiciary threatening to restrict judicial review by legislation and the accusations in response of potential despotism by the judges: 'That such a controversy could arise over this very issue in a country which cradled the common law and judicial independence is hard to believe'.[11]

But despite the strong opposition of the judges to many of the administration's policies in the area of sentencing and the legal system and the poor relations which existed between the two branches of government, the judges were generally at pains to emphasise that the conflict was not based on any attempt by the judges to seek to extend their constitutional role into the field of policy-making. Whilst objecting to the substantive proposals on sentencing, and in particular the reduction of judicial discretion, the judges were keen to assert that Parliament was quite within its powers to transfer power from the judges to the executive. Lord Donaldson, former Master of the Rolls, was one of the strongest critics of Government policy. In 1995 he claimed that any attempt by the government to limit the scope of judicial review would be the act of a despotic power:

> It is one thing to be governed by the rule of law. It is quite another to be governed by a despotic, albeit no doubt benevolent, Government. And any Government which seeks to make itself immune to an independent review of whether its actions are lawful or unlawful is potentially despotic.[12]

Nevertheless, despite this strength of feeling against Government policy, Lord Donaldson also stressed that whatever law Parliament saw fit to pass the judiciary will: 'as always, loyally conform'.[13] Similarly Lord Taylor, whilst objecting strongly to the sentencing proposals, argued that the executive was entirely within its constitutional rights to introduce them and accused *The Times* of a 'gross libel' for suggesting that he had ignored the provisions of the 1991 Criminal Justice Act.[14] The perspective of Lord Woolf and Mr Justice Laws was therefore an unprecedented challenge to the view that parliamentary sovereignty dictated that the judges would 'loyally conform' by upholding any statute passed. Moreover, in debate in the House of Lords in 1996 Lord Woolf appeared to distance himself from his earlier comments and offered a far more tempered perspective on the role of the judiciary, stressing the orthodox line that the function of judicial review was to uphold the sovereignty of Parliament by ensuring only that the acts of the executive were lawful.

Outside the judiciary the arguments of Lord Woolf and Sir John Laws also attracted criticism. John Griffith argued that they amounted to a claim that the jurisdiction of the courts extends to challenge the constitutional settlement on which the current balance between Parliament and the judiciary rested. He described the arguments of Sir John as: 'a take-over bid which may, if it fails, devalue the reputation and trustworthiness of the judiciary' (Griffith, 1997, p. 306). Others argued that it ran this risk even if it succeeded, since it would expose the judiciary to charges of supremacism (Lord Irvine, 1996a, p. 77). As a result of concern about the implications of the claims of Lord Woolf and Sir John Laws a debate in the House of Lords on the role of the judiciary was called by Lord Irvine in June 1996.[15] In his speech to the House he emphasised the principle of parliamentary sovereignty and stressed that in exercising their powers of judicial review the courts decide only on the legality of a decision, not its correctness. His views were shared by other participants in the debate which demonstrated a strong consensus both as to the desirability of the development of judicial review and the need to acknowledge the sovereignty of Parliament. Similarly Lord Steyn stated in 1997 that:

> The relationship between the judiciary and the legislature is simple and straightforward. Parliament asserts sovereign legislative power. The courts acknowledge the sovereignty of Parliament. And in countless decisions the courts have declared the unqualified supremacy of Parliament. *There are no exceptions...the judiciary unreservedly respects the will of Parliament as expressed in statutes* (Lord Steyn, 1997, p. 85, emphasis added).

Such assertions directly contradict the suggestion of a higher law or principles superseding parliamentary sovereignty. Lord Steyn went on to state that unless statute makes 'crystal clear' provision to the contrary judges are entitled to assume that Parliament would not wish to make unjust laws (Lord Steyn, 1997, p. 85). The consequence being that if Parliament explicitly states that it intends to pass an unjust law the judges would enforce it. This is, perhaps, another variation of the fairy-tale of judicial restraint. It is unconscionable to believe that the judges would, in practice, uphold a law, however clear-cut its wording, removing all the courts' power of review as in Lord Woolf's example or stripping citizens of some fundamental human right, as in Sir John's example. Though perhaps the fairy-tale is a relatively harmless one since, as John Griffith points out, the question of what the judges would do in the event of such a constitutional revolution would be the least of our worries.

In addition, the immediacy of the tension which had generated this level of debate about the fundamental relationship between the judiciary, Parliament and the executive was diffused by the appointment of Lord Irvine as Lord Chancellor in 1997. Shortly after coming to office he told the judges that he regarded it as of the first importance that their views be taken into account on proposed changes to legislation. He acknowledged that it was widely perceived by the public that: 'relations between the Government and the judges had sunk to an all time low' and he emphasised the need for a good dialogue between the two branches.[16] The change which was ushered in by the appointment of Lord Irvine suggests that despite the fact that the debate on the role of the judges in the 1990s raised critical constitutional questions, the conflict between the judges and the Conservative Government was less about such fundamental issues and more rooted in the particular policies and relationships of the time. The sentencing provisions introduced by the Conservative Government had been as offensive to the judges as any equivalently radical proposals from a Government of the left would have been. The election of the Labour Government in May 1997 represented a move back towards the centre ground in justice policy-making. A place in which senior judges tend to feel comfortable. This change, therefore, heralded a retreat from aggressive judicial activism:

> Activist judges, by definition, may be expected to take every opportunity to use their decision-making to expand the policy values they hold dear. But when those values are *consistent* with the values dominating majoritarian institutions, there will be much less incentive for activist judges to seek to judicialize a political process that is already producing such good policy results (Tate, 1995, p. 34).

On this analysis, judicial activism is understood as instrumental, expanded by the judges when it will advance their values and avoided when it is not needed. As the values of the executive and the judges move closer, so the degree of conflict is likely to ease, as it appears to have done between the judiciary and the Labour Government. It should also be remembered that the conflicts between the judiciary and the Government in the 1990s are not unprecedented. Robert Stevens has stressed that such strains have a long pedigree. In 1929 the Lord Chancellor's Permanent Secretary, Sir Claud Schuster wrote to the Lord Chancellor warning him of the expansion of judicial power and the growing hostility of the judges towards the executive: 'in recent years...the weight of prejudice against the State in the minds of many members of the Court of Appeal and Judges of the High Court has been such as seriously to affect the Administration of Justice' (quoted in Stevens, 1996, p. 1).

But while political relations between the judges and the executive may ebb and flow, there is general agreement that the underlying trend is for the courts to be drawn further into political life (Sunkin, 1995, p. 75). The result of this process will be that the debates raised by the claims of Lord Woolf and Sir John Laws will resurface as the exact limits of judicial power continues to be redefined. In order to assess the likely future development of judicial activism it is useful to consider the reasons why it has arisen during the last thirty years.

Explanations for the development of judicial review

A number of different explanations have been put forward for the rise of judicial review. Lord Wilberforce suggested three: first, the great increase in the amount of legislation being passed, some of which was poorly thought-out or phrased; second, the number of gaps in the legislation which were left to be filled by judges; and third, the growing public demand for limiting the power of the executive.[17] Linked to this last point is the increasing difficulty of obtaining redress through the parliamentary system. The chances of a person persuading his or her MP to challenge a minister over an administrative decision and ensuring a full, open and impartial review of it in Parliament is increasingly unlikely. These arguments have not gone unchallenged. In 1997, Anthony Holland and Robert Stevens dismissed as highly unlikely the claim that legislation was more poorly drafted in the 1970s than the 1940s, or that there were more legislative vacua for the courts to fill (Holland and Stevens, 1997, pp. 699-700).

There is more agreement over the role played by individual judges in the process of expansion. John Griffith has highlighted the influence of Lord Reid in advancing judicial review in the 1960s: 'He pulled public law out of the doldrums in which it had become becalmed and set it on a new course'. Griffith argued that this process was extended by Lord Woolf in the early 1990s (Griffith, 1997, p. 293). The expansion of judicial power in other countries has similarly been marked by the influence of certain individual judges - most obviously, the role of Earl Warren in the development of activism in the US Supreme Court in the 1960s. In Australia, Justice Lionel Murphy has been attributed with expanding the role of the court in the 1980s (Galligan, 1991, p. 80) while Lord Cooke has been similarly assertive in New Zealand.

The most controversial explanation concerns the extent to which the development of judicial activism was a response to the particular political landscape of the 1980s and 1990s. Lord Donaldson suggested in 1995 that the greater willingness on the part of the judiciary to scrutinise the actions of government had partly arisen because one political party had been in power for an exceptionally long period.[18] Robert Stevens similarly suggested that the creation of a power vacuum in the political centre had been instrumental in the expansion of judicial power (Stevens, 1996, p. 14). Some senior judges have sought to distance the developments of the courts from any immediate political circumstances. The argument that the judges came to form some sort of quasi-opposition has been dismissed by Lord Nolan as 'fanciful' (Lord Nolan, 1997, p. 73). Most judges have preferred to describe the growth of judicial review express as connected to the rise of executive power generally rather than the policies of one particular Government.[19] The judges are also often at pains to emphasise that the judiciary did not initiate this growth of power voluntarily but that they were obliged to take on these new powers to check administrative action as a result of the inability of Parliament to do so. In 1996, in a parliamentary debate on the judicial role Lord Williams cited recent decisions concerning the termination of life support to coma patients and the sterilisation of mentally ill patients as examples of ones which judges would have preferred not to make:

> no judge whom I have ever spoken to is greedy to take [these powers].
> They are obliged to take these powers because Parliament has been too
> busy, too supine or too fearful to define the limits of these activities.[20]

This view of the judges taking up powers by default is widely
accepted. It is common for commentators in England and Wales and in
other countries to talk of the judges being 'thrust' or 'dragged' into
activism (see, for example, Waltman, 1991, p. 34). The claim that the
judges have been reluctant to expand their powers to decide on sensitive
moral issues is highly plausible. However, these reservations should be
distinguished from the argument that they had no choice but to take on new
powers. The judges were quite at will to refuse to expand their role, as they
had done between the 1880s and 1950s when they 'retreated into almost
complete passivity' (Waltman, 1991, p. 36). In the years since then the
judiciary has taken on a greater role because the opportunity to do so
presented itself and because certain individual judges, in particular, chose
to do so:

> judicialisation develops only because judges decide that they *should*
> participate in policy-making that could be left to the wise or foolish
> discretion of other institutions...(Tate, 1995, p. 33).

Certain judges might have preferred that circumstances had not
provided them with the choice, but the fact that the conditions were there
for expansion did not make it inevitable. It is important to acknowledge the
free will of the judges in expanding their role, even while accepting their
genuine reservations. The image of the judges as unwilling participants
obliged to undertake their new powers is dangerous because it serves to
divorce the judiciary from the responsibility for the consequences of its
actions. Increased scrutiny and accountability can be rejected or minimised
on the grounds that the judges should not be subject to the same checks as
those who actively seek power. Whilst it may be true that had other checks
existed the judges would probably not have developed their powers, it is
also true that they were under no obligation to do so. In many instances
over the years individual judges have declined to extend the role of the
courts. Where they have done so, this had been done consciously and
intentionally with awareness, at least in general terms, of the
consequences. Lord Diplock was not the only judge who has regarded the

increased control of administrative action by the courts as: 'the greatest achievement of the English courts in my lifetime'.

Global judicialisation

The explanations for the development of judicial review are not restricted to the particular context of the political and legal history of England and Wales. The increasing judicialisation of political life has been a feature common to all liberal democracies in recent years. It is a change which affects not just the legal system and those who come before the courts but amounts to a redistribution of power throughout the political system in favour of the judiciary. As well as having important constitutional implications, this development inevitably affects the structures and processes of the judiciary itself.

The increasing tendency for judges throughout Europe to meet and exchange views and ideas has been identified as one factor in the global increase of judicial activism (Cornish, 1997, p. 364). Judges are generally much more aware of and influenced by international developments than they once were. A particularly important facet of this process of judicial exchange is the role of international human rights documents. As judiciaries are called upon to interpret and implement these conventions and declarations so they increasingly draw upon a global jurisprudence. The critics of global judicial culture see it as responsible for the worst effects of judicialisation:

> The development of a kind of world-wide constitutional jurisprudence with judges following each other across the globe in defying the will of their respective legislatures is one of the more haunting aspects of our new pseudo-democratic world (Gearty, 1996, p. 8).

Nor is the process of increasing judicial power vis-à-vis the executive and legislature limited to countries with common political structures. Judicialisation has been noted in such diverse countries as Holland, Belgium, Sweden, South Africa, Namibia, India, Israel, the US, Australia and Canada (Shetreet and Deschelle, 1985; Tate and Vallinder, 1995, p. 4). As early as 1979, a US commentator wrote that the judges appeared to be acting: 'as an accelerator rather than a brake' (Kaufman, 1979). By 1984, the growing role of the judiciary had been noted by the UN based International Association of Judges: 'All over the world the trend seems to be towards a strengthening of the judicial power...'[21] In

New Zealand the rise of judicial activism was noted by Sir Geoffrey Palmer, a former minister of Justice and Professor of Law:

> There can be little doubt of the importance of judges in terms of the role they have in society and the public power invested in them. The club they wield may not be as dangerous as that carried by actors from other branches of government - ministers and MPs - but it is still capable of delivering a hefty clout, and it is growing bigger all the time (Palmer, 1993, p. 4).

Similarly, the New Zealand Minister of Justice, Paul East, wrote in 1992 that:

> ...decisions in relation to administrative review have increasingly placed judges ever closer to making decisions about administrative decision-making itself, something which, on the pure doctrine of the separation of the powers, falls to be a matter exclusively for the executive (East, 1992, p. 1).

In Australia, Justice Lionel Murphy stated in 1980 that: 'Judges used to pretend that they only interpreted the law, never made it. But the law-making role of the judges is now openly accepted all around the world' (quoted in Galligan, 1991, p. 80). In some countries, such as Australia, the changes came later than in England and Wales while in others, such as the US and Canada, they were experienced earlier. The comparative review of the Courts in the US and England in 1980 by Shapiro is informative about the different pace of change. Even at that relatively late stage he regarded the English courts as deeply passive:

> The process of both parliamentary and judicial abdication has gone so far that there are serious doubts about whether the rule of law survives in England at all. And if it does, it must do so as the ideological commitments of the executive elite itself rather than in the constraining powers of the courts...[The state] apparatus is essentially immune from judicial scrutiny so long as it stays within the bounds set by Parliament (Shapiro, 1980, p. 124).

This is an interesting perspective for two reasons. First, it highlights the relativism of judicial activism. Shapiro was writing at a time when most English commentators would have argued that the era of passivity was long gone. Second, it serves as a reminder of how far the boundaries of activism were pushed in the 1980s and 1990s since this commentary was written. As late as 1985 one international commentary which ranked judiciaries on a scale of 'most' to 'least' active placed England ninth below such countries as France and Japan (Dhavan, 1985, p. 2). A similar exercise today would undoubtedly find the English judiciary ranked several positions higher, while in ten years time it is quite possible that it would be listed near the top with the US and Canada.

From a global perspective it would appear that in the short to medium term judicial activism is on a steady, perhaps accelerating, upward trend. However, the experience of the US judiciary suggests that in the long term the pattern may be less predictable. Since the Supreme Court first expanded its powers of judicial review in the early 19th century, the judiciary has gone through periods of restraint as well as activism (Gearty, 1996, p. 9). After an upsurge of judicialisation in the 1950s, 1960s and 1970s the Supreme Court adopted a more non-interventionist stance in the 1980s. Since then it has been suggested that: 'active judicial policy-making on major political issues seems to have plateaued or to be slightly on the wane' (Shapiro, 1995, p. 64).

In England and Wales the pendulum is still swinging firmly towards increasing activity. The conditions which have been identified as giving rise to judicialisation around the world are becoming stronger in England and Wales. Some of these have traditionally existed, such as strong judicial independence, the absence of separate administrative courts, a competitive party system and relatively easy access to the courts (Tate, 1995, p. 29; Edelman, 1995, p. 412; Shetreet, 1985, p. 594; Dhavan, 1985, p. 7). Others have, to date, been absent, such as federalism, a Bill of Rights and a written constitution. But these are being developed. Although England and Wales do not formally belong to a federal system, the growing role of the European Union has moved them closer in that direction. While there are no immediate proposals for introducing a written constitution, the Human Rights Act now provides a Bill of Rights through the incorporation of the European Convention on Human Rights - a document which has been identified as being responsible for spreading the 'gospel of judicialisation' (Tate and Vallinder, 1995, p. 3). The Act specifically requires judges to take account of the decisions of the European Court of Human Rights and Commission when interpreting the convention rights, thus incorporating not just the Convention, but the jurisprudence on its interpretation. The effect of the closer relationship with Europe is to draw the judges into a new role familiar to any judiciary in a federal state, of mediating the development of national policy-making with the overarching requirement of European law and human rights.

The Human Rights Act 1998

During the last thirty years many criticisms have been made of the rise of judicial activism but few today, on the political left or right, argue for a complete reversal of the expansion of judicial review. This consensus does not extend to incorporation of the European Convention on Human Rights which is widely recognised as a turning point in judicial activism.

The development of dynamic law-making

Not all commentators accept that the Human Rights Act will have a significant impact on the function of the judiciary. Some judges have suggested that incorporation will not expand judicial power:

> If I thought for one moment that such an enactment of the convention [into domestic law] would entail a great transfer of political power to judges I would oppose it. It will mean nothing of the kind. It will simply mean that issues of alleged abuses of human rights law will be tried in our courts rather than in Strasbourg (Lord Steyn, 1997, p. 94).

Others observers have argued that incorporation will only have a marginal affect (Rozenberg, 1996). But these views are in the minority. Amongst supporters and opponents of incorporation alike there is general agreement that incorporation represents a significant stage in the expansion of judicial power. Lord Irvine has acknowledged that because the judges will be called upon to make decisions as to whether a UK statute comes up to the standards of the Convention or not, incorporation will involve: 'a very significant transfer of power to the judges' (1996, p. 18). Robert Stevens suggested in 1993 that it may necessitate fundamental constitutional changes:

> A new vision of judicial independence and a further rewriting of the separation of powers may be on the way. The idea of the judiciary as a co-equal branch of government is clearly the goal of some (Stevens 1993 p. 179).

The requirement that public bodies must conform to the provisions of the Convention in their decision-making will mean that judges will be required to consider the merits of executive decisions rather than the much more limited questions of their lawfulness, fairness or reasonableness. In the case of *Brind* in 1991 Lord Ackner suggested that incorporation would allow the judges to consider whether a minister's decision was 'acceptable', a question currently outside the scope of the courts' powers.[22] Under the existing arrangements, Lord Templeman stressed that: 'the courts must not substitute their own view for the informed view of the Home Secretary'.[23] Whilst critics such as John Griffith may argue that they have regularly done just this, no judge would accept that such decision-making forms part of their current role. In the case of *Smith*, Lord Justice Brown regretted that he could not find the decision to discharge gay personnel from the army unlawful or irrational. He envisaged that incorporation would give the courts the freedom to review that decision on its merits.[24]

Critics of this development argue that the expansion of judicial activism through incorporation will fundamentally undermine the relationship between the judges and Parliament by substitution of the will of the judges for the will of Parliament (Gearty, 1996, p. 4). Although the senior judges generally support incorporation, some have concurred in this view. Lord Mackay, when Lord Chancellor, expressed strong concerns about the expansion of the judges' role which it would entail. These fears were first aired by Lord Devlin in the 1970s on the grounds that promoting the law-making role of the judiciary above that of the democratic process was a first step to totalitarianism. His analysis drew a distinction between judicial 'activism' and 'dynamism'. The former described the process whereby judges develop the law in line with the changing social consensus - a judicial function which Devlin considered to be quite legitimate. By contrast, dynamism arose when judges pushed the boundaries of public opinion by giving: 'a touch of the whip to hasten laggards'. Devlin regarded this function as being for the legislature alone (Devlin, 1976). ⤬ This analysis can be criticised on the grounds that is based on an overly simplistic view of social consensus. Nevertheless, the distinction is a useful one in recognising the qualitative change in the role of the judiciary which comes about when judges are required overtly to exercise value judgments.

The effect of the model of incorporation

During the debate on the Human Rights Bill much time was spent on the question of what model of incorporation should be adopted. Few commentators supported an entrenched Bill of Rights as in the US or South Africa where the judiciary has the unqualified power to strike down any legislation which breaches its provisions. Much more support was attracted by the Canadian model. Under the Charter of Rights and Freedoms passed in 1982 the courts can declare that any law which is in breach of its provisions is 'of no force or effect'. Under clause 24(1) the judges may apply any remedy which they consider appropriate and just in the circumstances. However, clause 1 provides a limitation clause which allows for provisions to be held to be valid which breach the Charter where they can be 'demonstrably justified in a free and democratic society'. This has been used in a number of instances, for example allowing legislation in breach of the Charter in relation to restrictions on Sunday shopping, prostitution and pornography. In addition, clause 33 allows Parliament to pass an Act which is valid notwithstanding the fact that it breaches the Charter. Such an Act can be passed with a simple majority vote of Parliament and can relate to virtually all of the Charter's provisions. At the time the Charter was passed it was widely expected that this section would significantly limit its scope. Indeed, the Prime Minister, Brian Mulroney, stated in 1989 that the 'notwithstanding' clause was such as to render the Charter 'not worth the paper it's written on'. But in practice use of Clause 33 has been limited, having only once been applied outside of Quebec (Russell, 1995, p. 138, 146).

There is a wide difference of opinion on the extent to which the Charter has lead to an expansion of judicial power, largely dependent on the ideological perspective of the commentator. Those hostile to judicial activism argued that the Charter has given powers to the judiciary which were rightly the responsibility of Parliament: 'The power to dispense with statute law that was claimed by Stuart kings and extinguished by the Bill of Rights in 1689 has now been resurrected for the judiciary' (Ison, 1997). Similar claims have been made by critics of incorporation in England and Wales:

> Canada has embraced an American style Charter of Rights which has transformed its political system and brought as much havoc to many areas

of public policy as it has political power and financial remuneration to many lawyers (Gearty, 1996, p. 8).

In contrast, others have claimed that the Charter has been too restricted to have much effect (Baar, 1991). More detailed review of the Canadian Supreme Court's activity suggests that it has not been uniform. There is now general agreement that after an initial upsurge of activity the court has adopted a far less interventionist stance in recent years (Beatty, 1997). Moreover, the Court's record has been very different in different areas. At least 80 per cent of decisions have been in the field of criminal justice, where the judiciary has traditionally fulfilled a policy-making role (Russell, 1995, p. 141). In this area the Supreme Court has produced some far reaching judgments such as the strict enforcement of fast trial provisions which jeopardised the disposal of thousands of criminal prosecutions in Ontario. However, in other areas their intervention has been much more restrained. The Chief Justice, Antonio Lamer, commented in 1992 on the tenth anniversary of the Charter:

> In 1982 when the Charter came in, governments were watching the courts to see what they would do. I think now they realize we haven't gone berserk with the Charter and we aren't striking down laws left and right (quoted in Russell, 1995, p. 145).

This claim is supported by the relatively modest success rate of Charter cases before the Court. Of its first 100 cases claiming breaches of the provisions heard between 1982 and 1989, a total of 36 were upheld. In general, looking at the judges' record during the first fifteen years it can be concluded that the Canadian Supreme Court has proved itself a restrained policy-maker which bears little resemblance to its US cousins: 'The shift has been from a small-c conservative to small-l liberal approach to the law and politics of constitutional jurisprudence' (Baar, 1991, pp. 60-61). Where the Court has been seen to be particularly active, the approach of individual judges have been influential. Madam Justice Bertha Wilson has, for example, been recognised as responsible for initiating a new activism in relation to women's rights and gender discrimination (Baar, 1991, p. 66).

Despite the rather moderate record of the Canadian experience, the model was rejected on the grounds that it threatened parliamentary sovereignty. Instead, the courts in England and Wales are given the more limited power to declare that a statute is incompatible with convention rights. The intention is that such a declaration will present the government with a moral and political onus to amend the law through the fast track provisions which the Act provides.

The UK model is closer to that of New Zealand which passed the New Zealand Bill of Rights Act in 1990. Under that provision the courts, similarly, have no power to rule a statute unlawful. During Parliamentary debates it was described as a 'toothless' bill, but has generally been regarded as relatively effective (Zander, 1996, p. 48). By 1993 the Courts had considered over 200 cases, and the judges' approach had given rise to some criticism of excessive activist:

> The Courts have not been timid in their application of the legislation and, in some ways, the approach has dimmed the doctrine of parliamentary sovereignty (Palmer, 1993, p. 12).

Although the Human Rights Act does not give the courts the power to strike down legislation, and is therefore weaker than many supporters of incorporation would have liked, it is in other respects a document which goes further than had generally been anticipated in strengthening the role of the judiciary. The Act imposes on judges in all levels of court, from the magistrates' court to the House of Lords the duty to ensure that all public authorities (which includes the courts themselves) act in accordance with the convention. This provision means that the number of cases in which human rights issues can be raised is potentially enormous and judges may be asked to apply broad value judgments in scrutinising the acceptability of a very wide range of public decision-making. In may be, therefore, that the restriction on striking down legislation will prove to be much less relevant than it first appears in restricting the expansion of judicial activism.

Moreover, the ultimate effect of the model of incorporation on the courts' approach to their role in enforcing human rights may be less relevant than the wider political context in which the judiciary operates. The Hong Kong Bill of Rights is, for example, generally regarded as relatively ineffectual not because of the wording of the provisions but because the judiciary is not secure enough in its powers to undertake a robust approach to its human rights role (Ghai, 1997). In contrast, the new Constitutional Court in South Africa has taken a proactive approach to the new Bill of Rights. Most strikingly, it has ruled that capital punishment was a breach of the convention, at a time when rising fear of crime was producing strong public support for its retention. Whatever the exact model of incorporation, a Bill of Rights give judges a broad discretion to lay down the parameters of important areas of social and political life. Whether or not the judges choose to push these powers to the limit or to exercise them with restraint depends largely on the political culture of the judges. The new conservatism of the Canadian Supreme Court is a reflection of the changing ideology of recent appointments. The radicalism of the current South African Constitutional Court is, similarly, a natural consequence of the appointment of judges with a history of active commitment to the promotion of human rights during the years of the apartheid regime and a strong culture of human rights in the new order (Cockrell, 1997).

The effect of the Human Rights Act in England and Wales can only be predicted in the light of the attitudes of those judges who will interpret it and the political context in which they will operate. The recent history of judicial activism suggests that the current judges are unlikely to adopt a passive approach. The present trends are such that in order for incorporation to have little or no effect the judiciary would need to apply a brake to the process which was already underway before incorporation. The experience of other countries and the recent history of judicial activism in England and Wales therefore suggests that the effect of incorporation will be to expand judicial power. How extensively this will be in the long term is less easy to predict. What is certain, is that if the Human Rights Act continues the expansion which is already underway, the politics of the judiciary will become of increasing public interest and its decisions will attract more controversy. A key issue is what effect this change will have on public confidence in the judges. Since, ultimately, their authority rests on public support, the relationship between activism and confidence is a critical one for the future of the judiciary.

Public confidence and increasing activism

In recent years there has been a marked increase in public criticism of the judiciary both in England and Wales and in many other countries.[25] But despite this development, judges still command relatively high levels of public confidence around the world (Waltman, 1991, p. 45; Dhavan, 1985, p. 165). In France, a recent survey found that 69% of the public thought that the judges carried out their functions satisfactorily or very satisfactorily (McKillop, 1996, p. 24). Similarly, judges in Canada and

New Zealand receive high marks on opinion polls when compared with politicians, teachers or clerics (Nejelski, 1985, p. 52; Goldfinch, 1993, p. 164).

It is these relative levels of public confidence which are particularly relevant for the development of judicial activism. Judges will be encouraged to expand their activities into those areas traditionally delineated for the executive and Parliament when they are considered more trustworthy than politicians. Although the level of public support for the judges may have fallen in absolute terms they are still generally better regarded than politicians: 'distrust of ministers and MPs is now more marked than distrust of judges' (Tate and Vallinder, 1995, p. 3). This relative popularity provides an explanation for the public tolerance for judicial activism and incorporation:

> When the public and leaders of interest groups and major economic and social institutions view the majoritarian institutions as immobilised, self-serving or even corrupt, it is hardly surprising that they would accord the policy-making of judiciaries, who have reputations for expertise and rectitude as much or more legitimacy as that of executives and legislatures (Tate, 1995, p. 31).

Opponents of incorporation who regard the expansion of judicial power as fundamentally undemocratic, have expressed surprise that there has been so little opposition from the general public for the transfer of power away from the elected branches of government:

> How, having fought so hard over such a long time and so bloodily for democratic advancement as a nation, can it now be that we seem so willing to give it all up? (Gearty, 1996, p. 6).

The answer to this question is that those who support incorporation, even if without any detailed understanding of its implications, recognise that the powers of MPs to check executive action exists more in theory than in practice. Parliament itself has fewer and fewer means of applying its own mechanisms of accountability to check the government and is increasingly reliant on the courts to apply them on its behalf. Unless or until there is the option of a real increase in parliamentary power vis-à-vis the executive exists, the decision to support judicial expansion can be seen as an entirely rational means of achieving the goal of checking the abuse of executive power.

As judicial activism expands after the enactment of the Human Rights Act, the confidence enjoyed by the judiciary will increasingly depend on the perceived political complexion of its decisions. From the mid 1980s, the judges have come to enjoy the confidence of the political left as it has become persuaded of their more liberal record by a greater willingness to strike down ministerial decisions. This confidence in the judges has grown in direct proportion to the increase in judicial decisions against the Conservative administration (Zander, 1997, p. 89). It is likely that if the judges show a similar strength of purpose towards Labour ministers in the coming years their popularity will wane with the left and rise with the right as it has done in the US.

The popularity of activist courts is not only dependent on the way in which its decisions are regarded along the political spectrum, but is also strongly linked to the type of issue they are asked to decide. There is an important distinction to be drawn between the activist judge's role in checking the power of the executive and in checking the will of majority public opinion, which may be, but are not necessarily the same. Support for expanding the judicial role is also closely linked to an awareness of the imperfection of the democratic process in protecting minority rights. If the definition of democracy is taken to incorporate respect for minorities then achieving this can be done through the use of an unrepresentative or unelected body is consistent with the broad aims of democracy:

> The very purpose of a bill of rights was to withdraw certain subjects from the vicissitudes of political controversy, to place them beyond the reach of majorities and officials... (Jackson J. quoted in Kentridge, 1997, p. 105).

This approach recognises that an activist judiciary is a strong anti-majoritarian element in the system; that its very purpose in a democracy is to restrain the will of the majority as expressed through the executive and legislature. A judiciary enforcing a Bill of Rights may be required to protect the interests of individuals and minorities even in the face of political opposition from the majority. To its opponent this amounts to 'judicial dictatorship' (Quirk and Bridwell, 1997); to its supporters this is its very strength.[26]

In England, the role of the judges' in defying majority opinion where this impinges on minorities' rights is not generally stressed by supporters of incorporation. But the implications for the public confidence are significant. If the judges adopt an activist approach to this role they are very likely to incur greater unpopularity:

> At present judges are more popular than politicians, but this may not remain so. The more power the judges have the more likely their exercise of it will be called into question (Palmer, 1993, p. 46).

As Lord Devlin pointed out as long ago as 1976, enthusiasm for an institution usually coincides with enthusiasm for what it is doing (Devlin, 1976, p. 7). The more extensively the judges use their powers the more political they seem and the weaker their claim to judicial independence becomes (Shapiro, 1995, p. 62). Judicial politics can be said to balance on this razor's edge of confidence (Volcansez, 1992, p. 7).

Where activism is used primarily to check the executive in the illegal, unfair or irrational use of its powers, as has been the case in England and Wales to date, the judiciary is likely to command widespread public support for many of its decisions, for the simple reason that government action of whatever kind is often unpopular. Sir Stephen Sedley has pointed out that whilst the judiciary lost public confidence as a result of the miscarriages of justice cases, they gained it for their willingness to curb governmental abuse of power (Sedley, 1995, p. 386). Similarly, where judges uphold the rights of vulnerable individuals and minorities, such as the rights of a child seeking costly medical care, pensioners or the disabled against perceived heavy-handed treatment by the executive, the courts will often command the support of the public since these groups do not threaten the interests of the majorities and often command widespread sympathy.

But this consensus is much weaker when the courts are asked to decide not between the individual and the state but between minority and majority views on controversial social or ethical issues. In the US, decisions of the courts concerning such matters as the death penalty, religious worship in school, or discrimination on the grounds of sexual orientation invoke strongly held competing values. Many state legislatures have left the area of abortion for the courts to decide because it is regarded as a political minefield (Tate, 1995, p. 32). This process of leaving controversial social issues such as immigration, pornography, euthanasia and abortion to the courts has already begun identified in Europe (Volcansez, 1992, p. 5). In England and Wales many of the areas which have come before the courts for judicial review in the 1990s such as broadcasting the views of terrorist sympathisers, hunting bans, and the disposal of nuclear waste, are all highly controversial:

> You cannot construct a litany of the subject matter of modern judicial review without being struck by the fact that time and again it engages questions upon whose merits the politicians (and others) are in rancorous disagreement (Laws, 1995, p. 74).

The areas which politicians wish to delegate to the courts are those which are seen as 'lose-lose' issues (Russell, 1995, p. 145). It is these areas in which the judges, if they carry out vigorously the job given to them under the Bill of Rights and protect the rights of unpopular minorities and individuals, face increased public censure. In such cases, whatever decision the judges reach there will always be strong support for an equally valid alternative view which might rest as much on the personal perspective of the judge as the objective merits of a case. Sir Stephen Sedley recognised this dilemma in the case of *Bland* where the judges had to decide whether to allow artificial feeding to be withdrawn from a victim of the Hillsborough stadium collapse:

> I would venture the view that they acquitted themselves extremely well in grappling with a series of profound moral and ethical questions....but there are plenty of people who would dispute this; and it is impossible not to speculate what the equally conscientious judgement of a Roman Catholic judge would have been in the *Bland* case (Sedley, 1997, p. 316).

The economic impact of judicial activism

The expansion of judicial decision-making into controversial and sensitive social and political issues may have ramifications for the popularity of the judges, but it is much less clear that this change will have any significant economic implications. In many respects, as Lord Denning recognised, the role of the judges in economic policy-making is very limited:

> [The judges] cannot direct the government to spend money on this or that. They cannot do anything to help the poor or the unemployed. They cannot provide housing for the homeless (Lord Denning, 1985, p. 4).

Many essential areas of public and economic policy such as health, housing and education are largely untouched by the judiciary. In 1996 Lord Irvine suggested that in cases which involved national economic policy, the judiciary would exercise the highest degree of self-restraint: 'The House [of Lords] did not go so far as to hold that such decisions are non-justiciable but powerfully indicated that, in practice, they will be, unless in the most exceptional circumstances' (Lord Irvine, 1996a, p. 66). Most commentators would agree that the effect of this restraint is that the judges still do little more than 'patrol the boundaries' of government activity (Drewry, 1992). This assessment is shared by most commentators on other judiciaries. It has been said that 'judges have penetrated the political arena, but still sit at the outer edges, they are but bit players in the main drama' (Waltman, 1991, p. 48). Another commentator has noted that even activist judiciaries: 'rarely reach the truly fundamental social economic, or political questions' (Dhavan, 1985, p. 10).

The experience of the US, however, suggests that activist judiciaries can, over time, exert influence over areas which have traditionally been the preserve of the legislature and executive. In recent years, it has been argued that the US courts are making decisions which have major budgetary and tax consequences for state governments (Shapiro, 1995, p. 50; Jacob et al., 1996, p. 17). Virtually every American state had been forced by the state or federal courts to revise its policies governing the provision and funding of basic state services of one kind or another, an example given being the state of Texas where the State Supreme Court had declared the system of funding public education to be in conflict with the requirements of the state's own constitution (Tate and Vallinder, 1995, p. 2). How great this economic impact is as a proportion of total national government spending is not easy to assess. It may be that it still represents a relatively small element of economic activity. Nevertheless, this degree of activism would amount to a significant increase in economic intervention if adopted in England and Wales.

Whether or not this form of economic activism develops around the world depends to a large extent on whether the growth in positive rights, currently still embryonic, continues. To date, the rights which are protected by activist courts tend to be negative rights; the freedom from interference in relation to such areas as a person's possession of property, personal liberty and privacy, rather than the positive right to material advantages such as housing, welfare, education and health services (Dhavan, 1985, p. 3). The most recently drafted bills of rights, such as that of South Africa, do include some positive rights such as education and housing, although conditional on the existence of sufficient government resources to fund them. This change may be currently intended to be little more than an expression of expectation with limited effect on government policy-making, but in future years these new rights may take on a real significance. If individuals on a large scale sought to claim these rights, and if courts upheld them, this would result in a vastly expanded role for the judges. Such a role would then bring the judiciary much closer to the other branches of government and so would undermine the basis for any differentiation in the approach to the judiciary's composition and the control of its power (Bell, 1985, p. 55). The way in which judges are chosen, their make-up and training and the methods by which they are held accountable for their actions would become increasingly the subject of legitimate public scrutiny.

Summary

The judges have gradually cast off their 'fairy-tales' and 'fig-leaves' and acknowledged the political role they play in shaping the law, public policy and the principles upon which judicial review rests. There can no longer be any doubt that judges are active policy-makers and the experience of other countries with activist judiciaries suggests that this role is very likely to increase. The ultimate implications of this change for broader policy-making questions are not yet possible to determine, but the implications for the judiciary itself are unquestionably significant. The way the judges are appointed, the training they receive and the processes for scrutinising their work will need to be rethought in the light of the expansion of their political power. One significant effect of the developments throughout these areas is that the tension between the demands of judicial independence and accountability will increase.

Notes

[1] *Liversidge v. Anderson* (1942) A.C. 206. See also Waltman, 1991, p. 36.
[2] *The Law Journal,* 1944, p. 351. Quoted in Griffith, 1997, p. 290.
[3] Quoted in CoHL.er, 1989, p. 163.
[4] *Conway v. Rimmer* (1968) A.C. 147.
[5] *Council of Civil Servants Union v. Minister for Civil Service* (1984) 3 ALL ER 935.

6 In *Council of Civil Servants Union v. Minister for Civil Service* (1985) 1 A.C. 374.

7 *Ex Parte Bennett* [1994] 1 A.C. 42, p. 62.

8 Lord Ackner in *R v Home Secretary ex parte Brind* [1991] 1 A.C. at 757.

9 *R v Secretary of State for Home Affairs ex parte the Fire Brigade's Union and others* [1995] 2 ALL ER 244.

10 See chapter three below.

11 Quoted in Lord Bingham, 1996, p. 3.

12 Lord Donaldson, *The Guardian,* 11 December 1995.

13 *Ibid.*

14 See chapter three below.

15 Hansard HL. 5 June 1996 col. 1255.

16 Speech at the Lord Mayor's Mansion House dinner. 24 July 1997.

17 Quoted by Lord Ackner, *The Guardian,* 12 November 1996.

18 *The Guardian,* 11 December 1995.

19 *Ex p. Fire Brigade Union* [1995] 2 A.C. 513 at p. 567.

20 Hansard HL. 5 June 1996 col. 1307.

21 International Association of Judges, 1984, p. 7.

22 *R v. Secretary of State for the Home Department ex parte Brind and Others* [1991] 2 WLR 588 at 606.

23 *Ibid.* at 595.

24 *R v. Minister of Defence ex parte Smith and others* [1995] 4 All ER at 427.

25 See chapter six below.

26 One Tennessee Supreme Court judge recently ousted by voters who objected to her ruling in a death-penalty case summarised this aspect of the judicial role: 'Those who want judges to rule based on majority public opinions have never been in a minority' (American Bar Association, 1995, p. 2).

3 Accountability and Independence

A dominant feature of the current developments in the judiciary is the increasing pressure for greater accountability. This trend is not unique to England and Wales but is evident in many other judiciaries around the world. As the role of judges has expanded in liberal democracies in consequence of their increasing numbers and influence on policy-making, the demands for greater political and social accountability have grown. To date, the development of mechanisms of accountability has been strictly limited by the competing requirements of judicial independence which has traditionally been taken to require that judges must occupy 'a place apart' in the social and political world (Friedland, 1995). The judiciary has argued strongly for the application of a very wide definition of the principle in order to ensure that judges are independent in both an individual and a collective sense 'from all sources of influence', whether internal from other judges or external from government, the media or others. The effect of this approach has been to exclude most forms of accountability by which decision-makers in other spheres of public service explain their actions and answer for the consequences. Because accountability has been viewed as posing a threat to judicial independence, its introduction in the judiciary has been slower and more controversial than in other areas of public life.

As the pressure for the judges to adopt a more responsive and answerable approach to their work has grown, the underlying tension between the requirements of independence and accountability has surfaced. The debate over the scope of judicial independence and its relationship to accountability exerts a strong influence on the changes to the way in which judges are appointed, trained and scrutinised reviewed in the following chapters. Since the development of accountability is affected by the demands of judicial independence, the outcome of that debate is of great significance in determining the structure and style of the judiciary in the years ahead. This chapter analyses the relationship between the two principles and argues for the application of a more qualified definition of judicial independence which protects essential judicial impartiality but allows for the introduction of new mechanisms of accountability which are necessary for the development of the new judiciary.

Mechanisms of accountability

Accountability can be defined as the duty of a public decision-maker to explain, legitimate and justify a decision and to make amends where a decision causes injustice or harm (Dhavan 1985 p. 167; Oliver and Drewry, 1996, p. 134). This requires, ultimately, that ministers must account for their actions to the legislature which may remove them from office if it disapproves of those actions and that members of the legislature, in turn, must account to the electorate at regular elections and may, similarly, be replaced by the voting public. This form of 'hard' political accountability, whereby decision-makers may be removed from office, is an essential but relatively crude means of checking officials. Its main failing is its limited effectiveness as a means of imposing ongoing duties on the decision-maker concerning the way in which decisions are taken. To provide this type of control, alternative 'soft' mechanisms of accountability are needed, in particular those of openness and representativeness. These build on the requirement that decision-makers justify and explain their decisions by demanding that such decision-making is procedurally transparent and sensitive to the interests of different groups in society and changing social conditions. A key feature of such soft mechanisms of accountability is that they are a two way process whereby decision-makers explain themselves to the public while also responding to the changing needs and opinions of the communities they serve. For this reason the media plays an important, but not unique role in transmitting information and opinions back and forth between decision-makers and the public. Another way in which responsiveness can be demonstrated is by ensuring that the decision-makers are representative or reflective of the community they serve. This can be seen as a form of social as opposed to political accountability since it is concerned with who the decision-makers are, demographically and culturally, rather than the nature of their structural relationship to the electoral process. The distinction between these hard and soft mechanisms of accountability in the judiciary is a particularly important one in the light of the role of judicial independence.

Hard political accountability

The prioritisation of the principle of judicial independence over accountability has meant that most of the methods by which individuals in public office are held politically accountable for their actions are not applicable to the judiciary. Judges cannot be dismissed simply because the public or politicians do not like their decisions. Nor can they be called before Parliament to explain their actions. Alternative mechanisms for responding to errors in decision-making such as disciplinary proceedings, public censure, civil or criminal liability are also, to a less or greater extent, constrained. Traditionally, this restriction has been justified on the grounds that the open nature of court proceedings and the structured appeal process provide sufficiently strong mechanisms for checking judicial decision-making. A court's judgments are public and a judge is generally obliged to give written reasons for them. The decisions are then normally reviewable by a higher court which can correct them if they are found to be wrong. However, these mechanisms, although significant, do not amount to a comprehensive system of accountability. The appeal process is an internal mechanism by which judges review the decisions of other judges. Its purpose is to maintain consistency and accuracy in the law, both substantive and procedural. It does not incorporate any element of external accountability which could link the judiciary to the electoral process and applies only to those categories of errors which are determined by the courts themselves to be appealable.[1]

Despite these limitations of the appeal process, the scope for scrutiny via other mechanisms remains strictly limited. Until recently, the Lord Chancellor's Department was largely free from the normal system of parliamentary scrutiny. It was not until the early 1990s that the Department became subject to review by the parliamentary Select Committees and acquired for the first time a minister in the Commons to account for its activities. This change has had a significant effect in opening up the work of the judiciary and the courts to external review. During the last few years the Public Accounts Committee has examined the Legal Aid means test system while the Home Affairs Committee has scrutinised the judicial appointment process and the role of freemasonry in the judiciary.[2]

These changes have gone some way towards bringing the Lord Chancellor's Department into line with other ministries and it can be said that there is now a clearer line of accountability to Parliament. Lord Mackay, when Lord Chancellor, was keen to emphasise the importance of this responsibility. For example, he objected to a change in the appointments process on the grounds that it would reduce accountability since he was personally and directly answerable to Parliament for his appointment decisions. However, criticisms have continued to be voiced about the effectiveness of parliamentary scrutiny of the judicial system. In 1998, a Commons motion signed by 50 Labour MPs called for the Lord Chancellor to be replaced by an elected Minister of Justice directly accountable to the House of Commons. This move may have been inspired as much by disapproval of the personal political style of Lord Irvine as by a carefully thought out response to the constitutional structure of the office of Lord Chancellor. Nevertheless, its expression clearly demonstrated the underlying dissatisfaction with the constitutional position of the Lord Chancellor's Department and the weakness inherent in the traditional system of judicial accountability. The tension which underlies the present arrangements was noted by one Canadian commentator:

> In studying the recent English comments on the Lord Chancellor, I have been struck by the number of attacks on his office by reputable individuals, including a number of judges. Once it is felt that the emperor cannot wear three hats, it is likely that there will be pressure for change (Friedland, 1995, p. 114).

Similar concerns have been expressed about the practical effectiveness of the department's financial accountability. In 1997, the Public Accounts Committee of the House of Commons heard evidence about the refusal of the National Audit Office to grant the Lord Chancellor's Department an audit certificate for the fifth year running on the grounds that the Legal Aid means test was not being properly applied in the magistrates' courts. The failure of the courts to take action to correct this situation was regarded by the Committee as an example of the fact that the judiciary was 'totally unaccountable to anyone'.[3]

Thus the scope of the Lord Chancellor's accountability to Parliament is limited to those areas, such as the appointments process, for which he has direct responsibility. The effect of the principle of judicial independence is such that he cannot be held directly answerable for the actions of the judges since he has no control over them. He may not even have ultimate control over his own decision-making since the courts may overturn them if challenged through judicial review. An example being the decision of the Divisional Court reversing the Lord Chancellor's reductions in the exemptions to court fees. Theoretically, this same inhibition affects all ministers where judicial review of their decisions has financial implications. It could be said that the nature of judicial independence is such that it provides the judiciary with a roving mandate to affect the spending plans of all departments without being required to account, collectively or through the Lord Chancellor, for these decisions to Parliament.

Soft accountability

If traditional mechanisms of hard political accountability can have only limited application in relation to the judiciary then alternative soft methods of openness and representativeness may be developed which would compensate for this gap in its accountability audit. To date, the judiciary's record as an open and representative body has not been good. The most common public criticism which is currently made of the judges is that they are socially unaccountable in that they neither reflect nor respond to the needs and interests of the people they serve. Its representation as an 'out of touch' body is probably the judiciary's most widespread and enduring public image today. The public nature of court proceedings is not enough to counter this limitation since openness as a function of accountability requires more than merely stating formal decisions in a forum to which the public have access. It is a far-reaching requirement which demands that decision-makers actively engage with the communities they serve, both directly and via the media. This duty stretches beyond the delivery of a judgment, the end product of a decision-making process. It encompasses the judges' participation in wider debate about all aspects of the work it does, the way it does it and why. It also requires that judges are collectively receptive to criticism.

Traditionally, the judges have regarded their removal from such interaction as being a positive virtue. Maintaining a distance from the day-to-day pressures of social and political life was viewed as a means of reinforcing judicial independence. As a result of this culture of disengagement, the judiciary has been reluctant to adopt a more open and responsive approach and actively to promote a more demographically reflective make-up amongst its members. By necessity, this perspective is changing as the demands for greater accountability grow.

The rise of judicial accountability

Until relatively recently, the limitations placed on both hard and soft accountability were widely regarded as an appropriate price to be paid for securing the independence of the judiciary. But during the last thirty years or so a number of different factors have come together to increase the pressure on the judiciary for the introduction of greater accountability. Some of these are not specific to the judiciary. The general political reforms which began in the mid 1980s designed to enhance the position of the public as 'consumers' of services have gradually affected all areas of public life (Oliver and Drewry, 1996). These changes both reacted to and reinforced the increasing expectation of a greater degree of openness in government. The introduction of Users' Charters, more open complaints processes and greater accessibility of information about public service are all indicative of this wider trend. As citizens throughout liberal democracies have developed increasing expectations of this type of consumer-led accountability from their public bodies the judiciary has gradually come to be perceived as lagging behind (Nicolson J, 1993, p. 413).

Related to this development has been the growth of public pressure for greater social accountability amongst decision-makers in the form of greater representativeness. Demands that members of public bodies should be demographically and culturally reflective of society have affected all areas of government. The make-up, background and social attitudes of decision-makers such as MPs, ministers, civil servants and police officers are now widely scrutinised. The extent to which those who exercise power are seen to be drawn from the communities they serve and 'in touch' with current social norms is one important measure of the extent of their potential for responsiveness and thus their social accountability.

Other factors which have contributed to the growing pressure for greater judicial accountability are particular to the judiciary. The rise in the political role of the judges examined above has inevitably increased demands that judges should be subject to greater public scrutiny. As the decisions the courts make increasingly affect all aspects of individuals' lives, demands have grown for the quality of the decision-making and the background and views of the decision-makers to be subject to scrutiny. A driving force behind this pressure is the increase in the spending power of the courts. The key rationale which underpins public accountability is that those who are responsible for spending public funds must account for their decisions:

> ...those who are entrusted with the use of public resources should not only act in the public interest but should be seen to do so; and should be subject to public censure if they do not (Downey, 1987, p. 2).

In the past, the Lord Chancellor's Department was regarded as a small and relatively low-spending department. But by 1997, its annual budget had grown to £2.3 billion, largely as a result of the expansion of legal aid. As the Lord Chancellor's Department's spending requirements have moved closer to that of other departments, its use of resources has come to have a significant impact on the level of public funds available for other services. Now that it is competing for a significant proportion of the public finance budget it can no longer claim the insulation from the normal rigours of financial accountability mechanisms which it once enjoyed.

The combined effect of these external and internal factors has been to undermine the traditional judicial insulation from accountability. Whether or not it is appropriate to increase hard or soft mechanisms of accountability in order to respond to these developments depends on the view which is taken of the role of judicial independence.

The scope of judicial independence

A useful starting point for examining the role of judicial independence is the extensive body of international jurisprudence in the form of treaties, conventions and declarations which seek to articulate and protect the principle.[4] Although the texts of these documents differ in detail, they share an approach which defines judicial independence in very broad terms to ensure the protection of the courts from actual or apparent interference of any kind. Such generalised wording provides little practical guidance on the scope of the principle in practice. In common with the provisions of all constitutions and international conventions those relating to judicial independence are drafted widely in order to set out common standards which can reconcile the different historical and cultural traditions of the citizens and signatories which they cover.

This requirement of general applicability is illustrated by the approach of the international conventions to arrangements for judicial appointments. Most state that in deciding whether the processes are consistent with the requirements of judicial independence account must be taken of the different appointment methods, different tenure arrangements (such as fixed term contracts or life tenure), and different remuneration arrangements which currently exist in the signatory states. Alternatively, the documents set down a general requirement and then allow for an exception. For example, the International Bar Association code states that the requirement of judicial independence is such that the appointment of judges should be vested in a judicial body, but that the use of appointment by the executive or legislature is allowed where this is justified by long democratic tradition, so legitimising the arrangements in such countries as England and Wales and Australia which would otherwise be in breach of the code (Shetreet, 1987, p. 769).

Until recently these generalised approaches were sufficient for their purposes since the parameters of the principle of judicial independence were relatively uncontroversial and there existed a broad consensus between the judges and commentators that it should be defined in wide and unqualified terms (Armytage, 1996, p. 10). However, the growing pressure for increasing accountability raises questions about the exact boundaries of the principle and the limits of its practical application. A particular subject of debate has been the relationship between impartiality and judicial independence. From the international jurisprudence it is unclear whether impartiality is an inherent feature of judicial independence or a separate principle in its own right. Many conventions, including the European Convention on Human Rights, grant the right to a fair and public hearing within a reasonable time by an independent and impartial tribunal. This wording suggests that there is a distinction between the two. The same phrase is included in the Canadian Charter of Rights and its meaning has been the subject of review by the Supreme Court in Canada. In the 1983 case of *Valente* the Canadian Supreme Court drew a distinction between them. Le Dain J stated that although there was a close relationship between impartiality and independence, the two were separate and distinct values:

> Impartiality refers to a state of mind or attitude of the tribunal in relation to the issues and the parties in a particular case... the word independent connotes not merely a state of mind or attitude in the actual exercise of

judicial functions, but a status or relationship to others, particularly the executive branch of government...[5].

This distinction can be expressed in another way as being between collective and individual independence. Judges must approach each individual case with an impartial state of mind while the judiciary as a body must maintain a structural or constitutional independence from the other branches of government. The distinction between collective and individual independence, one which is often blurred, requires some careful critical analysis. It is an important one because the two-pronged definition is a reflection of the fact that the judges simultaneously fulfil two separate roles. Their constitutional function as one branch of the state counterbalancing the interests of the executive and Parliament can be distinguished from their social service role of resolving disputes and allocating fault between parties carried out in their day to day work in the courts.[6] These two functions are often not clearly separated in discussions of the role of the judiciary which allows the principle of judicial independence to be spread generally over both, so avoiding the need to define precisely in what way any particular action or process impinges on the principle. The claim to collective independence is one often made by senior judges and yet the justification for the principle as being based on a constitutionally distinct branch of state is hard to establish when examined closely.

Collective judicial independence

The separation of powers

The principle of collective judicial independence is founded on the idea of the separation of powers between the executive, legislature and judiciary. The principle holds that judges, as one branch of the state play a role in balancing competing interests at a constitutional level. In the US, where the concept of the separation of powers is strong, judicial independence is defined as ensuring that: 'judges are free from potential domination by other branches of government' (Roseberg, 1992, p. 370). In England and Wales there is a surprising lack of agreement about the role which the separation of powers plays in the constitution. In 1991 Lord Mackay, then Lord Chancellor, declared that:

> Our constitution, unlike that of, for example, the United States, is not built on the principle that the legislative, the executive and the judicial powers should be separate and equal (Lord Mackay, 1991, p. 258).

However, in 1996, Lord Irvine, shortly before replacing Lord Mackay as Lord Chancellor stated during a parliamentary debate on the constitutional role of the judiciary that: 'it is time to return to first principles. The British Constitution, largely unwritten, is firmly based on the separation of powers'.[7]

The practical division of roles between the branches of government tends to support Lord Mackay's view with numerous examples of the overlap between the functions of the executive, Parliament and the judiciary.[8] According to the Lord Chief Justice, Lord Bingham, the fundamental reason why the principle of judicial independence cannot be rested on any classical doctrine of the separation of powers is because the executive appoint and pay for the judges (Lord Bingham, 1996, p. 5). At an even more basic level, the fact that the most senior judges are all members of the House of Lords is itself a direct contradiction of the principle, while the Chancellor is the greatest offender in breaching all three boundaries - head of the judiciary, he is also the speaker of the House of Lords and a member of the Government.[9]

To an American citizen, used to the much sharper separation between the three branches of government, such a figure is an anathema. However, even in the US it is accepted that judicial independence does not require that the different branches are 'hermetically sealed-off' and there is a measure of overlap between them (Rosenberg, 1992, p. 371). One test of whether the separation of powers is sufficiently substantial upon which to rest the principle of judicial independence would be to ask whether the overlap is kept to the minimum necessary for the functioning of the state. In England and Wales this cannot be maintained and indeed, the overlap between the executive and the judiciary has, if anything, increased in recent years in ways which are not obviously constitutionally necessary. The development of the appointment of judges to head inquiries when started in the 1960s has raised concerns about breaching the boundary between government and judiciary (Stevens 1993, p. 169). Although judges have generally been held to have functioned competently and fairly in this capacity, anxieties are still expressed, from both on and off the bench, about the constitutional blurring of roles which such judicial inquiries promote: 'There is a risk that judges who engage in inquiries or other tasks on behalf of Her Majesty's Government are being seduced into a dangerous liaison' (Munro 1992, p. 23).

These examples suggest that in so far as the principle of collective judicial independence exists at all it does so despite, not because of, the distribution of powers between the three branches of the state. Nevertheless, the notion of the constitutional separation between the judiciary and the other branches retains a strong hold in debates on judicial independence both in England and Wales and internationally and is the basis for a number of claims regarding the domain of the judges and the need for a wide measure of autonomy in a range of different areas.[10] At its most general, it has been suggested that collective judicial independence requires that the scope of the courts' authority should not be reduced. Under the Australian Declaration of the Principles of Judicial Independence the principle was held to encompass the requirement that: 'the judiciary has jurisdiction, directly or by way of review, over all issues of a justiciable nature'.[11]

In Canada, concern has been expressed over the creation of administrative agencies and other alternatives to adjudication such as arbitrators. The basis for this fear being that the judges could be punished by the executive for unpopular decisions under the guise of a reform creating an alternative means of dispute resolution (Nejelski 1985, p. 52). In England and Wales, by contrast, there appears to be very broad support for the expansion of the work of tribunals and alternative dispute resolution mechanisms such as mediation with little concern that such processes threaten judicial independence. The reason for this may be less to do with principle than pragmatics, in that the expansion in the criminal and civil processes of recent years ensures that there is no danger of any net erosion of the judicial sphere in terms of the quantity and nature of business coming before the courts. The greater problem facing the judiciary, as attested by the Woolf proposals for reform of the civil system, is, rather, how to manage the increased caseload more cheaply and efficiently.

Administrative and financial control of the courts

A more controversial area which the judges have claimed falls within their domain under the principle of collective judicial independence is the administration and financial management of the courts. The link between administration and judicial independence has been widely asserted. A draft written constitution proposed by the Institute for Public Policy Research in 1991 enshrined the principle of judicial control of court business on the grounds that it would conflict with the principle of judicial independence if the allocation of cases to particular judges was to be carried out by a civil servant (IPPR 1991, p. 20). Shimon Shetreet has suggested that: 'collective independence requires that the Executive's control over matters of judicial administration must be limited to those areas where the system of government deems it indispensable' (Shetreet, 1984, p. 992). The international jurisprudence on judicial independence similarly recognises the requirement that the judiciary should retain control of court administration. The Montreal declaration on the Independence of Justice, for example, gives the main responsibility for court administration to the judiciary.[12] In some jurisdictions, this principle is strictly respected in practice. In Australia, under the High Court of Australia Act 1979 the judiciary was given financial and administrative responsibility for the High Court and similar powers were given over the federal Family Court in 1989 (Goldfinch, 1993, p. 160). Similar arrangements exist in the US. Since 1939 federal judges have had responsibility for drawing up their own budgets and presenting them directly to Congress (See Shetreet, 1985, p. 592).

The potential threat to judicial independence from executive control of the administration of the courts lies, at the most extreme, in the power to refuse to appoint judges or provide courtrooms or staff to service the courts. In Malta a court was closed down by the Government in 1981 the day before it was due to hear a case challenging a decision of the Prime Minister (Shetreet, 1985, p. 608). Similarly, the Government in Bulgaria attempted to expel the constitutional court from its quarters in 1995 (Melone, 1996). The decision as to where a judge sits can also undermine judicial independence. In India, for example, it has been claimed that the use by the executive of powers to transfer judges has been used as a de facto form of removal.[13] While crude interference in the court system seems unlikely in England and Wales at the present time, the danger of indirect intrusion by the executive into the administration of the courts in order to influence individual cases, particularly those which are politically sensitive, clearly exists. One potentially powerful method by which the executive can influence judicial decision-making through the administrative process is by control of the allocation of judges to particular cases. The decision as to which judge is to hear a case is often regarded as critical to its outcome: 'Lawyers sometimes cheer, or as the case may be, groan, when they learn who is to sit in the case' (Zander, 1989, p. 106). In 1991 Lord Mackay, then Lord Chancellor, argued that such administrative decisions as the listing of cases must remain in the hands of the judges in order to protect against the danger of an 'unscrupulous executive' seeking to influence the outcome of cases.[14] It has been suggested that in 1984 just such a situation arose in the case of Clive Ponting, a civil servant charged with breach of the Official Secrets Act by providing information to a newspaper about the sinking of the Belgrano in the Falklands war. It was claimed at the time that Margaret Thatcher, then Prime Minister, had commented that 'an appropriately severe member of the judiciary would be on hand to hear the case'.[15] In the event, Clive Ponting was acquitted by a jury and there was no suggestion that judicial independence was in fact undermined by the case but such examples serve as a reminder of the vulnerability of the principle in times which are politically charged.

It was for these reasons that proposals for creating a ministry of justice based in the Home Office during the 1860s and 1870s were opposed by the judiciary on the grounds that this would impinge upon their independence. Although in England and Wales the degree of autonomy enjoyed by Australian or US judges has never existed, until relatively recently the judges exercised a wide degree of administrative control. The creation of the Lord Chancellor's Office represented a compromise which ensured that the administration remained in the hands of a judge, in the person of the Lord Chancellor while allowing for the chain of accountability to run through him to Parliament.[16] The fact that the Lord Chancellor's Department was originally known as the Lord Chancellor's Office illustrates its separate status in the government structure. Through the Office's early years the judges retained a strong degree of control of the administration process and finance and until relatively recently all its staff were lawyers.

The Courts Act of 1971 transformed the Office into a department and brought it closer into line with all other government departments by handing a wider measure of control to the civil servants representing a marked shift towards greater executive control (Stevens 1993 p. 181; Browne-Wilkinson 1988, p. 46). According to the Lord Chief Justice, Lord Bingham, the relationship between the Administration and the judges since then has not always been easy with many judges resenting what they see as: 'the Administration breathing down their necks, treating them as pawns on a bureaucratic chess board' (Lord Bingham, 1996, p. 12). An underlying difficulty which gives rise to tension in this area is the fact that there is not, in practice, a neat distinction between administrative and judicial functions. The structure, resources and procedures adopted in the courts all have a direct bearing on the type of justice received. Its speed, the level of experience of the judge allocated to a case, the scope for appealing and the extent of legal advice and assistance can all be described as administrative decisions yet they are all factors which can affect the ultimate decision.

A recent example which demonstrates this problem arose in 1994 when Lord Mackay, then Lord Chancellor, wrote to Sir John Wood, then president of the Employment Appeal Tribunal, demanding that he should follow certain procedures in deciding the appeals criteria and if not, that he should 'consider his position'. The letter which Sir John wrote in reply stated that he considered that the Lord Chancellor had demanded that he exercise his judicial function: 'in a way in which you regard as best suited to your executive purposes'. He concluded that he could not comply with the demand since he did not regard it as conducive to justice.[17]

Most commentators have viewed this exchange as an example of the threat posed to judicial independence by the executive undermining judicial discretion. But equally it can be seen as an attempt to enforce administrative control by the minister responsible to Parliament. The issue turns on whether the action in question is viewed as administrative or judicial. In this case, at least, the Lord Chancellor ultimately accepted the judge's insistence that the application of the appeals procedure was a judicial and not an administrative decision. This division between the judicial and administrative duties of the courts is not therefore an easy one and the tension between the two has a long history (Purchas, 1994, p. 1306).

By the 1980s this tension had surfaced after some strong expressions from some senior judges that the loss of judicial control in the finances and administration of the courts threatened judicial independence. One of the triggers for this conflict between the executive and judiciary was the proposals for changes to the rights of audience in court. The head of the Chancery Division, the Vice-Chancellor, Sir Nicolas Browne-Wilkinson, (now Lord Browne-Wilkinson) argued in 1988 that the rules governing these arrangement had traditionally been made by the judges and were being altered by the executive as part of a government efficiency drive (Browne-Wilkinson 1988, p. 50). Ultimately his fears over the loss of control by the judges in this area proved unfounded as the reforms were effectively scuppered by the united opposition of the judges (Zander, 1989). Nevertheless, the strength of feeling on the part of the judges over the proposals went so far as to suggest implicitly that they represented a fundamental threat to the democratic fabric of society. Lord Lane argued that they amounted to a threat to the very liberty of the individual:

> Oppression does not stand on the doorstep with a toothbrush moustache and a swastika armband. It creeps up insidiously; it creeps up step by step; and all of a sudden the unfortunate citizen realises that it has gone.[18]

By 1988 Sir Nicolas Browne-Wilkinson suggested that there was an atmosphere of: 'mutual suspicion between the judges and the Lord Chancellor's Department' (1988, p. 50). In 1994, Sir Francis Purchas, a retired Court of Appeal judge, claimed that the period was one which had witnessed the 'final domination' of the judiciary by the executive (1994, p. 1306). It is difficult to reconcile proposals which, whatever their merits or failings, were designed to end restrictive practices and extend rights of audience to solicitors with the totalitarianism of the Nazi regime or the collapse of the constitutional arrangement of the past four centuries. Nevertheless, the strength of language which Lord Lane employed highlights the extent to which the judges sought to equate their control of the court system with the fundamental principles of democracy. It also illustrates a recurring theme in judicial discourse on judicial independence, that the threats to the principle are not direct but are of: 'insidious erosion, of gradual (almost imperceptible) encroachment' (Lord Bingham, 1996, p. 12. See also Sir Francis Purchas, 1994, p. 1306).

In the 1980s and early 1990s the judges believed that this erosion was occurring as a result of the prioritisation of cost savings over the needs of justice. Sir Francis wrote that: 'Constitutional independence will not be achieved if the funding of the administration of justice remains subject to the influences of the political marketplace' (1994, p. 1324). According to Lord Bingham, his claims represented the high-water mark in the argument that collective judicial independence required substantial control over the administration of the courts (Lord Bingham, 1996, p. 4). In so far as all economic choices as to the allocation of resources can be described as political, Sir Francis's statement is accurate. But it is misleading in so far as it implies that the Government's aim in introducing the changes was to curb the power of the judges. The underlying reason behind the increasing interference in the administration of justice by the executive was not essentially an ideological power struggle between the executive and the judiciary but the more prosaic one of cost-cutting. The changes had taken place at a time when demands on the courts had grown very significantly with the result that for the first time judges were not being given the resources which in their view were required.

Like any other government minister the Lord Chancellor must go to the treasury to obtain funding for the department, arguing his cases for his budget. In the past, this arrangement has, in practice, caused few problems. The Lord Chancellor's Department was generally given the funds it asked for. However, the dramatic increase in the costs of Legal Aid and the expansion in the size of the court system, combined with a tightening of public expenditure across all government departments led to significant change. Browne-Wilkinson acknowledged this development. He argued that in the past this overlap between the executive and the judiciary had operated smoothly: 'When England was a rich country with a broadly stable society there was never any real conflict as to the allocation of funds' (1988, p. 45). He went on to claim that developments in the 1980s had brought about a real friction between the executive and the judiciary which threatened judicial independence. These changes were, he argued, the result of financial pressures and the introduction of a system of funding which was 'value for money' led and incompatible with the unique status of the Lord Chancellor's Department:

> The requirements of judicial independence make the Lord Chancellor's Department wholly different from any other department of state. It is not for the executive alone to determine what should be the policy objective of the courts. It is not for the executive alone to determine whether or not a particular judicial procedure provides 'value for money'. Justice is not capable of being measured by an accountant's computer (Browne-Wilkinson, 1988, p. 48).

Sir Nicolas further claimed that judicial independence was threatened by the fact that decisions about efficiency and spending priorities were being taken by civil servants without reference to the judges and that this had led a number of judges: 'to consider that there is some form of civil service conspiracy designed to erode the independence of the judiciary and their powers' (1988, p. 51).[19] He himself did not subscribe to this conspiracy theory but nevertheless regarded the threat as a real one, and drew upon the common theme of the silent erosion of judicial independence: 'To my mind nobody is trying to erode the independence of the legal system: it is happening unperceived and unappreciated' (1988, p. 51).

These fears expressed in 1988 were partly confirmed in the early 1990s when the senior judiciary and the executive came into conflict over judicial manpower. According to the former Law Lord, Lord Ackner, between 1989 and 1993 judges repeatedly stressed the urgent need for the appointment of more High Court judges. The failure of the Lord Chancellor to increase appointments to the bench lead Lord Lane, then Lord Chief Justice to warn in 1992 that the administration of justice was 'in peril'. Similarly Lord Taylor when Lord Chief Justice claimed that the waiting list for trials was becoming 'a national disgrace'. A year later the necessary appointments were made.[20]

The conflict between the judiciary and the executive over resources has continued. The increases in court fees in 1996 by Lord Mackay raised even stronger objections from the judiciary over what some senior judges saw as executive interference in the running of the courts. In 1997, the Divisional Court upheld a challenge to the Government's decision to abolish exemptions from, and remission of, High Court fees and refused leave to appeal.[21] As a result the exemptions and remissions were reintroduced, although the increased fees remained.[22] In the face of continuing criticism of the rises, Lord Irvine, on appointment as Lord Chancellor, agreed to consider extending the exemptions. Whether or not the change of Government and the greater avowed willingness to consult with the judges, which has been expressed both by Lord Mackay at the end of his period as Lord Chancellor and Lord Irvine at the start of his, will end this period of tension over court administration remains to be seen. As long as public spending constraints are felt by the judiciary to impact upon the work of the courts the conflicts of recent years are likely to reoccur in other areas of the legal system.

Concern about the extent of executive control over the administration of the courts is not unique to England and Wales. Shimon Shetreet noted in 1985 that: 'the overall assessment of executive control over the judges suggests that in many countries the executive has too much power over the judiciary' (Shetreet, 1985, p. 658). In Canada the absence of judicial control by the judges has been described as a threat to judicial independence (Nejelski, 1985, p. 51) while in Israel similar concerns have lead to proposals to give judges greater administrative control (Shetreet, 1984). In New Zealand the Royal Commission on the Courts in 1978 held that the 'prime duty of a judge is to hear cases and not to administer'.

Despite this conclusion there has remained support for greater judicial control of the administration of courts on the grounds of judicial independence (Goldfinch, 1993, p. 156).

The underlying economic tensions which have affected all these jurisdictions in which the cost of the legal system has grown are unlikely to disappear. If the judiciary wishes to maintain a degree of control over the budgets and administration of the courts at a time when all public spending decisions are highly political it will necessarily be drawn into political debate. The judiciary and the executive have, for the first time, disagreed about the necessary minimum level of resources needed by the legal system. The question of what constitutes adequate funding is a political question since, as the judges themselves have acknowledged, the legal system is just one of a number of areas of social life which require funds. Despite arguing for greater judicial control on courts administration, Browne-Wilkinson conceded that the legal system is not inherently more important than other social services such as health and education and that the judges, like doctors and teachers, must accept that they will not have all the resources which they ask for. Similarly the Lord Chief Justice, Lord Bingham, commented in 1996 that the justice system had no greater claim to resources than other areas and that judges could not be left to determine the appropriate level of funding:

> Even we cannot overlook the existence of other pressing claims on finite national resources. We would all recognise the defence of the realm as a vital national priority, but I suspect that we would shrink from giving the chiefs of staff *Carte Blanche* to demand all the resources which are judged necessary for that end (Lord Bingham, 1996, p. 4).

The increased politicisation of budgetary decisions has been identified by some judges in other jurisdictions as a reason not to adopt a greater role in decisions about financing the legal system. The Chief Justice of British Columbia, Allan McEachern, argued in 1996 that it was the right of the legislature to decide how public money is to be spent.[23] He commented that: 'if mistakes are to be made in budgeting or financial operations, it is better that they be made by someone other than the judiciary'.[24] In New Zealand some judges have expressed similar arguments that being removed from the administrative function allows the judiciary to reach decisions with reference to the law alone, free from the 'niggling concerns' of case loads, administrative efficiency and the demands on court budgets (Goldfinch, 1993, p. 164). The dilemma faced by judges who seek more extensive control of administrative and financial matters is that the greater judicial independence from executive control which it provides must go hand-in-hand with greater accountability to Parliament. How this works in practice is uncertain. In Australia, the way in which the Chief Justice or the Chief Executive Officer who is answerable to him are accountable to Parliament is said to remain unclear (Church and Sallman, 1991, p. 50). One model of judicial-led control of the courts suggests that the judges would be required to appear before select committees on a regular basis (Goldfinch, 1993, p. 164). Such a suggestion is not a popular one with judges in England and Wales.

The claim that justice cannot be run by accountants only goes so far since where public resources are limited, a price has to be put on the funding of the courts. This means that priorities must be made as to where the money should go and the public is entitled to scrutinise and criticise these decisions:

> Voters have a legitimate concern about how the tax they pay is spent. They also have a legitimate concern that some person is held responsible for how this money is spent. It is difficult to reconcile ministerial responsibility with a system of court administration that would entrust considerable amounts of taxpayers' money to unelected and largely unaccountable hands (Goldfinch, 1993, p. 167).

The change which has occurred in recent years is that the court system has joined other areas of public life in the arena in which hard fought battles over funding levels and priorities are played out. The level of autonomy which could be enjoyed by the judiciary at a time of broad consensus government, free from chronic public spending pressures no longer exists and is unlikely to do so again. Whether or not this matters depends on the view taken of the definition of judicial independence. As a wide constitutional collective, any reduction impinges on the principle:

> Whilst the independence of the judiciary is protected only in so far as the actual trial and its immediate listing penumbra is concerned, the judiciary cannot be seriously considered as an effective constitutional element in the concept of the separation of the powers (Sir Francis Purchas, 1994, p. 1324).

If a narrower definition is applied, the erosion of judicial control at a wider level only breaches the principle if it directly or indirectly reduces the impartiality exercised by the individual judges in hearing the cases before them. This position was summarised by Ian Greene writing in relation to the Canadian system:

> The bottom line for judicial independence is whether a particular administrative decision taken outside the judiciary may have a direct or indirect impact on adjudicative impartiality (Greene, 1995, p. xvii).

The listing of cases is clearly open to this danger and for this reason the Canadian Supreme Court in the *Valente* case stated that judicial control over the assignment of judges and sittings of the courts was the minimum requirement for collective independence.[25] Similarly, the threat to withhold payment of judicial salaries is a powerful tool which could be used to manipulate judicial decision-making, which is why judges are paid out of the Consolidated Fund rather than departmental budgets. But it is much harder to sustain the argument that political decisions about the prioritisation of spending between different public services and the overall fixing of the budget has an empirical connection to judicial impartiality at an individual level. The standards of justice may be poorer in terms of such matters as delay and standards of legal advice if less resources are available, but that need not affect the independence of the judges. Impartial judges can dispense justice under the proverbial palm tree.

Sentencing and penal policy-making

In the area of judicial administration the potential for conflict between the judiciary and the courts may have grown, but there is general agreement in principle that the judges must have some measure of control over the judicial process in order to fulfil the minimum requirements of judicial independence. By contrast, a more problematic area in which collective judicial independence is sometimes claimed by the judiciary is that of sentencing and penal policy-making. Although the original doctrine of the separation of powers as proposed by Montesquieu and others did not encompass the field of sentencing, the gradual growth in judicial discretion in sentencing has caused the development of a convention that the sentence of the court should be for the judge alone (Munro 1992, p. 27).[26]

However, this principle remains constrained by the fact that this broad area of policy-making is also the responsibility of government. Indeed, Sir James Stephen argued in 1885 that if the judiciary were to take on the task of formulating principles of sentencing they would be assuming a power which the constitution did not give them.[27] It was not, for example, suggested in 1965 when the death penalty was abolished, that Parliament was acting outside the scope of its authority and impinging on the realm of the judiciary. More recently the principle that policy-making is the responsibility of the executive was reiterated in the 1990 White Paper, *Crime, Justice and Protecting the Public,* which formed the basis of the Criminal Justice Act 1991. It stated that: 'sentencing principles and sentencing practice are matters of legitimate concern to government'.

The curtailment of the judges' discretion in sentencing is neither new nor constitutionally questionable. As Munro notes: 'A judicial monopoly [on sentencing] should never again be advocated on the bases of misunderstandings of legal history and misrepresentations of constitutional theory' (1992, p. 30). However, the uncertainty over the boundary between the two branches of the state in this area has the potential for conflict. Since the 1980s this potential has, arguably, been realised. For most of the period after the Second World War the division of responsibility for sentencing matters between the executive and judiciary was relatively uncontroversial with a wide measure of discretion given to the judges justified by reference to judicial independence. For the third quarter of the twentieth century Parliament adopted a minimalist approach to sentencing, generally restricted to setting relatively high maximum sentences and occasionally introducing new penal measures (Ashworth, 1995, p. 40). Increasingly, however, it has become a source of conflict in which the boundaries and requirements of judicial independence have been contested. The reason for this change lies primarily in the increase in the amount of new legislation in the area of penal policy as a result of the dramatic growth in importance of 'law and order' on the political agenda and the growing cost of the penal system.

Whilst generally accepting that Parliament has the constitutional right to legislate on sentencing policy, the judges have considered it within their domain to influence these changes whether from within Parliament or from outside.[28] For example, a proposal in 1981 by William Whitelaw, then Home Secretary, to reduce the prison population by introducing automatic parole for shorter sentence prisoners who had served one third of their sentence was dropped in the face of opposition from a group of Court of Appeal judges who had agreed that if the plans were implemented they would scupper them by awarding proportionately higher sentences (Munro 1992, p. 14).

During the latter 1980s and 1990s the forum for the judges' opposition to government proposals in the field of penal policy shifted to the legislature, partly as relations between the judges and the Conservative administration deteriorated and consultation became less common. In 1991, the Criminal Justice Act was passed in an attempt to impose a structured approach to sentencing. It set out a framework for the exercise of sentencers' discretion which aimed to promote a more coherent system, ensure greater consistency and reduce the use of custody for minor offences. The reduction in the scope of judges' sentencing discretion which the Act necessarily entailed was a cause of criticism on the part of the many senior judges who played a leading part in the debates on the bill. Some central features of the bill in particular attracted criticism (such as the requirements that previous convictions be disregarded in determining the seriousness of an offence) but it was never suggested by those who took part in the debates that Parliament did not have the power to legislate on the subject.

A much more intense debate about the boundaries of judicial independence in the area of sentencing was provoked by the passage of the Crime (Sentencing) Act 1996 which introduced new mandatory minimum sentences and mandatory life sentences. In response to the proposals set out in the Conservative Party conference in 1995, Lord Taylor issued a press statement arguing against the introduction of the new measures.[29] During the passage of the legislation a number of senior judges joined Lord Taylor in criticising the proposals. His objections were based on the arguments that they were unnecessary, unjust and ineffective. Nevertheless, he openly acknowledged Parliament's constitutional right to pass them and emphasised that if passed the judiciary would implement them faithfully - a view which was supported by Lord Irvine before his appointment as Lord Chancellor.[30] He argued that the separation of powers demanded only that the executive and Parliament must avoid interfering with the role of judges in interpreting the law as passed by Parliament. Conversely, it may be argued that judges must avoid interfering with the legislative role of Parliament by challenging its right to pass whatever law it considered fit. Similarly Lord Bingham stressed that while he personally did not support the proposals, the Government was quite within its powers to pass the necessary legislation: 'As Parliament can prescribe a maximum penalty without infringing the constitutional independence of the judges, so it can prescribe a minimum' (quoted in Steven, 1996, p. 32). On this interpretation, parliamentary sovereignty allows that legislation restricting the sentencing discretion of judges does not breach the principle of judicial independence. Such a breach would only arise if Parliament or the executive sought to interfere with the right of the judiciary to apply that law.

However, not all the senior judges drew such a clear distinction between the content of the legislation and the right to pass it. Some went further than Lord Taylor had done by suggesting that the proposals constituted a breach of judicial independence on a constitutional level by impinging on the constitutional division between the branches of state.[31] Lord Donaldson, former Master of the Rolls, argued that the proposals limited the powers of the courts to decide, by means of judicial review whether the executive was exceeding the powers granted to it by Parliament.[32] Lord Ackner, a former Law Lord, argued that the tension between the executive and the judiciary, which was healthy in a democracy up to a certain level had become excessive and that the reason for this was the government's failure: 'properly to understand the breadth of the concept of judicial independence and therefore properly to protect it'.[33]

The strength of feeling expressed by the judges during the passage of the 1996 Act was rooted in a conflict between the two branches of government which lay beyond the particularities of the sentencing legislation and should be seen in the context of the period of conflict between the judiciary and the Conservative administration during the 1990s. The commitment of Lord Irvine, when appointed Lord Chancellor to ensuring that the judges were brought back into the process of consultation during the early stages of the formulation of penal policy did much to re-establish harmony between the two branches. This change of approach may have been a politically astute means of diffusing the tension which had arisen between the judges and the executive, and may also have been a good use of judicial knowledge and experience, but it cannot be claimed to be a necessary element of the principle of judicial independence as some judges have sought to suggest. In Australia, where a similar conflict took place in the mid 1980s over changes to the parole system, one commentator described the argument that the proposals represented a breach of the principle of judicial independence as: 'both an appalling historical amnesia and a flagrant attack on parliamentary sovereignty' (Brown, 1986, p. 351). Much the same could be said of some of the

comments made by senior judges over the Crime (Sentencing) Act 1996.[34]
The claim that collective judicial independence provides the judiciary with
a mandate over sentencing policy, or any other policy aspect of the legal
system, is not sustainable: 'The principle of judicial independence is a
principle of impartiality in administering justice, not a principle which
demarcates a certain sphere of policy-making as the province of the courts'
(Ashworth, 1995, p. 44).

The tension over the respective spheres of the executive and
judiciary in the field of penal policy-making is equally apparent in the
realm of individual sentencing. The division which was commonly drawn
in the debates on recent sentencing legislation between the responsibilities
of the executive for policy-making and the judges for determining
individual sentences is not as clear-cut as it seems since the executive has
traditionally had an important role to play in the sentencing process. By
virtue of the Royal Prerogative of Mercy the Home Secretary has the
power to grant a full or conditional pardon or to order the remission of a
sentence. He may also alter the parole arrangements and order executive
release. It has never, to date, been seriously suggested that these powers
are unconstitutional and similar arrangements exist in many other
jurisdictions. The principles of judicial independence set out by the UN
Centre for the Independence of Judges and Lawyers specifically state that
the general rule that decisions of the courts should not be subject to
revision is without prejudice to the mitigation or commutation of sentences
by competent authorities (1990, p. 18).

One reason for this attitude may be that these prerogative powers
are, in practice, used sparingly and attract relatively little public attention.
But the same cannot be said for the Home Secretary's power to determine
the length of sentence served by life sentence prisoners. There are two
aspects to this power; the right to set the tariff period which must be served
to fulfil the requirement of deterrence and retribution and the decision to
determine whether or not to order release after the expiry of the tariff in the
light of the threat posed by the prisoner to public safety. This aspect of the
sentencing system is a particularly high profile one since life sentence
prisoners are often the subjects of intense public interest. As a result,
successive Home Secretaries have taken a direct and personal role in the
release decisions in high-profile cases. Traditionally, the judges have
accepted this incursion into their domain. However, in recent years the
courts, both domestic and European have begun to challenge the rights of
the executive to participate in this judicial function. In 1991, the European

Court of Human Rights held that the involvement of the Home Secretary in setting the tariff for discretionary life sentences was contrary to article 5 of the European Convention on Human Rights which requires that a detained person should be able to challenge the lawfulness of his or her continued detention in a judicial forum.[35] In response to the European Court's decision s. 34 Criminal Justice Act 1991 places the duty on the court to specify the period which should be served before the offender can be considered for release by the parole board. The Home Secretary retains a more limited role in approving any recommendation for release made by the board after the expiration of the tariff.

Restrictions have also been placed on the discretionary powers of the Home Secretary to set the tariff for children and young people sentenced to detention during Her Majesty's pleasure. In the case of *Venables and Thompson*, the two boys convicted in 1993 of the murder of two year old James Bulger, the decision of Michael Howard, then Home Secretary, to set the tariff at 15 years was overturned by the Divisional Court in 1996. The Court of Appeal upheld the High Court's decision that the Home Secretary had acted unlawfully in setting the tariff at 15 years after the trial judge had recommended a minimum of eight years and the Lord Chief Justice, ten years. Lord Woolf, giving judgment, explained that in setting the 15 year tariff the Home Secretary had deprived himself of the essential discretionary review power which was inherent in the sentence of detention at Her Majesty's pleasure.[36]

In July 1997, the House of Lords held that the Home Secretary could not reach a decision on the period to be served in relation to a mandatory life sentence which effectively increased the tariff period set previously.[37] The issue of increasing tariff in mandatory life sentences is currently under review in the case of Myra Hindley.[38] The Court of Appeal upheld the right of the Home Secretary to increase the tariff from a fixed period to that of her whole lifespan on the grounds that she had not been officially notified of the original tariff.[39] However, in reaching that decision Lord Bingham made clear his concerns about the more general question of whether the executive should be involved at all in the release dates of prisoners. The case has been granted leave to appeal to the House of Lords where that issue may well be addressed more fully.

Although none of these cases removes the Home Secretary's involvement in the determination of the release date of life prisoners, they curb the degree of discretion which he can exercise and reflect an increasing willingness on the part of the courts to fetter executive involvement in this area. This trend is mirrored in another area in which the Home Secretary has had a judicial role; his right to refer back alleged miscarriages of justice cases to the Court of Appeal. In the Criminal Appeal Act 1995 this power was handed to a new body, the Criminal Cases Review Commission. The removal of this power from the Home Secretary came about largely because of concerns that it was constitutionally inappropriate for the executive to be involved in such judicial decisions (Malleson, 1995).

These changes indicate that the courts have been prepared to strengthen judicial control in the field of sentencing and the penal system and draw a sharper demarcation between the functions of the executive and the judiciary in matters of justice. Some measure of tension between the two branches of government in this area is likely to remain. But the emerging consensus appears to be that it is for Parliament to legislate on matters of policy while the judges may legitimately seek to influence the proposals it puts forward from within Parliament or from outside. The determination of the outcome of individual cases should, in contrast, be primarily for the judiciary alone and where an external check on the sentencing and penal system is required this should be provided by non-governmental public bodies such as the Parole Board or the Criminal Cases Review Commission. These organisations give rise to separate constitutional problems in that they reduce direct accountability to Parliament, but being removed from day-to-day executive control they pose less of a danger of offending against the principle of judicial independence.

But despite such changes, the broad overlap between the functions of the judiciary, the executive and Parliament will continue so that a definition of judicial independence as a constitutional requirement based on the separation of powers cannot be sustained. Instead, the rationale behind the principle of judicial independence must be found in the more limited role of the judge as adjudicator.

Individual judicial independence

One reason why judges have argued the case for collective judicial independence is the concern that individual judicial independence fails fully to protect the judiciary from interference in its decision-making. Lord Oliver has argued, for example, that the definition of judicial independence as freedom from interference in a particular individual case would not cover the situation which arose in Germany in the 1930s when the Government instructed the judiciary as a whole not to decide disputes in favour of Jews or against party members.[40] This argument is persuasive only if the term 'individual' is taken as meaning limited to the decision in a *particular* case. A more plausible definition of individual independence would cover individual cases generally. The example given of the instruction to the judiciary in Germany in the 1930s would impinge on individual judicial independence so defined because it would be an interference in the way each judge decided the individual cases before him or her involving the proscribed parties, and so would affect each judge's impartiality.

It is the notion of impartiality which is the defining feature of judicial independence. If an action by the executive, Parliament or any other person or body constitutes a restriction on the impartiality of a judge or judges in hearing the cases before them, whether in the present or the future (as in Lord Oliver's example), it would constitute a breach of individual judicial independence. If this definition is adopted, then the concept of collective judicial independence only has relevance if it impinges, directly or indirectly, upon judicial impartiality in individual cases:

> It is the independence of the judge that we are concerned with. Strictures on the collectivity of the courts or the judicial institution are only relevant insofar as they act upon the judge in adjudication (Marshall, 1995, p. 18).

Where the judiciary is, as a body, institutionally independent it may be more likely that in determining individual cases the judges will be more impartial. But collective independence has no justification separate from its relationship to individual impartiality. This view of judicial independence as essentially bound to impartiality in individual cases was advanced by the 1990 White Paper on Crime, Sentencing and Protecting the Public which stressed that judicial independence demanded that no Government should try to influence a decision of the courts in individual cases.

Collective independence may help to promote this individual impartiality but it does not guarantee it. A judge operating in a judiciary which is institutionally independent may still demonstrate partiality when adjudicating in court. That is because the danger from interference is not limited to government. Judicial independence requires that judges are protected in their decision-making from interference by the state and '... *all other influences that may affect their impartiality*' (emphasis added).[41] A judge, like anyone else, is subject to influences from a wide range of sources - family and friends, the media, academic debate and the political discourse in its widest sense - any of which may undermine impartiality as effectively as governmental pressure.

A particularly important potential source of influence comes from other judges: 'The independence of the judiciary must connote not only independence form the executive but also that of one judge from another' (Lord Mackay, 1996). Lord Taylor when Lord Chief Justice objected to the introduction of performance appraisal on the grounds that it would: 'clearly endanger the fundamental independence of individual judges, not only from the executive *but also from each other*' (emphasis added).[42] In the Canadian case of *Bearegard* the court held that:

> Historically, the generally accepted core of the principle of judicial independence has been the complete liberty of individual judges to hear and decide the cases that come before them; no outsider - be it government, pressure groups, individual or even another judge - should interfere in fact, or attempt to interfere with the way in which a judge conducts his or her case and makes his or her decisions.[43]

The dangers of interference by the executive or other judges are linked since the improper exercise of control by senior judges over the junior ranks may provide a backdoor route to executive interference (Russell, 1996a).

Although there is a wide range of sources from which influence may flow, whether or not this amounts to a breach of judicial independence depends on the nature of the influence. Not all influences which affect judges in their decision-making can be termed improper so that a distinction must be drawn between proper influence and improper interference. The difference between the two is found in the distinction between issue and party impartiality (Russell, 1996). Judicial independence requires that judges are as impartial as is humanly possible as between the parties. It does not oblige judges to be impartial in relation to all issues which might be raised in court. Traditionally it has been suggested that judges should purge their minds: 'not only of partiality to persons, but of partiality to arguments'.[44] This unqualified view of partiality suggests that judges should come to court with no prior ordering of values or priorities. Not only is it, in practice, impossible to undertake such a purge, neither is it desirable. In relation to matters of justice and ethics there is a positive expectation that judges will be partial - for example, in favour of truth over dishonesty, equality over discrimination and fairness over unfairness. In contrast, judicial independence places judges under a duty to come to court with an open mind as to the strengths and weakness of the different parties' cases in relation to such issues. In differentiating between the two, the key question to ask is whether an influence may affect the party impartiality of a judge in his or her decision-making. If so, it is improper since all interference with party impartiality is a breach of judicial independence.

While some aspects of issue partiality may be positively desirable, as in the examples given above, others may be more questionable and deciding where the line should be drawn is difficult. It cannot be possible, or even desirable, for judges to be removed from all outside influences and judges come to the bench with personal views: 'if we are to have a judiciary with both intellectual depth and public awareness, we surely would not want it otherwise' (Russell, 1996, p. 156). The question is whether judges should attempt to distance themselves from their views as they relate to particular social practices. All judges will have particular opinions on such issues as labour relations, taxation, education, abortion, parenting and marriage which may influence them in favour of one or another argument in any particular dispute. Even assuming that it is humanly possible for an adjudicator to strip away these beliefs from his or her decision-making, there is clearly room for disagreement as to whether or not it is appropriate for the judges to be influenced by them. This is the boundary at which the limits of impartiality can be contested, in contrast with the sphere of party impartiality which can be proposed as an absolute requirement of the rule of law and the essence of judicial independence.

The central role of party impartiality is illustrated by the fact that it is articulated by each judge on taking office in the words of the judicial oath. He or she promises to decide every case without 'fear or favour, affection or ill-will'. In order to promote this form of impartiality attention must be paid to the structural and cultural pressures which bear on judges. To encourage party impartiality it is necessary to ensure as far as possible that judges should have: 'nothing to lose by doing what is right and little to gain by doing what is wrong'.[45] This neutral environment in terms of cost benefits is most difficult to achieve in cases which involve unpopular parties, and it is therefore in such hard cases that the principle of judicial independence is put to the test:

> Judicial independence is hardly needed to protect the interests of the powerful, the politically well-connected or the interests of the majority. Like free speech, its only value lies in protecting the unpopular, the disliked and the others outside the mainstream (Rylaarsdam, 1993, p. 1655).

In deciding such cases, pressure from government, the media, the general public, other judges, friends and family, and the judge's own prejudices are likely to be greatest. In an open democracy it is not possible or desirable to shield a judge from all public and private pressure but it is essential to ensure that these do not have a practical effect on a judge's party impartiality. One retired US Supreme Court judge, when asked what effect he believed political criticism would have on the decisions of the courts replied: 'it is difficult to ignore a crocodile in your bathtub when you are shaving'.[46] However, it is the fear of being bitten rather than the presence of the proverbial crocodile which undermines judicial independence. Judges can only be expected to withstand the inevitable approval or disapproval which may be expressed about their decisions if they can be sure that no consequences, either good or bad, will flow for them personally as a result of making them.

Whether or not this protection exists depends not on the constitutional arrangements between the branches of state but the practical conditions of judicial service. It is quite possible to have a system with a limited collective judicial independence, as in England and Wales, and yet still demonstrate high levels of individual independence because those conditions do not allow for the erosion of party impartiality. The way in which judges are appointed, promoted, paid, disciplined and dismissed all provide the potential means for punishing or rewarding judges for their decisions. In all these areas the executive and/or Parliament currently play a role, to a greater or lesser extent. In addition, in some of these areas the senior judges also contribute and so provide, potentially, a route to the erosion of individual independence by other judges. But whether or not a threat exists in practice depends on whether or not there is a relationship between these processes and the judges' decision-making.

A good example of this distinction is found in the arrangements for setting and paying judicial salaries. Constitutionally, the judiciary is wholly dependent on the executive for its income and since the 1970s the executive has had the right to set judicial salary levels without recourse to Parliament (Stevens, 1993, p. 12). Just as the government must decide on the allocation of funding for court administration, so it must determine the salary levels of the judges. However, because this area provides an obvious route for influencing judicial decision-making, arrangements have been devised which are intended to minimise that risk. Salaries are paid out of the Consolidated Fund while the rates of pay are recommended by a body independent of government, the Top Salaries Review Body. This system does not guarantee the pay levels recommended, indeed in 1992 John Major rejected the proposed judicial pay rises, but it does provide a buffer between the Government and the judiciary which mitigates the danger of judicial salary levels being manipulated by the executive as a means of ensuring a compliant bench. But despite these safeguards, the constitutional settlement allows the executive, ultimately, to control the judges through their pockets. In practice, however, there does not appear to have been any serious suggestion that the government has sought to influence the judges either collectively or individually in this way. Although the judiciary and the government have periodically come into conflict over the appropriate salary levels, attempts to keep down pay rises have been driven by the same cost-saving urge which affects all those in the public sector rather than any more sinister motivation.

This conclusion as regards salaries is equally true for the other areas in which there is scope for controlling the judges. Most commentators both on and off the bench would agree that under the current arrangements in England and Wales the relationship between the conditions of judicial service and their decision-making is weak. The notable absence of allegations of bribery and corruption amongst the judiciary compared with other professional groups suggests that judges feel that they have little to gain and much to lose by selling their decision-making. Security of tenure and income combined with a generally high level of respect for judicial independence in English political life has eliminated such crude forms of interference. Lord Mackay, when Lord Chancellor, commented in debate in the House of Lords:

> I certainly do not know of anyone who has successfully attempted - or indeed has attempted without success - to influence the decision of the judges in the cases committed to them.[47]

Similarly, in 1988 Sir Nicolas Browne-Wilkinson commented that no one had ever sought to apply pressure to him to decide a case in a particular way and nor had he heard of any other judge coming under such pressure (Browne-Wilkinson 1988 p. 44). The absence of any evidence to the contrary would seem to support this claim. However, the absence of blatant attempts to undermine judicial party impartiality does not necessarily rule out more subtle forms of manipulation:

> Influence may however take a more insidious form than direct pressure on the judges; attempts to manipulate the listing of cases; political statements of the law which set the agenda for public debate and legal argument in politically convenient terms; the exposition of government policy in terms which suggest that there is no realistic alternative (Oliver 1986, p. 238).

Dawn Oliver suggested that such tactics were effectively used during the miners' strike in 1984-5 to exert improper influence on the judiciary. The difficulty with such allegations is that by the very nature of their subtlety they are hard to substantiate. Similar problems arise in assessing whether or not the internal threat to judicial independence from other judges materialises in practice. If such interference does take place it is unlikely to occur in a crude form, such as punishing or rewarding a judge for a decision through recommending or withholding support for promotion, but rather through more subtle cultural pressures. The norms and values of any occupational group can have a strong influence on its members. This is particularly true of the judiciary which has traditionally operated as a relatively closed order. While this approach has served to protect the judges against improper external influences it has, paradoxically, exposed them to a greater risk of the internal erosion of judicial independence.

Such pressure need not involve the expression of overt prejudice against a particular party in a case, but it is possible to imagine the effects of generalised disapproval by fellow judges of an unpopular cause which is supported by a party to an action, or criticism of the actions of a group of which he or she is a member. The effect of such pressures is not easy to define and in many cases they may fall into that grey area between acceptable influence and improper interference. Moreover, even if judges did feel improperly pressurised by such influences, few would be prepared to object publicly to the behaviour of their brethren. Like any other whistle-blowers, the fear of being blacklisted by colleagues for exposing the institution to criticism may be a very powerful restraint.[48] Since detection is so difficult, preventing such subtle internal interference is not easy. The introduction of great accountability, in particular soft mechanisms of openness and representativeness may mitigate the problem. By promoting greater interaction between the judges and the wider community and the creation of a judiciary with a more representative make-up, it is possible to discourage the expression of inward-looking prejudices which can flourish in a closed institution. Increasing accountability by opening the judiciary to more outside scrutiny increases the opportunity for exposing such internal interference where it does occur. Thus, far from undermining judicial independence, this example demonstrates the potential of increasing accountability to strengthen it by tackling some of those factors which undermine party impartiality.

The relationship between independence and accountability

Thus far I have argued that claims to collective judicial independence are generally weak since constitutional separation is neither a necessary nor sufficient condition for protecting party impartiality in individual cases. The key to promoting this goal is the maintenance of conditions of service for judges which minimise the danger that their decision-making will give rise to consequences for them personally as a result of improper interference from either internal and external sources. The advantage of this qualified definition of judicial independence is that it allows judicial accountability to play a stronger role. Until relatively recently it was not generally questioned that independence should be the defining and dominant feature of the judiciary, in order to ensure that the judges were 'institutionally insulated' from outside interference (Rozenberg, 1992, p. 370).

One reason for the general acceptance of such an unqualified definition of judicial independence has been the 'brooding omnipresence' of the principle, which hovers over the judiciary, inhibiting intelligent questioning and promoting a 'say no more' effect (Stevens, 1993a, p. 5; Brown, 1986, p. 354). The authoritative and powerful role of the principle in the legal culture has resulted in it being often used in support of arguments against change since few would argue against it, anymore than one would argue in favour of injustice (Ashworth, 1995, p. 44). This 'trumping' value therefore makes it a forceful card for judges to play when opposing any innovation in the judiciary. Like any other powerful elite, the judiciary has its own vested interests to protect which might be threatened by the introduction of greater accountability. English judges may be known for their lack of corruption and high intellectual standards but their collective motives and needs are not significantly different from any other occupational group. Because the principle of judicial independence can shield judges from critical scrutiny and responsibility for poor performance it can serve as a protective cloak. Anthony Holland and Robert Stevens have argued that the definition of judicial independence relied upon by the judiciary is often used for self-serving purposes. An example being the judges' opposition on the grounds of judicial independence to the provisions of the Courts and Legal Services Act 1990 extending rights of audience in the courts:

> To seek, radically, to change that which the profession could not, or would not, for the benefit of the ordinary citizen has nothing whatsoever to do with judicial independence, however defined. To suggest otherwise is, we suspect more to do with the protection of vested interests than serious analysis (1997, p. 700).

It is notable in the discourse on judicial independence that it is usually described as a principle required to protect the judiciary from oppressive action by the executive and others. This is something of a distortion of its original meaning. According to Montesquieu, the need to ensure separation of the judicial authority from the executive authority arose because: 'if the [judicial] power were combined with the executive power, the judge would be able to act as an oppressor' (Montesquieu, 1961, XI, VI). The notion that judicial independence exists to protect the public against oppression from judges is not a perspective which is often stressed by the judiciary.

None of this, however, undermines the essential importance of judicial independence. Claims that it has been used to serve the interest of judges can be accepted whilst also acknowledging that the principle is a fundamental requirement of a just legal system and a unique and important feature which differentiates the judiciary from other political institutions (Russell, 1987). Like many important principles, judicial independence can be adapted to a variety of purposes:

The constitutional guarantee of independence stands guardian not only of the fearless judges but also of the judge who cannot or will not properly discharge the functions of his office.[49]

The application of an unqualified definition of the principle has been instrumental in allowed it to be misused in this way. The redefinition proposed here seeks to preserve the principle for protecting the fearless judge (and perhaps even more so, the genuinely fearful) while removing the insulation of the judiciary from the necessary and legitimate demands of accountability to which those in public service are subjected. Paradoxically, the judges have been at the forefront of the process of increasing accountability in public life through the expansion of the scope of judicial review. Yet the judiciary itself is one of the last institutions to feel the impact of this change as a result of the limiting influence of the principle of judicial independence. While the judiciary fulfilled a relatively passive role in policy-making and a limited role in the lives of individuals the relative restrictions on accountability and the wide scope of judicial independence could be justified. The emergence of pressures for greater accountability described above has created a tension between the two principles which requires a reconsideration of the relationship between them.

It is often said that judges find themselves increasingly torn between the need to preserve judicial independence and to provide accountability to the community (Armytage, 1996, p. 11). The latter is sometimes described as the price which the judiciary must pay if it wishes to continue to enjoy independence (McKillop, 1997, p. 133). A common response to the problem is to suggest that the divergent requirements of the two principles must be reconciled in a way which provides an acceptable balance between their conflicting demands (Lord Hailsham, 1979; Gleeson, 1997, p. xi; Mason, 1997 p. 2). Thus independence and accountability are seen as two competing qualities which are traded-off in a search for the correct balance. However, if the more qualified definition of judicial independence is adopted of freedom from improper interference which would undermine party impartiality, then the two concepts are not necessarily in conflict. There is no reason why the mechanisms of hard and soft accountability described above should necessarily affect party impartiality. They are only inherently in conflict if judicial independence is defined very widely as an institutional freedom from interference, whether or not related to the question of impartiality in decision-making in court.

If it is accepted that judicial independence can be redefined as an individual requirement then the concepts of independence and accountability are not incompatible. Further than this, it can be argued that accountability actually reinforces independence; the link between the two being public confidence which is the bedrock upon which judicial independence rests (Goldfinch, 1992, p. 12). Alexander Hamilton recognised in the 18th century that judges have no physical force or financial means to enforce their will and are thus dependent on public support for their legitimacy (Hamilton, 1788 p. 437). This is no less true today. Judges are well aware of the fact that if either of the other branches of the state decided to disregard the decisions of the judiciary they would become paper tigers (Mahomed CJ, 1997). The ultimate protection which the judges have against this event is public regard which is itself based largely on the extent to which the judiciary is seen to be independent. (Marshall, 1995, p. 18).

There is some evidence that public confidence in the independence of the judiciary from the executive has fallen. Gallup polls carried out in 1969 and 1985 showed an increase in the proportion of people who thought that the judiciary was influenced by the government from 19 per cent to 43 per cent (Oliver, 1986, p. 237). This development, if indicative of a continuing trend, has worrying implications for judicial independence since loss of public confidence in its freedom from government may leave the judiciary more exposed to threats to its independence because there is less to lose by being seen to attack the judges. The media, the executive and Parliament will tread less warily in crossing the grey line between proper influence and improper interference in judicial decision-making where there is less of a price to be paid in terms of public disapproval.

Accountability has an increasingly important role to play in this process by providing a tool for the judges to increase public confidence. Public support rests on legitimacy and increasingly in liberal democracies legitimacy is dependent on the demonstration of accountability, in particular, soft accountability. The current drop in public confidence in the judiciary is not restricted to concerns about the extent of government influence on the judges but is strongly linked to a perception of the judiciary as unresponsive, unrepresentative and 'out of touch' in a way which renders it socially unaccountable. By increasing accountability the judiciary has a means of countering these complaints and so restoring a degree of public confidence which is essential for the maintenance of its independence.

The argument that accountability can serve to reinforce judicial independence has begun to emerge in debates on the judiciaries around the world and the proposition that judicial independence requires that the judicial branch is accountable for its competency is now accepted as beyond doubt (Nicholson, 1993). As this approach gains ground the pressure for increased judicial accountability will become stronger and new mechanisms of accountability will develop. In order to assess whether or not these developments represent a breach of judicial independence the key question which must be asked is what effect the changes have on party impartiality. If it is directly or indirectly weakened, whether in a particular case or future cases in general, the changes would amount to a breach of judicial independence. If, on the other hand, the effects of increased mechanisms of accountability were limited to the way in which the judicial process operates and the general approach of the judges to their work there would be no objection to their introduction. If, for example new mechanisms of accountability sought to promote more openness, efficiency, competence and responsiveness in the judiciary, either collectively or individually, then such developments would be entirely compatible with the demands of judicial independence.

Summary

Because judicial independence can be used to protect the vested interests of the judges, it is easy to regard sceptically the claims which the judiciary make for it as the bedrock of the rule of law. This is particularly true in a society which is relatively politically stable. While the work of the judges is generally routine or uncontroversial and there is a high level of political consensus between the branches of government, judicial independence can appear to be little more than a troublesome smokescreen for shielding the judges from democratic scrutiny. But judicial independence is itself an essential feature of a modern liberal democracy. As long as the judiciary may reach judgments which are unpopular with individuals, the public, the media, pressure groups, the legislature or the executive, the danger of improper interference in its decision-making will be present. Moreover, as the role of the judiciary expands in the field of human rights the scope for reaching controversial social or political judgments which incur the disapproval of one group or another will increase significantly.

To know that judges can be trusted to decide cases impartially as between the parties, whoever they might be, is an essential requirement of a just legal system. But as the judiciary grows more powerful the application of an unqualified independence which does not sufficiently recognise the claims of accountability can itself undermine democracy (Russell, 1996a). The change of approach which is necessary in order to acknowledge these claims can only be achieved if the traditional understanding of the scope of judicial independence is challenged. Its broad definition as a constitutional imperative based on the separation between the branches of the state must be replaced by a more limited interpretation which regards the concept as a means to the end of ensuring party impartiality in individual cases.

The effect of redefining judicial independence as a qualified principle is to challenge the notion that independence and accountability are irreconcilable, or even necessarily in tension. A narrower definition recognises that some forms of influence are acceptable and even desirable, The essential distinction is between proper influence and improper interference. The latter may come from a wide range of different sources, both internal and external to the judiciary; it may take the form of crude oppression or subtle cultural pressure. But the feature which is common to all improper interference is that, in contrast to proper influences, it threatens party impartiality in individual cases.

The areas of training, appointments and scrutiny reviewed below are those where mechanisms of accountability are emerging which expose the judiciary to many different types of scrutiny from a wide range of sources. In each area these developments must be assessed in terms of the direct or indirect effect which they have on party impartiality in order to distinguish a proper influence from an improper interference. The cloak of judicial independence can no longer be spread so widely as to inhibit the development of legitimate mechanisms of accountability. There are many aspects of judicial performance which can be promoted through increasing accountability without undermining party impartiality. Some are collective, such as the need for the judiciary as a body to be open, responsive, representative and efficient. Others are individual, such as the requirement that each judge should serve the public with fairness, courtesy, speed, competence and sensitivity. Mechanisms of accountability, whether hard or soft, which seek to promote these qualities are an essential means for the new judiciary to demonstrate its democratic legitimacy and the key to retaining and strengthening public confidence and so reinforcing judicial independence.

Notes

[1] In the criminal appeal process these categories are generally limited to errors of the judge on questions of law and procedural error which are reviewable from the trial transcript. Complaints about other aspects of the judge's performance such as rudeness, inattentiveness and other non-verbal inappropriate behaviour which may have affected the trial are rarely reviewed (Malleson, 1991).

[2] In 1998, the Committee came into conflict with the judiciary over its demands that the United Grand lodge, the freemasons' governing body, should provide names of sitting judges who were freemasons. The Council of Judges objected to the initiative on the grounds that it represented a breach of the judges' freedom of privacy and association but ultimately conceded its permission for the names to be revealed (see *The Guardian,* 20 March 1998).

[3] See *The Lawyer,* 'Commons Committee Slams Legal Aid Test', 25 February 1997.

[4] The main examples being the International Bar Association Code of Minimum Standards of Judicial Independence developed in Lisbon and Jerusalem and confirmed in New Delhi in 1982; The UN Basic Principles on the Independence of the Judiciary adopted at the Seventh United Nations Congress on the Prevention of Crime and the Treatment of Offenders in 1985; the Universal Declaration on the Independence of Justice adopted at Montreal in 1983: the Syracuse Principles adopted by the International Commission of Jurists; The Tokyo Principles adopted by LAWASIA (the Law Association for Asia and the Western Pacific).

[5] *Valente No. 2* (1983) 2 C.C.C. (3d) 417. Quoted in Friedland, 1995, p. 8.

[6] For a fuller discussion of the distinction between these roles see Stevens, 1993.

[7] Hansard, HL.. 5 June 1996 col. 1254.

[8] For a fuller discussion of this problem see Munro, 1992.

[9] Lord Steyn has recently argued that, for this reason, the head of the judiciary should be the Lord Chief Justice (1997, p. 91).

[10] See, for example, Shetreet, 1985, p. 590; Lord Irvine, Hansard, HL.. 5 June 1996 col. 1254.

[11] A similar provision is included in the UN declaration as to the principles of judicial independence (see Centre for the Independence of Judges and Lawyers, 1990, p. 18).

[12] Article 2.4 - 2.43.

[13] Shetreet, 1985, p. 608.

[14] Quoted in Lord Bingham, 1996, p. 4.

[15] *The Times,* 14 September 1984.

[16] See Stevens, 1993.

[17] See the comments of Lord Ackner on the case, *The Guardian,* 12 November 1996.

[18] Hansard, HL.. 7 April 1989 col. 1331

[19] This claim was supported by Lord Bingham in 1996 (Lord Bingham, 1996, p. 12).

[20] *The Guardian,* 12 November 1996.

[21] *R v. Lord Chancellor ex p Witham* (1997) *The Times,* 13 March 1997.

[22] See *Legal Action,* May 1997, p. 25.

[23] Paper delivered to the 11th Commonwealth Law Conference, Vancouver, August 1996. Quoted in Lord Bingham 1996, p. 4.

[24] Quoted in Lord Bingham, 1996, p. 4.

[25] *Valente No. 2* (1983) 2 C.C.C. (3d) 709.

[26] As Munro points out, there was very little sentencing discretion to be exercised before the abolition of minimum sentences in the nineteenth century (Munro, 1992).

[27] Quoted in Munro, 1992, p. 28.

[28] Although Lord Hailsham claimed in 1989 that the formulation of sentencing policy was properly a matter for the judiciary. As Andrew Ashworth rightly suggests, this notion does not bear scrutiny since it would follow that Parliamentary changes to sentencing would be unconstitutional (Ashworth, 1995, p. 42).

[29] For a full review of the conflict over the proposals see Rozenberg, 1997, pp. 51-68.

[30] Hansard, HL.. 5 June 1996 col. 1256.

[31] See the comments of Lord Ackner, Hansard, HL.. 24 October 1996 col. 38.

[32] *The Guardian,* 11 December 1995.

[33] *The Guardian,* 12 November 1996.

[34] An interesting question arises as to whether the incorporation of the European Convention on Human Rights will provide a means for the judges to challenge legislation which restricts their sentencing discretion. In Canada similar provisions to those of the 1996 Crime (Sentencing) Act which imposed minimum seven year sentences for importing narcotics were struck down by the Supreme Court as being in breach of the convention on the basis that that sentence was too high when imposed on all offenders. *Smith* (1987) 34 C.C.C. (3d) 97, [1987] 1 S.C.R. 1045.

[35] *Thynne, Wilson and Gunnell v. United Kingdom* (1991) 13 E.H.R.R. 666.

[36] For a full review of the politics of the case, see Rozenberg, 1997, pp. 103 - 109.

[37] *R v. Secretary of State for the Home Department, ex parte Pierson, The Times,* 25 July 1997. The Home Secretary was proposing to uphold a 20 year tariff after acknowledging that the basis on which it was set was incorrect in that it had wrongly been assessed as a double premeditated murder rather than a single incident which was unpremeditated. The Court held that this amounted to an increase in the length of the tariff.

[38] Myra Hindley was sentenced to life imprisonment in 1966 and the trial judge recommended a tariff of 25 years. This was increased to 30 years in 1985 by Leon Brittan, then Home Secretary. She was twice recommended for release by the parole board and both times the recommendations were rejected by the Home Secretary. In 1990 David Waddington, then Home Secretary, determined that a life sentence should mean her natural lifespan and this decision was confirmed by Michael Howard when Home Secretary.

[39] *R v. Secretary of State for the Home Department ex parte Hindley* [1998] 2 WLR at 505.

[40] Hansard, HL.. 27 April 1994 col. 779.

[41] The Right Hon Sir Ninian Stephen, quoted in Goldfinch, 1993, p. 155.

[42] From a speech at the London School of Economics, 27 July 1993.

[43] Quoted in Marshall, 1995, pp. 29-30.

[44] Lord Macmillan, quoted in Wilson, 1992, p. 94.

[45] R. MacGregor Dawson quoted in Friedland, 1995, p. 1.

[46] Quoted in Rylaardsdam, 1993, pp. 1655-1666.

[47] Hansard, HL. 5 June 1996 col 1308.

[48] Recent research by David O'Brien and Yasuo Ohkoshi into the Japanese judiciary and by Todd Foglesong into the Russian judiciary has demonstrated the presence of this form of internal interference where there is no overt and direct threat to judicial independence through external interference (see Russell, 1996a).

[49] Mr Justice Kirkby, quoted in Brown, 1996, p. 354.

4 Appointments

Of the three areas examined in this work it is the appointments process which has been subject to the greatest pressure for change as a result of the effects of expansion and the growth of judicial activism. The increase in the numbers of judges has meant that the informal appointments system which could operate when the judiciary was a small institution in which the Lord Chancellor knew personally or by reputation every appointee has become unworkable. By necessity, it has had to be replaced by a more professional and structured process. At the same time, the growth in judicial power has drawn public attention to the political importance of the appointments process. As the functions of the judiciary have moved closer to those of the other branches of government claims that there should be more similarity in their selection methods have grown stronger (Bell, 1983, p. 269). Recent constitutional reforms designed to increase the representativeness of the political process, such as Scottish and Welsh devolution and restructuring of the House of Lords, have further highlighted the undemocratic nature of the judicial appointments process. The incorporation of the European Convention on Human Rights adds a new dimension to this process. The expectation that judges will shortly be called upon to decide on a range of social and political questions previously outside their remit has turned people's attention to the question of who judges are and how they are appointed. In 1997, when Lord Irvine gave evidence before the Home Affairs Select Committee on the work of his department, he stated that there was no work to which he devoted more attention than the 'vexed question' of judicial appointments.[1]

In the light of these developments, the need to increase openness and accountability in the appointments process, whilst at the same time maintaining a high degree of judicial independence has been the driving forces behind a number of recent changes to the system. The experience of many other common law countries including the US, Canada, South Africa, New Zealand and Australia as well as the civil law jurisdictions in continental Europe, suggests that as the power of the judges grows the pressure for structural change to the appointments process increases (East, 1995). In addition, the growing policy-making role of the judiciary raises questions about the selection criteria which should be applied in order to identify judicial candidates who are fitted for their new and more diverse roles. When the Home Affairs Select Committee examined the judicial appointments process in 1996 it acknowledged this need: 'The kind of judges that are chosen in future will have to reflect the new role which society expects the judicial system to play'.[2] This chapter examines the changes which have taken place, and those which are likely to be introduced in the judicial appointments process as a result of these pressures.

The characteristics of the current appointments process

It is commonly said that England does not have a career judiciary. Traditionally the English bench has been distinguished from the judiciaries in other European jurisdictions because judges are chosen from barristers in practice rather than being specially trained for the bench. The origin of new appointees is not, however, the only feature of a career judiciary; the other important aspect being the system of promotion. The judiciary has prided itself on its freedom from a career ladder whereby a judge might be influenced in his or her decisions through the prospects of promotion. Lord Denning claimed that: 'Once a man becomes a judge, he has nothing to gain from further promotion and does not seek it' (Lord Denning, 1955, p. 17). If this was ever the case, it is no longer so. By the 1970s, the principle of non-promotion had been undermined by the introduction of part-time judges and the possibility of appointment from the circuit bench to the High Court (Stevens, 1993, p. 169). In the last twenty five years this process has accelerated. Much of the judicial work in the criminal courts is currently carried out by part-time Recorders and Assistant Recorders many of whom are seeking promotion to the full-time bench. The Home Affairs Select Committee report on the judicial appointments process in 1996 concluded that the English bench was already a career judiciary in the sense that there was a clear career path moving through successively higher ranks of court.[3] This view was shared by JUSTICE in its 1992 review of the judiciary:

The Assistant Recorder is clearly a training role for the Recordership, and promotion is based on reputed performance. District judges hope to become Circuit Judges and many Recorders are interested in becoming either Circuit Judges or High Court Judges. Circuit Judges are increasingly encouraged to think of the High Court as a goal (JUSTICE, 1992, p. 20).

Lord Mackay, when Lord Chancellor, commended this system as a means of testing the quality of potential appointees: 'I personally believe that this is an excellent method of selection since there is no better way of judging a person's qualification for a job than seeing how he or she performs in it' (Lord Mackay, 1994, p. 4). One consequence of this heavy use of part-time judges and the system of promotions from the part-time to the full-time bench, is that the scale of the appointments process is much larger than many other common law countries.

Yet despite this increasingly structured system of promotions the English appointments process has typically been characterised by its informality and lack of codification (Armytage, 1996). Until relatively recently very little was known about the process outside the Lord Chancellor's Department. Up until the late 1970s the Lord Chancellor was personally involved in selecting most of the judges. Lord Gardiner claimed to have interviewed applicants for the post of County Court judge (Shetreet, 1976, p. 397). This level of participation was possible because of the small size of the bench and bar. In 1970, there were 2,400 practising barristers and less than 300 judges, all selected from amongst senior members of the bar. By the mid 1970s, although the numbers of appointments had risen, there were still no more than 50 appointments made each year of both full-time and part-time posts (Shetreet, 1976, p. 396). The appointment process could operate on an informal basis because the pool of candidates for judicial office was small enough for the eligible candidates to be known personally:

The Lord Chancellor and members of his department and the judges would nearly all know a good deal about every member of the bar whose practice is big enough to justify his being considered for appointment to the bench (Henry, 1970, p. 13).

In 1973, Sir Robert Megarry, a High Court judge, explained that the emphasis on specialisation in the senior ranks of the judiciary and the bar reduced the pool of eligible candidates for any particular post to a handful. He suggested that if a vacancy arose on the Chancery bench there would be no more than three or four QCs of the right age bracket and experience who would be considered (Megarry, 1973, p. 102). The consequence of this small and personalised process was that there was little need for a formalised system. In 1976 Lord Justice Scarman (as he then was) wrote that: 'In the English practice of judicial appointment there is no systematised plan'.[4]

While it is still the case that the upper ranks of the judiciary remain relatively small and are drawn from a restricted pool of candidates, the same can no longer be said of the great majority of the judiciary. In 1978, the average number of new appointments made each year was between 60 and 80.[5] By 1997 this had increased to approximately 600 per year from over 60,000 barristers and solicitors.[6] The appointment of this number of judges from such a large pool of candidates has meant that the Lord Chancellor's Department has, by necessity, had to formalise and professionalise the appointments process. The early origins of this change can be traced back to the 1970s. The increase in the numbers of lower rank judges appointed after the creation of the Crown Court in the Courts Act 1971 meant that the role of the Permanent Secretary and his staff in selecting appropriate candidates increased significantly, with the Lord Chancellor generally only becoming involved at the latter stages of the process (Shetreet, 1976, p. 53). By the 1980s and 1990s, this pattern was firmly established and a number of further significant changes were introduced to handle the increased workload.

A particularly important development was the introduction of a system of interview panels. Each panel consists of a judge, a member of the Lord Chancellor's Department and a lay person appointed from the Advisory Committees of the Justices of the Peace by the Lord Chancellor's Department. Since 1994, all those appointed to the posts of District judge, Assistant Recorder, Recorder and Circuit judge have attended a formal interview before a panel. The views of the panel are relayed to the Lord Chancellor's Department to be taken into account in the selection decision in conjunction with other information gathered about the candidate through the consultation process. In 1997, the role of the interview panel was expanded to include the task of sifting initial applications for suitability. The panel is now sent a summary of the views expressed by members of the bar and bench about each candidate in order to assist them in screening the applications. In addition, in 1997 the number of lay people involved in the process was increased from 22 to 50, each undertaking approximately

15 days of interviewing per year. The role of the interview panels, both in terms of their workloads and the substantive role they play in selecting candidates, is therefore now very significant.

Other reforms introduced in the 1980s and 1990s include the public advertising of posts up to the rank of High Court judge, the use of annual competitions for the posts of Assistant Recorder and Recorder and the production of job descriptions for each judicial rank. These changes, which were initiated by Lord Mackay and continued by Lord Irvine, were partly a response to the practical demands of the increasing numbers of judges but they were also an attempt to address the growing criticisms of the process in the light of the expansion of judicial power. In particular, concern about the lack of openness and accountability and the potential threat posed to judicial independence by the involvement of the executive in the appointments process.

Judicial independence

The Lord Chief Justice, Lord Bingham, argued in 1996 that impartiality was the goal of the appointments process:

> The key to the successful making of appointments must, I would suggest, lie in an assumption shared by appointor, appointee and the public at large that those appointed should be capable of discharging their judicial duties, so far as humanly possible, with impartiality (Lord Bingham, 1996, p. 5).

According to Lord Bingham, the principle of impartiality, though not synonymous with independence, was its 'close blood tie' and therefore lay at the heart of a good appointments process. The Home Affairs Select Committee report on judicial appointments similarly claimed that the most important practical application of the principle of judicial independence is that members of the judiciary should not owe their office to a member of the executive.[7] If so, one would expect that the executive would play no part in selecting judges. Yet executive appointment is the commonest form of judicial selection method world-wide. Even in the US where the constitutional separation of the functions of the legislature, executive and judiciary is relatively strict, the federal judiciary is appointed by the President and the state judges are commonly appointed by the Governor. In England and Wales although constitutionally the responsibility for appointing senior judges is that of the Queen, the process is effectively in the hands of the Lord Chancellor. In the case of the Lords Justices and above the Prime Minister is responsible for making recommendations to the Queen on the advice of the Lord Chancellor. The constitutional justification usually proposed for the present arrangement is that although the Lord Chancellor is a member of the executive, it is in his capacity as head of the judiciary that he appoints the judges. Because decisions on appointment are not taken by the cabinet it can be said that they are kept under the direct control of the Lord Chancellor, thus ensuring that judicial independence is preserved.

Nevertheless, the current arrangement has frequently attracted criticism as incompatible with the demands of judicial independence. In particular, the promotions system has been identified as a source of weakness because the future employment of part-time appointments is dependent on the executive. The Montreal Declaration on the independence of the judiciary states that probationary appointments are inconsistent with the principles of judicial independence and should be phased out. Although the system in England and Wales may comply with the letter of this provision, the spirit is undoubtedly broken by the current use of part-time appointments as a testing ground for full-time appointments and it was for this reason that the Beeching Royal Commission Report on Assizes and Quarter Sessions in 1969 recommended a reduction in the use of part-time judges.[8] However, Lord Bingham claimed in 1996 that these dangers were was not a problem in practice:

> If any judge were to trim or tailor his judicial decision in order to ingratiate himself with, or avoid offending, any member of the executive who he thought would be influential in deciding on his future promotion...I would regard such conduct as a flagrant violation of judicial duty (1996, p. 7).

Lord Nolan has gone further and claimed that the reward for judges who reach decisions which thwart the interests of the Government is promotion:

> In some countries, less happy than ours, it may need great courage for a judge to decide a case against the government. In this marvellous country, all that happens if you decide a case against the government is that you get rather a good press and very possibly promoted (1997, p. 75).

A recent example which would seem to support this argument is that of Sir Brian Smedly who was trial judge in the Matrix Churchill case in 1992 which collapsed after he rejected the Government's claim to withhold material from the defence on the grounds of Public Interest Immunity. As a result of the evidence which emerged about official policy relating to the sale of arms to Iraq, the Scott inquiry was set up which lead to the criticism of ministerial decision-making. Despite this record, Sir Brian was appointed to the High Court from the Circuit bench, a move still relatively unusual. These individual cases do not, however, prove that there are not some judges who have been passed over as a result of unpopular views, but they do suggest that in recent years rulings against the government do not preclude advancement. The era of Lord Mackay was certainly widely regarded as one in which partisan politics played no discernible role in the appointments process. The promotions which he made as Lord Chancellor were generally regarded as extremely good ones. Although Lord Mackay was a member of a Conservative Government, a number of notably liberal promotions were made during his period. Nevertheless, the danger with the current system lies precisely in the exclusive authority given to one individual. Lord Mackay may have been a scrupulously unpartisan Lord Chancellor who appointed strictly on the basis of competence, but a future Lord Chancellor without his credentials could very easily manipulate the appointments system to his or her partisan political ends.

The argument that the separation of judicial and executive power can be effected by one person donning different hats to fulfil different constitutional functions is not, on the face of it, very convincing. Because this method of separation appears to be so vulnerable to abuse, the involvement of the Lord Chancellor in the appointments process has been the subject of some scrutiny. The Home Affairs Select Committee considered this issue in some detail in 1996 and a number of the witnesses called by the Committee criticised this aspect of the system, though very few of these critics suggested that, in practice, judicial independence was under threat. In general, the evidence received by the Committee expressed widespread praise for the quality of appointments in recent years. Lord Taylor, then Lord Chief Justice, in his evidence, summarised a common view of the role of the Lord Chancellor and the appointments process: 'Like a number of English institutions they may defy common sense but somehow they work'.[9] He pointed to the recent history of appointments as justifying his claim that the Lord Chancellor was not in any way influenced by political considerations:

> It would be invidious to mention names but when you look at some of the judges who have been appointed in the very last few years you can see that there have been those appointed who clearly could not be described as being of the same political colour as the Executive in power at the moment.[10]

The consensus which emerged from the Committee's deliberations was that the present system was exposed to the theoretical danger that a future Lord Chancellor who was politically motivated might undermine judicial independence but that this was, in practice, very unlikely to happen.

However, in relation to the appointment of Lords Justices and Law Lords the Committee recognised that the position was somewhat different in that the responsibility for recommending appointments to the Queen rests with the Prime Minister. This recommendation is made in consultation with the Lord Chancellor and it is now widely accepted to be the case that the Lord Chancellor's advice is not generally disregarded. However, this has not always been so and the Committee heard that Margaret Thatcher, when Prime Minister, did not necessarily accept the preferred candidate of her Lord Chancellor. Lord Mackay's characteristically diplomatic evidence to the Committee suggested that these rumours were correct:

> *Chairman*: I think you answered, just to confirm to Peter Butler, that all your recommendations [to the Prime Minister] had been accepted?
> *Lord Mackay*: I was careful not to say that. What I did say was that I make these recommendations in confidence to the Prime Minister. I have never been disappointed by any recommendation that the Prime Minister has made to Her Majesty during my time - neither surprised nor disappointed.[11]

On the basis of such evidence the Committee concluded that it was left with 'some qualms' about the role of the Prime Minister in the appointments process and questioned whether he or she should continue to play a part in the system.[12] This question is likely to become more critical as the political role of the senior judges grows. Because the restraint of the Prime Minister in judicial appointment is no more than a convention, and moreover one which is relatively new, it is fluid enough to allow for a future Prime Minister to take a significantly more active role in the process. The precedent of Margaret Thatcher suggests that there is considerable room for executive influence in the appointment of senior judges and it is hard to imagine how future Prime Ministers, faced with the selection of key policy-makers in the Court of Appeal and the House of Lords will be disinterested in the political persuasions of their appointees.

The role of the executive in the appointments process reinforces the arguments that the principle of judicial independence in a collective constitutional sense only applies, in practice, to a very limited extent. The judiciary is constitutionally dependent on the government for its appointments so that all judges can be said to owe their office to a member of the executive. Whether or not this arrangement runs the risk of undermining the impartiality which Lord Bingham rightly identified as the essence of successful appointments depends more on the general relationship between the executive and the judges. Impartiality in judicial decision-making will only be under threat if judges feel under pressure to promote the interests of those who appointed them. There is no evidence that, at present, the absence of constitutional independence in the appointments process impacts in any crude sense upon the decision-making of individual judges in court. This situation may, of course, change as the power of the judiciary expands and this is one strong argument for the introduction of some form of appointments commission, discussed below. But for now, it is equally possible to argue that the failure of the appointments process is not that it is not independent enough but that it is too independent in the sense that it lacks accountability.

Accountability

One of the first effects of the increasing political power of a group in a democratic society is a tendency to question how and by whom the members of the group are chosen. This change has been very evident in relation to the judiciary: 'Anxieties about the selection of judges increase - and rightly increase - in proportion to the amount of direct political power a society invites them to wield on its behalf' (Gearty, 1996, p. 3). Ordinarily, the greater the political influence of a public body the greater the pressure it faces to increase the accountability of its appointments process. However, this pressure has, to date, been largely resisted by the judiciary on the grounds that it is in conflict with the countervailing force of judicial independence. The tension between these two pressures is an increasingly dominant feature of the appointments process and requires some analysis of the two principles in order to identify where, in practice, the conflict lies.

The requirements of hard political accountability demand that, ultimately, a decision-maker can be removed from office because of his or her decisions. This form of accountability has only very limited application in the judicial appointments process. In theory, the Lord Chancellor might be forced to resign or be sacked from the government if his appointments (or the way in which they were made) were found to be flawed. However, even if this were to happen, as a member of the House of Lords the Lord Chancellor would retain his seat in Parliament irrespective of the wishes of the government or the electorate. In practice, such a scenario is highly unlikely since, to date, the appointment of judges has attracted very little public attention and is not included on the yardstick by which the performance of the government is measured. In practice, only a scandal of unprecedented proportion would bring about the Lord Chancellor's resignation or his dismissal from the government. Even if this situation changes as the role of the judiciary expands, and governments' reputations are affected by the quality of their judicial appointments, the fact that judges are appointed until retirement and tend to remain on the bench for a number of years means that many judges will not have been appointed by those currently in office. If, to take an extreme example, it was discovered that a previous Lord Chancellor and Prime Minister had sold judicial posts to the highest bidder, the current government could not reasonably be held accountable for that abuse.

In practice, therefore, the only meaningful form of political accountability in the appointment process is the more limited requirement that the appointor is called to explain and justify the basis of his or her appointments to Parliament. This covers both the decisions relating to individual appointments and, more generally, the criteria and methods adopted in the appointments process. Again, in theory, this form of accountability currently exists in England and Wales. Parliament can ask the Lord Chancellor to explain his decision-making in the same way as it can any other minister. Much has been made of this requirement by the judges. A common objection from the judiciary to any structural change in the appointments process which might remove the decision from the personal control of the Lord Chancellor is the argument that it would break the chain of accountability to Parliament. In evidence to the Home Affairs

Select Committee, Lord Mackay, when Lord Chancellor, confirmed that Parliament would, in his view, be entitled to ask him not just about the appointment process but also about a particular appointment which he had made. However, he went on to confirm that this had never, in fact, happened.

Thus, despite the formal existence of constitutional accountability there is clearly a strong convention which deters detailed investigation by Parliament into judicial appointments. The Home Affairs Select Committee's examination of the process in 1996 was careful to avoid any questions which might relate to individual appointments. Moreover, the extent to which the Lord Chancellor's Department is bound to explain the process itself is limited. During the evidence taken by the Select Committee, Chris Mullin MP attempted to identify exactly what the process consisted of by which the Prime Minister and the Lord Chancellor's Department negotiate the choice of the senior judges. Whether, for example, the Lord Chancellor presented the Prime Minister with a list or expressed a preference for one candidate or another. Neither Sir Thomas Legg, the Permanent Secretary, nor Lord Mackay were willing to provide information on this subject. Lord Mackay was at pains to stress that the discussions between himself and the Prime Minister were confidential and that he would not be drawn on the question of how the appointments were chosen between the two.

This refusal to account for the process went unchallenged by Parliament. It did not give rise to any constitutional strain between the executive and legislature over the issue of which branch should determine the limits of accountability as such an exchange might have done in another area of executive activity. The Committee effectively accepted Lord Mackay's implicit claim that the degree to which the appointments process was open to scrutiny was for the Lord Chancellor rather than Parliament to determine. The suggestion that the House of Commons is entitled as of right to know, in detail, how senior members of the judiciary are appointed is clearly not yet a widely accepted view in British politics.

The gap between constitutional theory and political reality in the field of accountability mirrors that identified in relation to judicial independence. In the present system, judicial independence appears weak because it is in the hands of a government minister and accountability would seem to be strong since Parliament has wide powers to scrutinise the system. In practice, the fact that appointments are effectively kept within the control of the senior judiciary results in strong judicial independence while the minimal scrutiny of the Lord Chancellor's work by the legislature means that there is very limited accountability.

A critical issue therefore, is whether accountability can be strengthened without weakening judicial independence since traditionally the justification for limiting accountability has been the need to avoid the danger of exposing the judiciary to improper influence. The answer to this question depends on the definition of judicial independence which is employed. When the principle is widely defined as a collective constitutional principle it is necessary strictly to limit accountability since it undermines the autonomy of the judiciary at a collective level. In order to ensure that the judiciary, as an institution, is free from any interference at all, however far removed from the individual decision-making of a judge in court, the process of selecting judges must not be open to outside influence. If the head of the judiciary must explain the appointments process and the reason for individual appointments to Parliament this might amount to pressure to do things differently.

However, if a narrower definition of judicial independence as freedom from interference in individual decision-making is adopted, the two principles of accountability and independence are not necessarily incompatible or even, in practice, in tension. Greater accountability can be achieved without inevitably sacrificing judicial independence. This change of perspective requires a different view of the judiciary, one which recognises its primary role as that of a public service. As such, it is not fundamentally different from any other public institution. It is funded from public money and the public are entitled to require that those resources are used efficiently and effectively to promote good judicial administration. On this basis, the claim that the judiciary should remain outside the ordinary processes of accountability to which other public services are subjected is much harder to sustain. The Law Society set out its approach to judicial appointments in 1991 as being: 'that judicial appointments are in principle, simply a category of senior appointments in the public service'.[13] If this view is accepted, the same standards of openness and parliamentary scrutiny are required to fulfil the demands of accountability. These mechanisms of institutional accountability are not designed to interfere with the individual decision-making of the judges. Provided accountability is concerned with the way in which the judges are chosen and the criteria used to appoint them rather than the decisions of those judges once appointed, the two principles of judicial independence and public accountability are not in conflict.

While this interpretation of the relationship between judicial independence and accountability is unlikely to find widespread favour with the judiciary, the judges have started to acknowledge that there is a need for greater accountability in the appointments process and that this can be achieved without threatening judicial independence. In October 1997, the Lord Chancellor, Lord Irvine announced that he would present an annual report to Parliament on the operation of the judicial appointments process starting in 1999. This change will provide a mechanism for an ongoing review of the process by Parliament and may encourage a more proactive approach to its task of holding the Lord Chancellor accountable for the way in which it operates and the type of appointments made under it.

Openness

If accountability is defined as the duty to explain and justify decisions, then increasing accountability inevitably requires greater openness on the part of the judiciary. There are two respects in which the appointments process may be judged to be more or less open. First, the extent to which the mechanics of the process and the selection criteria which are adopted are made known to the public and, second, the extent to which the candidates are informed about the basis on which decisions relating to their applications have been taken. Traditionally both have been very closed. In 1973, Sir Robert Megarry described the appointments process to an international symposium. He stated that he had no actual knowledge about the system but only intelligent guesses (Megarry, 1973, p. 105). This degree of ignorance, even from a senior judge who has himself been appointed through the system, was still unexceptional up until the early 1980s. Since then, however, some important changes have occurred which have opened up the process both for outside observers and for the applicants.

In 1986 The Lord Chancellor's Department published a guide entitled *Judicial Appointments: The Lord Chancellor's Policies and Procedures* setting out for the first time information on the way in which the system operated. This publication marked the start of a change in attitude within the Department which led to a gradual expansion in the range of information set out. Whereas once the duties of the different ranks of judges were known only by those who worked in the court system, there are now job descriptions for all posts. This has increased the knowledge of the system both for the public and for those who might be considering a career as a judge.

In addition, since 1994 posts have been advertised in an attempt to encourage a wider field of applicants. At first the system of advertising was opened up only to those posts below the High Court. It was argued that the traditional system whereby High Court applicants had to wait to be asked to apply was adequate because of the small pool of eligible candidates. However, the Lord Chancellor announced in 1997 that advertisements would be extended to the High Court so that: 'all with judicial ambition can be assured that their cases are properly considered'. In February 1998 the first such post was advertised. Lord Irvine has explained that this system is designed to supplement rather than replace the process of invitation which suggests that the old system by which candidates must wait to be asked to apply will still remain the ordinary route for appointment. But although it is unlikely that advertising High Court posts will have any immediate effect on the type of candidates applying for the position, it may be the first step in a change of culture which, in the long term, will increase the accessibility of the appointments process to a wider range of candidates. Experience in Canada suggests that advertising posts does encourage qualified candidates to apply who had previously considered the system to be closed to outsiders.

There have also been changes to the way in which candidates' applications are processed. In the past, applicants have waited many years after first applying while the Lord Chancellor's Department gathered opinions on their suitability. Lord Mackay explained that: 'for those who are seen as high fliers, the evidence often accumulates quickly; for those whose performance may be more standard it takes longer' (Lord Mackay, 1994, p. 4). During this time candidates were generally not informed of their progress. In 1996, the Lord Chancellor's Department tackled this problem by introducing an annual competition for vacant posts so that applicants are not left in a state of suspended limbo, unsure of how far they have progressed in their application.

As well as improving the amount of information which is made available about the system, greater openness has been encouraged through lay participation on the interview panels. To date, no research has been carried out to shed light on what role the lay members of the interview panels play in practice. Lord Taylor suggested to the Home Affairs Select Committee that they should be there only as an 'insurance policy' against anything being taken into account which shouldn't be and to give the public confidence in the system.[14] This view suggests a rather toothless and token contribution. However the extension of the role of the interview panels by Lord Irvine to the process of choosing candidates for shortlist suggests that they are playing a more important part in the process.

Despite these moves to open up the system of appointments the heart of the system is still closed. The most important stage in the process which will usually determine the fate of an applicant, is the consultation process whereby the views of senior members of the bar and bench as to a candidate's suitability are gathered by the Lord Chancellor's Department. The consultations are carried out by letter and in person. In 1973, Sir Robert Megarry described: 'a mysterious system of osmosis and grape-vine' by which the Lord Chancellor finds out about candidates (Megarry, 1973, p. 195). Today, the consultation system consists of a large scale and highly-organised operation. In 1997, over 1,600 people were consulted about 1,000 applicants in a process which generated over 8,000 comments. These numbers are evidence of the central role which consultations occupy in the appointments process.

Although the system is far more structured than it was in Sir Robert Megarry's day it is still largely hidden from view, hence the fact that the process is often referred to as one of 'secret soundings'. Lord Irvine has objected to this term on the grounds that since all lawyers are aware it happens it cannot be termed secret.[15] However, its critics would argue that it is not the existence of the system that is secret but the knowledge of how it operates in detail and the content of the information gathered. There is still no full information provided by the Lord Chancellor's Department setting out the lists of those who are consulted. Without this it is difficult for candidates to assess whether or not those with accurate knowledge of their work are being included. Once information has been gathered through the consultations, candidates can request a general overview of the opinions expressed by those consulted, but cannot be informed of who has said what. The argument for this level of secrecy is that those with knowledge of an individual must be free to give entirely candid opinions and to do this requires complete confidentiality. But its critics have described it as a left-over from times where government was conducted in smoke-filled rooms. In 1986 one observer described it as recalling the days of the 'rotten boroughs' (Harlow, 1986, p. 191). Ten years later the Home Affairs Select Committee noted that the consultation process remained the main focus for criticism of the procedure for appointment to the judiciary.[16]

There are a number of different strands to these criticisms. On grounds of principle it is argued that such secrecy is inconsistent with even the most moderate requirements of accountability and that it allows for bias and prejudice to creep into the appointments system. It has also been suggested that unsuccessful applicants are left with a sense of injustice (whether justified or not). Perhaps the most important criticism concerns the effect the system has on the make-up of the judiciary. Many commentators have argued that it encourages self-replication on the bench by excluding good candidates who do not share the same or similar characteristics as those whose advice is sought. This in turn skews the make-up of the judiciary and inhibits efforts to increase its representativeness (JUSTICE, 1992). In particular, it is argued that women, solicitors and members of ethnic minority groups are at a disadvantage as a result of the consultation process. The emphasis on the views of the judiciary and the senior bar inevitably excludes those who do not have a strong advocacy background and so are not known in the circles of those consulted. It also disadvantages those who do not have informal contact with judges and barristers through social connections where much networking goes on. Outsiders are inevitably at a disadvantage in a system which relies on the opinions of insiders.

In defence of the system, the Lord Chancellor's Department has stressed the breadth of different opinions sought and the fact that no one person's view is paramount however senior he or she might be. Lord Irvine has argued that the process is systematic and objective:

> To the sceptic I ask, what do you think happens at one of these consultation meeting? Do you honestly believe that my Permanent Secretary turns up at a senior judge's door asking whether old Copperfield is a good chap or whether young Pickwick is a bit suspect because, rumour has it, he voted for the Green Party at the last election? No, our consultations are not like that.[17]

As long as detailed information about how the system works remains secret, a sceptic might well be entitled to answer that something similar to the scenario dismissed by Lord Irvine might indeed occur. Without published guidelines stating who should be consulted in relation to which posts and what 'objective and systematic' methods are used, it is difficult to assess the Lord Chancellor's claim. Moreover, his argument is somewhat undermined by the evidence provided by Lord Taylor, when

Lord Chief Justice, to the Home Affairs Select Committee in 1996 during which he gave a thumb-nail sketch of the sort of comments made in the consultations process. He explained that a judge might say to his colleagues, in relation to someone being considered for appointment: "'I heard X the other day. He was absolutely super" or "I heard X the other day and I was very disappointed"'.[18] These unstructured, subjective and impressionist comments are not dissimilar to those dismissed as fanciful by Lord Irvine.

Despite these concerns, the Home Affairs Select Committee report gave its broad support to the existing system of consultations, arguing that it provided valuable information for the Lord Chancellor's Department. The report suggested only that the structure of letters sent to nominees of applicants for the post of Assistant Recorders should be improved so that they were clearer about the information being requested. It also recommended that an indication should be given by the Lord Chancellor's Department of the field from which consultations are taken.[19]

On coming to office in 1997, Lord Irvine moved to address some aspects of the criticisms aroused by the consultation process. He instituted a new rule that any allegation of misconduct on the part of a candidate made in the consultation process must be specific and would be subject to disclosure to the candidate. He also stated that in the long term he would be considering whether an ombudsman should be established with the power fully to examine complaints from any candidate who felt that he or she had been unfairly treated in the appointments process. The effect of such changes, when added to the range of reforms which have been enacted since 1986, are not merely window-dressing but represent real structural improvement as well as evidence of a greater culture of openness within the Lord Chancellor's Department. Nevertheless, the overall scope of the developments is still relatively limited and the public remains largely ignorant about the way in which judges are chosen. It is still very noticeable that the question of what type of judges we wish to select through which sort of process receives very little public attention. At a time when the role of the judiciary is changing rapidly, the answers to these questions are both increasingly important and uncertain.

The criteria for appointment

Devising an effective criteria for the appointment and promotion of judges raises the question - often only referred to obliquely if at all - of what constitutes a good judge. Defining the ideal judicial qualities is much harder than it might at first seem: 'Like the elephant, the judicial quality is easily recognisable but very difficult to define' (Megarry, 1973, p. 102). The three broad criteria on which judges might be appointed are those of merit, politics, and representativeness. The prioritisation and content of all three have become increasingly controversial.

Merit

When the question of the competence of the judiciary is raised amongst those who appear regularly before the courts, the conclusions are generally favourable. The Home Affairs Select Committee heard evidence from the Lord Chancellor, Lord Mackay, that he considered public confidence in the competence of the judges appointed to be strong. He based this view partly on the fact that judges were regularly called upon to undertake public inquiries and partly on the fact that he received: 'very very little in the way of complaint about the appointment of particular judges'.[20] It could be argued that the absence of complaint about judges' performance may merely reflect the fact that there is limited knowledge amongst the public about whom to complain to and/or little confidence that complaints will result in action. Likewise, the lack of complaints from barristers may reflect the common fears of whistleblowers that their future career, in terms of appointment to Silk or to the bench, will be jeopardised, particularly in the light of the central role which is played by the opinions of judges through the consultation process. Where there is no independent complaints and disciplinary procedure it is likely that there will be under-reporting of judicial incompetence. Nevertheless, the evidence heard by the Home Affairs Select Committee did suggest that judges were generally regarded as competent. The Commercial Bar Association and the Judges' Council both argued that the English courts were held in high esteem internationally in the business world. The opinions expressed by those off the bench were also broadly supportive of this view of judicial competence.

    At first sight, the suggestion that judges should be appointed on merit appears to be little more than a statement of the obvious. However, while there is universal agreement that judicial selection should be based on merit, there is limited agreement on what this constitutes. Livingstone Armytage argues that the difficulty of describing what we mean by a good judge arises because the nature of judging does not easily lend itself to clearly definable and objective factors: 'The essence or artistry of judging is too complex to be readily amenable to pre-determined behavioural criteria' (Armytage, 1996, p. 41). This claim would appear to be borne out by the published criteria of many judicial appointments processes around the world which tend to describe very generalised qualities. This is equally true of the system in England and Wales. The guidelines for judicial selection first set out in 1986 by Lord Hailsham, when Lord Chancellor, stated that the criteria for appointment were: 'personality, integrity, professional ability, experience, standing and capacity...'[21] With the possible exception of experience all of these factors are inherently difficult to measure quantitatively. More recently, those who gave evidence to the Home Affairs Select Committee on the criteria for appointment referred to a number of rather nebulous qualities. Lord Taylor highlighted the need for skills in 'court craft' and a 'judicial sixth sense' which facilitated for the control and good management of the court process.[22] Geoffrey Robertson QC emphasised 'chairpersonship'.[23]

The concept of merit is clearly not easy to pin down. This may be understood as the result of a genuine reflection of the diverse and complex work of a judge or of the traditional mystification which shrouds the work of judging which the judiciary has often perpetuated. The effect is that such imprecise criteria hamper the identification of what distinct qualities should be looked for when appointing judges. One way of seeking to identify what constitutes merit is to examine what it does not include. To date there has been almost universal agreement that merit does not include a candidate's political views.

Politics

It is common for senior judges to state that they know of no appointments which have been attributed to political motivation (Lord Nolan, 1997, p. 75). When Lord Bingham claimed in 1996 that no account was taken of a candidate's politics he did so by stating that there is virtually no evidence of appointments made otherwise than on the basis of merit (Lord Bingham, 1996, p. 5). Similarly, Lord Irvine in evidence to the Home Affairs Select Committee in 1997 stated that: 'Politics has never been a factor in appointment to the professional judiciary and as far as I am concerned it never will be nor should be'.[24] Implicit in these statements is the belief that the political views of appointees, by definition, plays no part in the assessment of their merit as a judge. When such commentators remark on the absence of politics in the process they are referring to politics in its limited sense of support for a political party. Today, if a candidate is an active supporter of a mainstream political party this appears to have very little relevance one way or the other for his or her chances of appointment. Although this is often presented, as in Lord Irvine's comment, as an entrenched feature of the appointments system it is in fact, relatively new. Before the Second World War party political support was considered an acceptable and open factor in determining the suitability of a candidate for judicial appointment. In 1973, Sir Robert Megarry claimed that this change could almost be pinpointed to the appointment of Lord Goddard as Lord Chief Justice in 1946 and, a few weeks later, that of Sir Donald Somerville, a Conservative Attorney-General, to the Court of Appeal by the Labour Government (Megarry, 1973).

The correlation between the removal of political patronage in the appointments process and the reduction in the activism of the judiciary after the War is very clear. As the judges distanced themselves from policy-making so their political allegiances became an increasingly irrelevant factor in their appointment. It is interesting that to date, the growth of activism appears to have had little effect in reversing this trend. This may, of course, change in the period after the Human Rights Act is passed. The incremental expansion in judicial power through judicial review is quite different from the sharp change in role which incorporation of the European Convention on Human Rights will bring. For critics of incorporation one of the strongest objections to the reform is that it will require a change in the appointment criteria of the judges by reintroducing scrutiny of the political stance of the candidates (Lord Mackay, 1996). Even those commentators who strongly support incorporation generally recognise that the political outlook of those appointed to the senior ranks of the judiciary are almost bound to be taken into consideration by the executive as the policy-making role of the judges increases (Kentridge, 1996). In the preamble to the draft written constitution for the UK produced by the Institute for Public Policy Research in 1991 it was argued that the increasing power given to the judges as a result of the adoption of a Bill of Rights of any kind would be likely to lead to the politicisation of the appointments process:

As can be seen from the experience of the USA, the power to appoint judges to courts with important constitutional powers can become a controversial political issue. If no changes were made to the present system of appointing judges, the temptation to depart from the recent tradition of impartiality in judicial appointments might become impossible to resist (IPPR, 1991, pp. 18-19).

Similarly, in a comparative study of judicial activism, Waltman has stressed the link between the judicialisation of politics and the politicisation of the judicial appointments process:

If courts are going to wade or be pulled into politically controversial areas, pressure will undoubtedly build to secure judges with 'acceptable' views, the definition of 'acceptable' varying widely, naturally, among MPs and various interest groups (Waltman, 1991, p. 46).

This trend of the politicisation of the appointments process accompanying the expansion of judicial policy-making role has been noted across Western Europe (Volcansez, 1992, p. 5). It has been argued that the way judges are appointed to the courts is, in practice, the determining factor in the effectiveness of a Bill of Rights (Beatty, 1997). Since there is broad agreement that politics is likely to find its way back into the appointment criteria in some form and to some degree, it is necessary to analysis more rigorously what is meant by politicisation in this context and what its effects might be.

Most commentators regard the removal of politics in the appointments process as an inherently good development and assume that its reintroduction would inevitably be a detrimental change in terms of the quality of the bench. Although this seems a common-sense assumption, it is surprisingly difficult to support this contention empirically. In the US and Canada, where politics has traditionally played a strong role in judicial selection, particularly at federal level, there is no clear evidence to demonstrate that this has, in practice, undermined competence or impartiality in decision-making on the bench. One explanation for this is the effect of permanent tenure. Where judges have security of tenure and do not look to the executive for reappointment, they are not under pressure to curry favour through their decision-making. Even where appointments are made which are overtly political, those chosen often, in practice, disappoint the expectations of the politicians who appoint them. President

Eisenhower, for example, claimed that the appointment of Earl Warren to the Supreme Court was the worst mistake of his presidency. Once appointed, the judicial culture of independence can be stronger than the previous political allegiances. As one South African Minister of Justice in the 1930s observed caustically: 'the trouble with political appointments is that after they have been on the bench for two weeks they imagine that they got there by merit'.[25]

If impartiality is not automatically at risk if the political views of judges are taken into account in the appointment process, the arguments in favour of de-politicisation grow weaker in the light of the growing policy-making role of the judges. As the judiciary is drawn into deciding a wider range of political controversial issues with long term implications for society it is reasonable to argue that they should be selected not just on the basis of legal skill or professionalism or even general temperament, but also on the basis on their political views:

> Aspects of a judge's experience, conduct and beliefs which would now be regarded as irrelevant to his fitness for the highest judicial office might well be of moment if he or she is to adjudicate on the constitutionality of legislation or even upon the constitutionality of executive action on a broader basis than is permissible under existing English administrative law (Kentridge, 1996, p. 260).

If, for example, a candidate has strongly racist, sexist or homophobic opinions, it would be valid to suggest that these would affect his or her ability to fulfil the judicial role envisaged by the Court under the Human Rights Act.

David Beatty argues, for example, that the reason why the judges' views on human rights should be scrutinised in the appointments process is not so much because they will exercise policy-making decisions but because they will exercise their discretion as to how broadly or narrowly to interpret the Bill of Rights (Beatty, 1997). In Canada, he argues, the judges have interpreted the Charter of Rights narrowly in a way which has failed to require officials and the government to respect basic human rights as envisaged by the Charter. Supporters of the Human Rights Act might argue that if the Courts are to apply its provisions meaningfully, it is necessary to ensure that the judges appointed are personally committed to the protection of human rights.

Moreover, the fact that there is currently no overt consideration of a judge's political views on appointment does not mean that they do not affect his or her decisions. The decision to support the status quo is, in itself, a political stance, lending legitimacy to the existing order (Volcansez, 1992, p. 2). There is no such thing as absolute political neutrality in a policy-maker. The issue is rather whether the appointor and the public should know something about the politics of the judges appointed and take this into consideration. Judges will carry their political views with them onto the bench whatever appointment process is used. It is arguable that the consideration of these views merely opens up to scrutiny what is currently hidden.

The US Senate confirmation hearings of federal judicial appointments before the Judiciary Committee are widely condemned in England for bringing politics into the judicial process. Yet the principle that a senior judge who may contribute to the formation of national policy-making should attend a public interview before appointment has much to recommend it. This is particularly true of Supreme Court judges. The Senate hearings require the judges to state their position on a range of critical issues in which their values may influence the social, political and economic life of the country. A similar process is carried out for judges appointed to the Constitutional Court in South Africa who attend a public interview before the Judicial Service Commission. Sidney Kentridge has described the process in the following terms:

> Many of the questions put to the judicial candidates were searching and some of them were personal. But the proceedings were nothing like the more exuberant proceedings in the Judiciary Committee of the United States Senate. I cannot say that any of the candidates enjoyed the experience but there is no reason to think that anyone has been put off high judicial office by the minor ordeal of the interview (Kentridge, 1996, p. 253).

Despite the initial misgivings which were expressed by lawyers and judges in South Africa about the use of such interviews, the general opinion now seems to be strongly supportive of their use as a means of identifying the broad approach of the candidates to the judicial role.

In England, senior judges are appointed without any equivalent method for the public expression of their values and beliefs. While their policy-making role was limited this was perhaps justifiable but it will become harder to defend once the judiciary are asked to decide a wide range of politically sensitive issues. Based on the experience of Canada, Beatty argues that rigorous questioning of a judicial candidate about his or her approach to the theory and practice of constitutional law on which the practical effect of a Bill of Rights will rest is essential if the underlying values of such a Bill are not to be negated (1997). Similar argument have started to be voiced in Australia as the political role of the courts has expanded. In 1998, a number of legal academics argued that prospective judges should be subject to a public interview.[26]

In England and Wales to date, any form of politicised appointments process is still widely regarded as a 'frightful prospect' (Drewry, 1992, p. 15). But this approach may be starting to be rethought. The inevitable result of the increased judicial activism which incorporation is likely to bring is that the boundaries which delimit the politics of the appointments process will need to be redrawn and the judiciary may need to reconcile itself to a more political selection process (Stevens, 1996, p. 43). The appointments of Lord Justice Millett and Lord Justice Hobhouse to the House of Lords in July 1998 led to unprecedented press criticism in both the popular and quality press about the lack of openness and accountability in the selection of such powerful public figures.[27] Equally, some politicians are starting to think the unthinkable. In 1998, William Hague stated that the Conservative Party was considering parliamentary confirmation hearings for judges: 'Just as the US Congress has a veto on senior appointments to the Supreme Court, so the House of Commons could have a veto on senior judicial appointments'. He argued that if the sovereign power of Parliament to make laws was removed, MPs should be given some say over who will exercise those powers. Such a move would appear to be some way off from being included in Conservative Party policy as Hague stressed that they would go down that route only if 'forced to'.[28]

One explanation for the continuing widespread resistance to the inclusion of a political element in the selection of judges is the tendency to interpret the notion of impartiality as an absolute requirement. However, if the distinction between 'party impartiality' and 'issue impartiality' is recognised and it is accepted that a measure of issue partiality is a necessary and desirable quality in a judge, the objections to consideration of a judge's political views in the appointment process are weakened. This is particularly so if a further distinction is drawn between politics in a wide sense as ideological views and in a narrow sense as party patronage. There is a strong argument for saying that whether a judge supports a particular party should not be relevant to his or her appointment. Even if such politicisation does not in practice undermine judicial independence, the link between party support in a system of executive appointment will undoubtedly undermine the appearance of judicial independence and so public confidence in the judiciary. There is certainly evidence for this contention from the US and Canada. However, if politics is defined more broadly to describe the values and beliefs of a judge, then a stronger case can be made out for including such considerations in the criteria in relation to the selection of senior judges. Using a broad definition of politics the criteria might cover such qualities as 'respect for minorities' and 'support for human rights' - topics on which we might expect 'issue partiality'. Being very general, these criteria begin to merge with broadly humanistic qualities which are increasingly being included on appointment criteria around the world. In one respect these can be seen as personal values but they also underpin the principles upon which the administration of justice rests and can be termed political in its broadest sense.

The adoption of this approach to the role of political considerations in the appointments process would affect the relative value ascribed to different selection criteria. To date, professional and technical skills have been highly prioritised by the judiciary while humanistic skill have often been regarded as almost incidental (Armytage, 1996, p. 50). However, as the judges become increasingly politically active, it will become harder to justify this weighting. The ability to do justice in the field of public policy does not primarily demand technical legal skills but political and humanistic ones. Indeed, there is no automatic requirement that senior judges who are responsible for public policy matters must exclusively be lawyers. By the 1980s voices were starting to be raised questioning whether eminence in the legal professions is really a *sine qua non* of judicial appointment (Harlow, 1986, p. 195). The passage of the Human Rights Act has brought a new force to this question: '...it is not self evident that it is only lawyers who are qualified to answer the moral and philosophical questions raised by a Bill of Rights' (Kentridge, 1996, p. 253). In Canada and South Africa the incorporation of a Bill of Rights has lead to a shift in the qualities which are looked for in a judge towards the humanistic and away from the forensic. The South African bench now look for such qualities as 'intolerance of injustice', 'emotional maturity' and 'the moral ability to distinguish right from wrong' (Mahomed CJ, 1997). Lord Nolan has similarly suggested that 'an understanding of human nature and the daily concerns of ordinary people' is also a key attribute for a judge (Lord Nolan, 1997, p. 71). Interviews conducted with Canadian judges in 1990 found that the attributes which judges most admired in their colleagues were the qualities of empathy, humanity, patience and courtesy above those of legal expertise. The researchers concluded that: 'this tendency is something the authorities responsible for judicial appointment should bear in mind' (McCormick and Greene, 1990, p. 117).

If the link between the increasing policy-making role of the senior judiciary and the redefinition of selection criteria is accepted in principle, its consequence would be to draw a sharper distinction between the qualities required of the senior and junior ranks of the judiciary. Although the Human Rights Act gives the courts at all levels the power to consider the effect of the European Convention on Human Rights, the system of appeal and precedent means that the ultimate decisions on the interpretation of the Convention will rest with the senior judges. In addition, it is only the High Court and above which has been given the power to declare legislation incompatible with the Convention. In the lower ranks, where judges primarily perform a social service role with very limited law-making or policy-making functions it is valid to argue that a candidate's political views should have less relevance. As John Bell has emphasised, the skills and characteristics required of judges are very different for different tasks (1983, pp. 1768-69). Rule determination requires good technical knowledge, dispute settlement requires fairness and social skills, and constitutional control requires an understanding of public policy considerations. The skills which need to be identified in appointing an Assistant Recorder may be increasingly different from those in appointing a Law Lord so that the definition of competence becomes more complex. It is therefore inappropriate to attempt to construct one set of criteria by which the suitability of all levels of judge can be assessed.

There is however, one possible exception to this argument. There is general agreement that the judiciary at all levels needs to be less 'out of touch' with the real world; a demand which relates less to competence and knowledge than to the question of the social background and 'life experience' of the judges. This issue raises the problem of whether social representativeness should be included in judicial appointment criteria.

Representativeness

The one aspect of the judiciary which almost all informed observers are aware of is the fact that judges are overwhelmingly made up of white, male barristers over the age of 50 who have been privately educated and are graduates of Oxford or Cambridge. This general profile is typical of many other common law systems (Shetreet, 1987). In New Zealand, for example, the background of a typical judge sounds strikingly familiar:

> ...the person appointed to be a judge in New Zealand in the years since the Second World War is a middle-aged Caucasian male; he is well-educated; and he is a successful and prominent member of the legal profession and, as such, is almost certainly wealthy, a member of the upper-middle class, and lives in an urban environment.[29]

In England, although there are now women and members of ethnic minorities on the bench, their numbers are still very small. Less than two per cent of the judiciary is non-white and only nine per cent of judges are women.[30] The educational background of the judiciary has changed very little over the years. If anything, the number of judges who are Oxbridge educated has risen slightly in the last ten years and now stands at over 80% compared with 76% in 1956.[31] Similarly, the average age of the judges has remained steady. The introduction of a mandatory retirement age has removed the very old from the bench but the age profile of the senior judges is still heavily weighted to late middle age and early old age.[32] The average age of a High Court judge in 1970 was 61 (Henry, 1970, p. 19). In 1996 the average age of both High Court judges and Circuit judges was 57.[33] The eligibility rules and selection criteria result in the exclusion of all those at the earlier stages of their career. Under the provisions of the Courts and Legal Services Act 1990 a candidate must have been in practice for ten years before he or she is eligible for appointment. This means that most candidates would not be able to apply to the bench before their mid thirties. In practice, it is very rare for a person to be appointed at that point. The job descriptions produced by the Lord Chancellor's Department set a normal minimum age of 38 for Recorders, 40 for District judges and 45 for Circuit judges. These requirements are designed to ensure that only experienced practitioners are appointed to the bench. This approach is reinforced by the economic structure of a career at the bar. The fact that the salary of a High Court judge is on average less than that of a successful QC encourages candidates to remain at the bar during their high earning years for as long as possible to provide a financial cushion against the cut in income which they are likely to experience on elevation to the bench.[34] This problem is accentuated by the relationship between retirement ages and pension entitlement. In 1993 when the retirement age was reduced to 70, the length of time which judges were required to serve before becoming entitled to their pension was increased to 20 years. This raised concerns amongst the judiciary that it would be difficult for barristers to complete this length of service since they would be obliged to give up a career at the bar at 50 just when their earning power was starting to reach its peak, so deterring high calibre candidates from considering a move to the bench (Lord Ackner, 1996, p. 1790).

Despite the growing public criticism of the unrepresentative background of the candidates chosen, the selection criteria do not include any reference to background except to emphasise its irrelevance in that appointments will be made of the candidate best qualified regardless of ethnic origin, gender, marital status, sexual orientation, political affiliation, religion or disability. In some countries the need for greater representativeness has been recognised as requiring a positive inclusion into the selection criteria. In Canada, the following broad statutory criteria must be applied by the Ontario Judicial Appointments Advisory Committee:

> Assessment of the professional excellence, community awareness and personal characteristics of candidates and recognition of the desirability of reflecting the diversity of Ontario society in judicial appointments.

Similarly, In South Africa, the Constitution states that: 'the need for the judiciary to reflect broadly the racial and gender composition of South Africa must be considered when judicial officers are appointed'.[35] Although there is no equivalent positive commitment to increasing representativeness incorporated into the selection criteria in England and Wales, nevertheless, both the judiciary and the Lord Chancellor's Department are increasingly aware of the extent of public concern over the background of the judges. From outside the judiciary there is now almost universal consensus that the judges needs to be more representative of society. Many on the bench would agree while those who do not would be very unlikely to say so publicly. Because the question of the background of the judges is so controversial this issue is likely to continue to dominate the debate on the reform of the appointment process and therefore requires some analysis.

Changing the make-up of the judiciary

Because there is such a widespread assumption that increasing representativeness in the judiciary is an inherently good thing it is generally regarded as either unnecessary or politically questionable to ask why the change is required. In fact, there are two quite different justifications which can be advanced for such a change. The first, and weaker claim, is based on the assumption that creating a judiciary with a more diverse background will improve the individual decision-making of the judges. The second, and stronger claim, is that wider participation in judicial decision-making will increase the accountability of the judiciary as a body.

Relevance of background to decision-making

To date, most research on the relationship between the background of the judges and their decision-making has sought to analyse the politics of senior judges. In *The Politics of the Judiciary* John Griffith concluded that: 'the judges define the public interest inevitably from the viewpoint of their own class' (1997, p. 327). As products of the upper middle classes he concluded that this class view was conservative. In the first edition of his book in 1977, Griffith argued that the judges' view of the public interest included the promotion of certain political values: 'normally associated with the Conservative party' (p. 195). By 1997, after relations between the Conservative administration and the senior judiciary had deteriorated, he suggested that the judges' conservatism was that of a small c variety:

> This conservatism does not necessarily follow the day-to-day political policies currently associated with the party of that name. But it is a political philosophy nonetheless (1997, p. 341).

Others have challenged this claim. Simon Lee, for example, questioned whether the case law did, in fact, show that the judges were particularly conservative in the areas of industrial relations (Lee, 1988). He suggested that the link between background and the politics of their decision-making was not a clear-cut one. The aristocratic background of Tony Benn, for example, would not have led one to predict his radical politics. Similarly, individuals from humble backgrounds who occasionally reach the bench have generally shown themselves to be as conservative as the most orthodox public school educated judge. Lee's point is that while background is an important factor which affects the judge's decision-making it is clearly not the only influence on their approach. Those who choose to be judges would be unlikely to hold views which rejected the status quo whatever background they come from. The retention of order is the essence of the law and those who support this goal generally tends towards conservatism.

Other responses to Griffith's work have raised questions about the nature of the strength of the collective judicial approach. Lord Devlin argued that despite the judges' common backgrounds their views were not, in fact, homogeneous and that there was considerable disagreement both between different levels of courts and between judges on the same bench. He also pointed out that even the same judge did not necessarily stay true to type, with individuals becoming more or less conservative with the passing of time (Devlin, 1978, p. 507).

Research in the US has similarly cast doubt upon the commonly held view that the political background of the judges affects their decision-making. A large study of federal cases found that there was little evidence that the political affiliations of the judges was reflected in their decision-making in the bulk of cases (Ashenfelter et al., 1997). The extensive literature in this area suggests that the effect of ideological differences is limited to a very small number of cases in which the law is unsettled.

These arguments highlight the fact that the relationship between the judges' background and the politics of their decision-making is not a straightforward, deterministic one. Nevertheless, the differences of approach which they demonstrate should not obscure the extent of the common ground which exists in the debate. There is widespread agreement with the essential point made by Griffith that the social and educational experiences of the judiciary are responsible for promoting a broadly conservative approach amongst the judges. Lord Devlin himself identified the relative old age of the judges as a determining factor in their conservatism: 'It is no use praying for the rejuvenation of the elderly' (Devlin, 1978, pp. 510-11). He argued that where decision-making falls into the hands of the aged it will tend to be directed by safe and orthodox people the result being an inevitable generation gap between the views of the judges and the wider community since societies composed of more than one generation are always changing. Thus, one of the main difference in the views of judges such as Lord Devlin and critics such as John Griffith lies in their assessment of the impact of the judges' conservatism on their decision-making. Griffith regards it as politically damaging whereas

Devlin saw it as an inevitable and, indeed, appropriate philosophical basis for a judge.

In the period since *The Politics of the Judiciary* was first published, the debate about the unrepresentative nature of the judiciary has shifted to some extent from questions of class to the social politics of race and gender but, in broad terms, the influence of background on decision-making is generally accepted. If a new judiciary were to be appointed tomorrow made up entirely of young black women from working-class backgrounds educated in state schools and the New Universities, it would be very surprising if they did not reach some strikingly different decisions. Of course, for the purposes of representativeness such a bench would be equally undesirable even if more palatable to the far left. The essence of a more representative judiciary is the need to cover a wider range of views not to replace one narrow perspective with another. This then raises the question of how, in practice, a more representative bench translates into better judicial decision-making.

The difficulty arises partly because of the over-riding requirement of impartiality in adjudication which is the basis of judicial independence. The principle of party impartiality demands that a judge in court does not identify with the interests of any of the parties in the case. In practice, of course, such detached neutrality may be impossible, but it is an essential principle on which public confidence rests. It would be wrong for any structural arrangement to be seen to undermine that ideal. It is for this reason that the notion of representativeness is potentially problematic when applied to the judiciary since it suggests that a judge might in some way have been selected to represent the interests of a particular group. The 1996 Home Affairs Select Committee report on the judicial appointments process stressed that the judiciary was not there to represent different constituencies: 'It is not the function of the judiciary to reflect particular sections of the community, as it is of the democratically elected legislature'.[36] It is arguable that this distinction between the function of Parliament and the judiciary will become much more difficult to sustain as the judges become more politically active.[37] As Professor Griffith pointed out in his evidence to the Committee, the fact that both branches of government exercise political power means that it is increasingly legitimate to expect them equally to constitute a 'fair reflection' of English society. The total sacrifice of representativeness in the name of merit which has been justified to date may be increasingly open to challenge as the political power of the judiciary increases.

But even if the notion of representativeness in adjudication could be reconciled with that of impartiality as a matter of principle, it is unsustainable in practice since a judge cannot simultaneously belong to all the cultural groups and backgrounds of the parties in every case. Each judge will be called upon to preside over many different cases involving a wide range of groups and individuals. Lord Taylor, when Lord Chief Justice, summed up this problem:

> No judge trying a case can be representative of all sections of the community. To take the gender issue, even with a judiciary of equal numbers male and female the judge in any given case can only be one or the other (Lord Taylor, 1992, p. 8).

In recognition of these difficulties, both of principle and practice, an alternative approach to the question of judges' backgrounds is gaining popularity in many jurisdictions. This replaces the concept of representativeness with the doctrine of 'fair reflection'. This more flexible principle holds that the judiciary: 'should reflect through its composition the interests of the community which it serves' (Armytage, 1996, p. 56). It moves away from the effect of the particular backgrounds of individual judges on particular decisions towards a broader approach which seeks to link the judiciary as a group to the society in which it operates. In so doing, it reduces the danger of offending against the principle of impartiality. Implicit in the 'fair reflection' argument is the notion that a more reflective judiciary will produce a better mirror of societal attitudes generally across the board. In each decision a judge sits as an impartial adjudicator who does not represent any interests other than those of justice. But as a body, the judiciary incorporates within it a wider range of social perspectives.

This new approach links in with a relatively old conception of the judicial function developed by Lord Devlin. He argued that the judiciary in its decision-making had a role to play in reflecting the social consensus. While rejecting the idea that judges should be 'dynamic' law-makers and seek to shape or lead societal values, he did believe that there was an activist role for the judiciary in bringing the law into line with the current consensus (1976).

Although Devlin's theory of consensus would appear to be a useful justification for the reflective approach there are a number of problems with its application. In order to fulfil the task of reflecting the social consensus it is obviously necessary for judges to be in a position to identify that consensus in the first place. Traditionally, judges have emphasised the role of 'common sense' in this process. Lord Reid was a classic supporter of this approach: 'We should, I think have regard to common sense, legal principle and public policy in that order' (1973, p. 25). Although the concept of common sense has not generally been acknowledged as being another way of describing social values, Lord Reid implicitly recognised the connection between common sense and consensus by stressing that in order for a judge to identify the common sense approach he required some connection with the world outside. For Lord Reid, this meant going to the 'grass roots' by having personal contact with different strata of society through some form of public service (1973, p. 27). For judges of Lord Reid's generation it was not thought necessary that the judges themselves should be drawn from these different strata but only that they should have some familiarity with those outside their own social world. The judges role was then to act as a conduit for the consensus they identified in the expression of what they regarded as common sense.

These traditional interpretations of the relationship between the judges' backgrounds and their decision-making adopt a relatively simplistic view of the social consensus; what it is, how it is found and applied. They side-step the problem that a judge's view of what is common sense is necessarily informed by his or her own value system: '... common sense is also a value. When a judge purports to rely on common sense as his guide, he relies on what he thinks is the consensus of the community on the subject' (McHugh J., 1988, p. 17). Once the subjective role of the judge's own values are acknowledged as an inherent part of the process of divining the consensus the unrepresentative make-up of the judiciary raises questions about its ability accurately to identify the consensus (Bell, 1985, p. 61).

A further problem arises from the notion of consensus itself. Part of the explanation for the apparent simplicity of the approach by the judges to the concept of consensus twenty or thirty years ago was that it was generally regarded as a less complex issue. It was assumed that there existed, in theory at least, a consensus in society at large for the judges to identify. If this was ever the case, it is much less clearly so today. The increasing heterogeneity of social structures and consequent diversity in attitudes combined with the acceleration of the pace of social change which has taken place since Lord Reid and Lord Devlin wrote, has served to weaken the very notion of common sense and consensus in many areas of social and political life. Moreover, as the role of the judiciary expands in the field of human rights, the issues which are coming before the courts are increasingly going to be those on the margins in which there are acute differences of opinions. In the near future judges will inevitably be called upon more frequently to decide on controversial ethical issues such as abortion or euthanasia in which the likelihood of a consensus is very remote. Similarly, if the courts continue to expand their involvement in the judicial review of policy issues in areas such as immigration they will increasingly be required to decide on the merits of cases which are highly politically divisive.

In addition to these external problems, the mechanics by which a more representative judiciary reflects social consensus in individual decision-making is far from clear. Even if the whole bench was a perfect representation of society and that society could be said to have some identifiable consensus on the issues before the courts, each case is decided by a judge or judges with individual background and views, not the whole of the judiciary or a distillation of their experiences. The fact that a judge personally may not come from a stereotypical judicial background and may be a member of a representative bench does not automatically equip that individual with the facility to divine the social consensus. It may be that a more representative bench would encourage a wider range of different approaches amongst the judges in the individual cases but on a case-by-case basis it is hard to see how this change could be said to reflect the consensus more accurately.

These difficulties which arise when trying to pin down the precise benefits in decision-making produced by a more representative judiciary undermine the suggestion that changing the background of the judges will automatically leave them better placed to identify the consensus or common sense view in the cases they hear. Such a claim can only realistically be expressed in the most general terms. It may be possible to argue that the creation of a more representative bench will lead in some incalculable and inexact sense to a more accurate reflection of the diversity of social attitudes in court. Paradoxically, however, the effect of a more representative judiciary may be to undermine the search for an elusive consensus towards an acknowledgement of the range of socially acceptable perspectives. The result may be that the law itself adapts to this more diverse approach. On this model, an unrepresentative certainty is replaced by a more unpredictable but accurate reflection of social reality. Mrs Justice Bertha Wilson of the Canadian judiciary has argued, for example, that the absence of women on the bench has skewed the law to a distinctly male perspective (Wilson, 1992, p. 94). She believes that more women on the bench will incorporate their perspective and so broaden the world view of the law to include these differences. Whether or not replacing the search for certainty and consensus with a more realistic reflection of social complexity can be said to improve the quality of decision-making is a question of political judgment.

These arguments undermine claims that by increasing representativeness the quality of judicial decision-making will automatically be improved. Nevertheless, there are strong grounds based on the requirements of accountability for saying that changes to the background of those appointed to the bench is desirable whether or not it has a positive effect on judicial decision-making.

Participation and accountability

In all liberal democracies it is regarded as an inherent good that different social groups should have the opportunity to participate in public life regardless of the objective quality of their decision-making. When South Africa dismantled the system of apartheid it did not do so because black people would inevitably make better decision-makers than whites, but because the system could not claim that it was accountable and therefore legitimate without the participation of that excluded majority. The same can be said of all the historical reforms which have taken place in England and Wales to extend the franchise and of the current constitutional changes being brought about in relation to devolution in Scotland and Wales and the reform of the House of Lords.

Such arguments have, to date, carried relatively little weight in relation to the judiciary because the job of a judge has been regarded as a legal rather than political one. The result has been that a strong emphasis has been placed on the need to prioritise a candidate's legal expertise over his or her social characteristics. The Home Affairs Select Committee concluded that the judges' role is: 'to administer justice in accordance with the laws of England and Wales. This requires above all professional legal knowledge and competence'.[38] In South Africa, the process of increased participation in decision-making has been rejected as a reason for appointing more black and women judges. The Judicial Service Commission selection criteria state that the constitutional requirement that the Judicial Service Commission must take account of 'the need to constitute a court which is representative in respect of race and gender' is for the benefit of the quality of justice and not to increase participation:

> The constitution maker is not here concerned with the interests of the individual, who by appointment to the court, might benefit from its instruction. Its concern is with the effectiveness of the Court as an instrument of justice.[39]

The criteria seek to resolve the dilemma posed by the question of whether, ultimately, individual competence should ever be sacrificed for representativeness, by arguing that the two concepts of competence and representativeness are not separate. The criteria reject an interpretation of the constitutional instruction as being the selection of such groups in direct proportion to their share of the national population. Instead the criteria argue that this amounts to a need to create a judiciary which can understand and relate to the experiences of all South Africans:

> Diversity, in other words, is a quality without which the court is unlikely to be able to do justice to all the citizens of this country. It is not an independent requirement superimposed upon the constitutional requirement of competence; properly understood it is a component of competence - the court will not be competent to do justice unless, as a collegiate whole, it can relate fully to the experience of all who seek its protection.[40]

This argument is perhaps disingenuous. The need to ensure the collective competence of the courts to do justice is distinct from the question of individual competence on a legal and intellectual level. The conflict between the requirements of competence in this sense and representativeness does in practice arise, both in South Africa and England and Wales. One way in which the stark choice between competence and representativeness can be mitigated is to broaden the definition of competence to include a wider range of humanistic characteristics, thus widening the pool of qualified candidates.

The claim that increasing representativeness amongst judges is a requirement of accountability rests on the assumption that the judiciary is a political body, in the broad sense of being an institution which exercises official power over individuals' lives. As such, it has a responsibility to promote the interests and ideals of the participatory democracy within which it operates. But the rationale based on accountability for increasing participation through a broader make-up of the judiciary does not rest solely upon the requirement of society at large, but can equally be argued to be in the interests of the judiciary itself. Whether or not the change has any positive effect on the judges' decision-making, increasing the representativeness of the judiciary can provide the judges with an essential opportunity to demonstrate their accountability and so secure public support. As public scrutiny and criticism of the judiciary increases, this means of regaining and maintaining public confidence will become increasingly critical. Since the judiciary cannot comply with the democratic requirements of electoral accountability, this method of social accountability amounts to an essential form of legitimacy. If this is recognised, then it can be argued that whether or not a more socially reflective judiciary produces a means to reflect consensus or common sense in its decisions, it is important and necessary to change the background of the judges for its own sake.

Mechanisms for change

In recent years there have been indications that the judiciary has come to accept the desirability and urgency of the need for change. In 1992, Lord Taylor, then Lord Chief Justice, claimed that reform was imminent:

> The present imbalance between male and female, white and black in the judiciary is obvious...I have no doubt that the balance will be redressed in the next few years...Within five years I would expect to see a substantial number of appointments from both these groups. This is not just a pious hope. It will be monitored (Taylor, 1992, p. 9).

He did not explain, however, how monitoring would, per se, bring about the increase in appointments of women and black people. Since 1992 the statistics which have been collected and, presumably, monitored show that the change which Lord Taylor predicted has not occurred. Although there has been some improvement in the figures in the last six years, with the proportion of black judges having risen from 0.9% to just under 2%, the total numbers are still very small. Numbers of women have similarly only shown a very moderate increase from 6.3% to 9.4%.[41] Although the rises were slightly greater in the lower ranks, these figures suggest that monitoring alone is insufficient to ensure that a significantly more representative judiciary is appointed. This then raises the question of whether more fundamental reforms to the system itself are needed. Whilst there is widespread agreement about the need for a more representative judiciary, this consensus breaks over the question of what action is required in the construction of the criteria for appointment in order to bring it about.

The trickle-up approach

The approach of the judiciary to this problem is firmly based on the premise that the make-up of the bench is not a product of the appointments process but a reflection of the background of the legal profession from which the judges are drawn. As the profile of the profession changes so will that of the judiciary and the under-represented groups will 'trickle-up' to the upper levels in increasing numbers. Lord Mackay summarised this position in 1994:

> Since the legal profession in this country is the base from which our judiciary is recruited, it follows that those making or recommending appointments are restricted by the nature of the members of the profession available for appointment. Over many years it had been difficult for women and members of the ethnic minorities to reach the senior ranks of the legal profession in the United Kingdom. This, I believe is in the course of changing, naturally and properly (1994, p. 9).

The consequence of the analysis of this change as being 'natural and proper' on the one hand, and dependent on the profile of the recruiting pool on the other, is that the greater representativeness of the judiciary is regarded as a change which will flow automatically, requiring little structural adjustment. The then Permanent Secretary of the Lord Chancellor's Department, Sir Thomas Legg, giving evidence to the Home Affairs Select Committee in 1996, argued that it was 'just a matter of time' before there were 'quite a lot of women judges'.[42] Similarly, in 1997 Lord Irvine emphasised the fact that the percentage of ethnic minority practitioners in both branches of the profession was rising, particularly in the junior ranks: 'While I am not complacent, I believe this is good news for the judiciary of the future'.[43] Lord Justice Sir Frederick Lawton has argued that the present over-representation of white men is simply a consequence of social and educational conditions of many years earlier, and that the Lord Chancellor cannot be expected to 're-write history'.[44]

The assumption which underlies these views is that the appointments process is a neutral conduit which identifies the most qualified members of the available recruiting pool. Appointments are made on merit alone and will include a proportionate number of qualified members of non-traditional groups once these reach the appropriate position in the legal profession. The most that is required of the system is to persuade women and members of ethnic minorities that the system is neutral and to apply. This is a strategy currently being adopted by the Lord Chancellor's Department. In an address to the Minority Lawyers Conference Lord Irvine stated:

> I will not be scattering promotions around like confetti - appointments must be made on merit. But I am determined to break down the culture of not applying because "they'd never have me or the likes of me".[45]

During the same speech Lord Irvine stressed the fact that prejudice does not exist in the appointments process and that the judges involved in the consultation process: 'go out of their way to be fair'. The effect of this analysis of the issue as being that of a 'culture of not applying' within a system free from discrimination is to transfer the problem away from the process itself and onto the applicants. Stressing the need to ensure that there should be no discrimination in the appointments process whilst emphasising that it has been free of discrimination suggests that the principle solution to the problem lies with the applicants readjusting their views of the system.

Structural and cultural barriers

This reliance on the 'trickle-up' model has its critics. In 1992, JUSTICE pointed out that the historical over-dominance of white males in the legal profession was ceasing to be a valid reason for the over-representation of this group. It argued that although there was some increase in the numbers of non-traditional appointees in the lower ranks, a smaller proportion of eligible women and members of ethnic minorities were being appointed to the first rank of Assistant Recorder and Recorder than the equivalent proportion of white men (JUSTICE, 1992, p. 13). Similarly, the make-up of those being appointed Queen's Counsel, which, under the 'trickle-up' model should be starting to reflect the changing profile of the legal profession has changed very little. In 1997, only one per cent of QCs were from an ethnic minority.[46] Moreover, during the 1990s the number of ethnic minority practitioners applying for Silk actually fell from 3.3% in

1992 to 2.4% in 1997. In evidence to the Home Affairs Select Committee the association of women barristers highlighted the 'obstinately small' number of women Silks and the disproportion between the number of women at the bar with over 15 years service and the 'tiny proportions of women on the bench'.[47] The continuing low number of women and members of ethnic minorities appointed as Queen's Counsel has a direct effect on the make-up of the senior bench because it is from this group that the majority of High Court appointments are made.

These figures suggest that the 'trickle-up' model fails to take account of the more complex cultural and structural reasons why women and members of ethnic minorities have failed to reach the judiciary. A number of witnesses before the Home Affairs Select Committee identified particular factors which they believed contributed to the under-representation of certain groups. In relation to both women and solicitors, the patterns of part-time sitting as an Assistant Recorder and Recorder was said to be problematic. The Law Society argued that women who took career breaks to have children found it difficult to complete the extensive period of part-time sitting. Similarly, solicitors found it difficult to take time out to sit for 20 days a year, since they were not self-employed but had to obtain the support of partners who would be financially carrying them for this period.

The experience of solicitors' attempts to gain access to the bench in recent years highlights the problems of the underlying resistance of the judiciary to change. Until recently only barristers were eligible for appointment to the senior bench. Under the Courts and Legal Services Act 1990 the potential pool of candidates was widened to include solicitors. The Act established a framework for expanding rights of audience and eligibility for the bench by creating different advocacy licences. The Bar's response to this change which threatened its advocacy monopoly was as aggressive as that of the solicitors to the equivalent removal of their exclusive control of conveyancing. However, the criticism from the judiciary to this change was equally strong (Zander, 1989, p. 18). Since all the senior judges were themselves drawn from the bar, it is not perhaps surprising that they should have supported the bar's position so unequivocally. Despite the intentions behind the Act, and because of the objections by the bar and the bench, the conditions upon which solicitors can qualify for extended rights of audience are stringent. As a result, eight years later only a few hundred solicitors have acquired rights of audience in the higher courts.[48] This means that solicitors are still only rarely eligible for senior appointments except via promotion from the circuit bench which is a comparatively rare route to the High Court. To date, only one solicitor has been appointed to the High Court although two solicitors were appointed as deputy High Court judges in 1997 by Lord Irvine who declared himself to have a: 'very, very progressive attitude to appointing suitably qualified solicitors to be deputy High Court judges and then High Court judges'.[49]

Despite these structural and attitudinal changes intended to open up the bench to both branches of the legal professions more equally, it is still strongly drawn not only from the bar, but from those barristers who have a strong advocacy record. In practice, many barristers as well as solicitors have 'paper' practices which involve very little appearance in court. These members of the bar are under-represented amongst the judges. Moreover, there is a further weighting to those with criminal experience. The emphasis on advocacy as a qualification for the bench was stressed by JUSTICE in 1992 as a structural barrier which was being placed in the way of solicitors:

> We share some of the concerns of the Law Society that the closer the solicitors' branch of the profession has come to being eligible for all levels of the judiciary, the greater has become the judiciary and bar's emphasis on advocacy as a *sine qua non* for judicial appointments (1992, p. 23).

Even if more solicitors acquire rights of audience in the higher courts, the strength of feeling against the breaking of the bar's monopoly amongst the judges suggests that such solicitor candidates for judicial office will not enjoy the same degree of support from the judges as their equivalent applicants from the bar. This problem is not only a problem for solicitors but has a knock-on effect across the range of under-represented groups. The solicitors' branch of the legal profession contains a much higher proportion of women, members of ethnic minorities people and those from more disadvantaged social backgrounds than does the bar. Increasing access for solicitors to the bench is an important means of increasing the pool of lawyers from non-traditional groups who are eligible for appointment.

Arguments which recognise the presence of structural factors in the appointments process as contributing to the unrepresentative make-up of the bench challenge the 'hands-off' approach of the judiciary which sees the question of representation as one which will resolve itself. In 1991, a leading solicitor, Geoffrey Bindman, suggested that the appointments process might amount to a breach of the Race Relations Act and Sex Discrimination Act which both prohibit unintended indirect discrimination. Bindman argued that the process of relying heavily on the opinions of other judges in the consultation process could be indirectly discriminatory and so illegal.[50] Lord Mackay, then Lord Chancellor, responded to that suggestion by seeking advice from counsel which, he claimed, showed that Bindman's argument was 'wrong in law and fact'. The strength of Lord Mackay's reaction suggests that by the early 1990s the judiciary had become aware that the unrepresentative make-up of the bench had become a highly sensitive issue which could no longer be ignored or treated lightly by the judges.

The clash between Geoffrey Bindman and Lord Mackay represented one of the first explicit acknowledgements of the different perspectives on how the problem of changing the judges' backgrounds should be approached. This conflict between the 'trickle-up' and structural explanations were again apparent in an exchange between Sir Thomas Legg and Chris Mullin MP regarding the appointment of Lord Justice Butler-Sloss (as she was then addressed) during the evidence taken by the Home Affairs Select Committee in 1996:

> *Chris Mullin*: I am sure that Lord Justice Butler-Sloss is a very capable judge who would have got to where she is on her merits, but she is also the sister of a Lord Chancellor and the daughter of a previous High Court judge, is she not?
>
> *Sir Thomas Legg*: Yes.
>
> *Chris Mullin*: Does it not strike you as remarkable that the only woman who has ever reached these rarefied circles, at the moment, appears to be extremely well-connected?
>
> *Sir Thomas Legg*: It does not strike me as particularly remarkable. It is a complete coincidence in her case.
>
> *Chris Mullin:* So a woman who was perhaps not the daughter of a High Court judge or a sister of a Lord Chancellor would have an equal chance of reaching the upper levels of the judiciary?
>
> *Sir Thomas Legg*: Absolutely.
>
> *Chris Mullin*: Has anyone ever done so?
>
> Sir Thomas Legg: Not yet.
>
> *Chris Mullin*: Thank you.

In a similar exchange with Chris Mullin, Lord Taylor claimed that a woman without Lord Butler-Sloss's connections could equally have made it to the senior bench, and he went on to promise that there would be many more senior women judges, and that not all of them would be the Lord Chancellor's sisters.[51]

Traditionally the judges have been dismissive of the argument that structural barriers exist for some who might seek appointment to the bench. Lord Taylor rejected the claim that women and solicitors were disadvantaged by the part-time sitting arrangement on the basis that this level of sacrifice was to be seen as a test of commitment to 'public service'. However, some recognition has been given to the particular position of women who take time out of their careers to raise children. Lord Mackay's policy was that such career breaks should be taken into account in making appointments:

> It is right to appoint the best person available at any particular time for the particular appointment. It is also right, in determining who that person might be, to take special account of the hurdles that individuals may have had to surmount in order to get to their present position in the profession (Lord Mackay, 1994, p. 10).

Lord Irvine took this process a stage further. In October 1997, he announced that there would be greater flexibility in part-time sitting arrangements to recognise the position of candidates who have taken a career break for family reasons. This would allow part-timers to concentrate their sittings into a shorter time. In addition, the age limit for appointment to Assistant Recorder was raised from 50 to 53 to accommodate such late entrants.

In addition to these formal structural barriers, informal processes have been identified as equally important in perpetuating the unrepresentative make-up of the bench. In evidence to the Home Affairs Select Committee a number of witnesses claimed that much depended on being 'seen' by members of the judiciary, both through formal interaction in court and informal contact through the social network. In 1973, before the relationship between the bar and the bench had become a sensitive topic, Sir Robert Megarry described the effect of judges and barristers sharing lunch in their Inns:

The atmosphere is one of ease and friendliness; and informal though it is it has a constitutional importance. It is in these regular contacts that we find so much of value rubbing off on each other (Megarry, 1973, p. 103).

These sorts of informal contacts are still very important in the light of the central role which the views of judges play in the consultation process. Solicitors are automatically excluded from these meetings while barristers from non-traditional groups who may not share the same social interests and background as the judges may be indirectly excluded. In view of the heavy reliance placed on the opinions of the judges in the appointments process those who miss such opportunities to be 'seen' are likely to be at a disadvantage.

Despite the recognition of these formal and informal structural barriers to appointment and the limitations of the 'trickle-up' approach to solving the problem, the proposal for introducing positive discrimination in any form attracts very little support both on or off the bench. Lord Taylor in his evidence to the Home Affairs Select Committee argued that his objection to such a strategy was widespread. He explained that he had attended an academic conference at which only one delegate amongst the three hundred present supported the principle of positive discrimination. Those who gave evidence before the Home Affairs Select Committee, including the Association of Women Solicitors and the Association of Women Barristers, equally opposed the introduction of affirmative action.[52] In 1997, Lord Irvine, in evidence to the Home Affairs Select Committee demonstrated the strength of feeling against such mechanisms for change:

> ...we cannot have affirmative action, we cannot have positive discrimination, and appointments must continue to be made on merit. You cannot have the judiciary as some kind of social experiment and you cannot run risks with the administration of justice for us all simply to correct gender or other imbalances on the bench.[53]

The almost universal rejection of any form of affirmative action appears to be based on a definition of the process as being the appointment or promotion of a less qualified person over one who is more qualified. Support for any form of preferential treatment is generally limited to the practice of actively encouraging one group to apply and appointing a member of that group over an equally qualified person from another group. Lord Taylor himself suggested that where two equal applicants were being considered, one a man and one a woman, it might be appropriate to appoint the woman.

Since there appears to be almost no support for any form of quota system or equivalent, much will depend on how effective the Lord Chancellor's Department can be in encouraging qualified candidates from under-represented groups to come forward and apply. The judiciary has traditionally argued that a pool of untapped talent amongst non-traditional lawyers does not exist. Similar arguments have been heard in other common law countries. The former Minister of Justice in New Zealand, for example, argued that during the time he spent appointing judges he had made considerable efforts to find qualified women and Maori candidates but that few were available (Palmer, 1993, p. 36). However, in other jurisdictions attempts actively to seek out under-represented groups have been more successful. For example, the Ontario Judicial Appointments Advisory Committee has had notable success in recent years in identifying well qualified women and black lawyers who had not applied in the past because they felt that they were not the type of candidates who would be appointed.

One response to the apparent dearth of qualified candidates from non-traditional backgrounds is to ask whether the qualifications required in the form of appointment criteria exclude such groups. If the appointment process seeks to find candidates who are identical in every way to those currently selected apart from their sex or race it is unlikely that many will be found. There are very unlikely to be significant numbers of women and members of ethnic minorities being passed over who have exactly the same type of educational background, years of advocacy experience, attitudes and values as those who are currently appointed. If judges from wider backgrounds are sought, then the criteria will have to be adapted to give recognition to the qualities which such candidates bring to the bench. The result might be gains in some areas and losses in others. In particular, the current balance in favour of forensic skills over humanistic skills discussed above might need to be reconsidered. We may, for example, reduce the proportion of judges who have first class degrees in law from Oxford or Cambridge and many years of advocacy experience, and so sacrifice some legal technical skills but increase the proportion of judges who have a broader range of 'life skills and experience' and so improve their awareness and sensitivity to the perspectives of those coming before the courts.

This change of emphasis would be consistent with international jurisprudence on judicial appointments in which the requirements of representativeness are increasingly being given priority. For example, article 2.13 of the Montreal Universal Declaration on the Independence of Justice states that: 'The process and standards of judicial selection shall give due consideration to ensuring a fair reflection by the judiciary of the society in all its aspects'.[54] Many national and state selection processes have similar statutory requirements. Yet despite the growing international support for the inclusion of representativeness as an independent criteria for appointment, there is resistance to such a change from within the judiciary. In evidence to the Home Affairs Select Committee the Lord Chancellor's Department rejected any structural attempt to change the make-up of the judiciary in such a way: 'The Lord Chancellor has no plans to reconstitute the professional judiciary to reflect the composition of society as a whole'. [55]

Comparative factors

Although all judiciaries are demographically unrepresentative to some degree, the extent to which this is the case in England and Wales is not paralleled in all other systems. It is therefore worthwhile examining those judiciaries where the balance is different in order to highlight those variables which appear particularly influential in determining the make-up of the judiciary.

Two generalisations can be made about the representativeness of judiciaries around the world. First, the more activist the judiciary the less representative it tends to be as a whole. Second, the higher the rank of the judiciary the less representative that rank will be. As a general rule, women feature in greater numbers in those judicial systems where judges have less power and prestige. In France, for example, where women make up nearly half the judiciary, judges are regarded as civil servants rather than a branch of the government and do not generally enjoy the equivalent status of an English judge. Moreover, it is notable that even in France the ratio of men to women changes at the higher, more powerful ranks, where men outnumber women 2:1 (McKillop, 1996, p. 24). The relevance of this rather simplistic correlation for England is that the external pressure for greater representativeness is growing at a time when the judiciary is becoming more powerful. The notion that women and black people will 'trickle up' to the senior ranks needs explicitly to address the fact that those ranks are becoming increasingly politically important. There will therefore be an inevitable conflict between the career paths of women and black people in the lower ranks and the traditional pattern of responsibility in public and professional life in which access to powerful positions is still largely restricted to white men.

In general there is a clear division between the make-up of the judiciaries in continental Europe and the common law countries such as New Zealand, Australia, South Africa, Canada and the US. The former are more representative, the latter much closer to the English model. In New Zealand, for example, the proportion of women is very similar to that of England and Wales. In 1993, they made up just under 9 per cent of the judiciary (Palmer, 1993, p. 46). This contrasts strongly with the position in other European countries such as France, for example, where women now outnumber men in the entrants to the judges' training school (Ecole Nationale de la Magistrature). A similar pattern exists in the Netherlands, Italy and Germany. The key variable in this difference is the fact that judges in these civil law jurisdictions are specially trained rather than being recruited from amongst practicing lawyers. Although the arrangements differ from country to country, judges attend some form of judicial college and generally start sitting in their early thirties. In France, 79% of judges are aged under 50 (McKillop, 1996, p. 22). The success of women under this system has been attributed to the emphasis on examination results in which women generally do as well, or better, than men.

A similar comparison with other professional and elite groups in England also demonstrates the effect of alternative appointments processes. Whilst middle aged, middle class, white men dominate most groups with power and status there are significant differences in the degree to which this pattern occurs which can be traced to differences in the way in which the individuals are appointed. Amongst doctors, for example, women make up 49% of GPs and 31% of hospital doctors.[56] In common with continental judges, doctors are specially trained and start practice relatively young with almost equal numbers of women and men entering medical school. MPs, in contrast, have traditionally had a very unrepresentative profile similar to judges. However, the 1997 general election resulted in a significant increase in the proportion of women in the House of Commons to 18%. This rise is almost all attributable to the much criticised women-only constituency shortlists adopted for a short period by the Labour party before the election. Another field which has seen an improvement in the position of women is the Civil Service where candidates are appointed through an open competition using formal panels and assessment methods which, it has been suggested, discourages the most obvious forms of self-replication.

These examples from different fields of public and professional life identify different structural factors which influence the proportion of women appointed. They suggest that early specialist training, the use of quotas and appointment by open competition can all be factors which improve the representativeness of a body. The fact that none of these structures is present in the judicial appointments process is undoubtedly a relevant factor in the continuing unrepresentative make-up of the judiciary.

The use of a judicial appointments commission

This review of the judicial appointments process thus far highlights that there are two aspects to the criticisms of the present arrangements; the failings of the system itself in terms of accountability, judicial independence and procedural openness, and its failings in terms of the type of judge appointed. The changes introduced to date have gone some way to addressing some of these problems. But the continuing lack of openness in the system and the very slow progress which is being made in increasing representativeness has fuelled calls for a more fundamental change. In particular, there is growing support for the adoption of some form of judicial appointments commission.

Proposals for establishing a judicial appointments commission have a long history, going back as far as *The Report of the Committee on the Machinery of Government* in 1918 (JUSTICE, 1992, p. 27). Before the War, the relative political passivity of the judiciary and the high level of public respect which it commanded limited the support for such a radical development. Within the last decade this has changed. Despite the reforms instituted by Lord Mackay during his period as Lord Chancellor designed to reduce the level of secrecy in the appointments process and to increase the representativeness of appointees, by the mid-1990s there was a widely held view that more radical changes were needed. In 1996, the Home Affairs Select Committee Report reviewed the pros and cons of adopting an alternative appointments process. The system of electing judges (as used in some US states) was dismissed out of hand as incompatible with the constitutional role of the judiciary.[57]

Fuller consideration was given to the possibility of establishing a career judiciary such as exists in many other European countries where judges are appointed after a long period of training and examinations. This system was supported by a number of those who gave evidence but was rejected by the Committee on the grounds that it would impose large scale change for no clear gain.[58] More detailed consideration was given to the proposal for establishing a judicial appointments commission. Whilst acknowledging the growing support for such a system and recognising its merits, the Committee concluded that creating a commission would not necessarily improve the quality of appointees and that the value of the consultation process would be diminished. This opinion was strongly supported by the judiciary. The Lord Chief Justice, then Lord Taylor, the Lord Chancellor, then Lord Mackay and the Council of Judges all strongly objected to the proposal. In contrast, the idea was supported in evidence by many other witnesses such as JUSTICE, the Law Society, NACRO and the Howard League for Penal Reform.[59]

In 1995, the Labour Party adopted the proposal for a judicial commission in its policy document *Access to Justice*. The election of the Labour Government in May 1997 therefore brought the implementation of the reform within sight for the first time. A month after coming to power, Lord Irvine, the Lord Chancellor, announced that he would be consulting on the merits of establishing a commission and commissioned research on their use in Europe and North America (see Thomas, 1997 and Malleson, 1997). However, in October 1997, the Government announced that the pressure of the workload of the reforms to the Legal Aid system and civil justice was such that it would be inappropriate for the Lord Chancellor's Department to take on any other major programmes. It was therefore decided to shelve the proposal for establishing a commission. Lord Irvine made clear that he did not reject the idea on substantive grounds and suggested that he did not rule out further changes in the future, so leaving the door open for its creation at some later date.[60]

In addition to the practical restraints of time and resources, the objections of the judiciary to the proposal were, no doubt, a significant factor in the decision not to proceed with a commission at that point. The new Government was likely to be particularly sensitive to the views of the judges in the light of the recent history of poor relations between the executive and the judiciary. One of the first speeches which Lord Irvine made as Lord Chancellor was a strong statement of his commitment to re-establishing the support of the judges and co-operation between the two branches of government. He might well, therefore, have wished to avoid an early confrontation on the subject of appointments particularly at a time when the support of the bench was needed if Lord Woolf's reforms to the civil process were to be instituted successfully.

Despite the decision not to proceed with the establishment of a commission in 1997, there are good reasons to believe that such a change is very likely in the future. The underlying reasons for the increasing popularity of an appointments commission will grow stronger in the years to come. The expansion of the judicial role through the incorporation of the European Convention on Human Rights is very likely to increase public concern about the current system so that the pressure for change will grow. This trend is not confined to England and Wales. The experiences of other judiciaries suggests that the link between growing judicial activism and the use of a commission is a very strong one. A recurring theme in many countries has been the pressure for the judicial appointments system to be secure from partisan political pressure while at the same time more open and accountable. The global response to these pressures has increasingly been to replace elections and exclusive executive appointment with some form of commission.

The current proposals in England and Wales have, for example, been mirrored in India, Australia and New Zealand in recent years (Palmer, 1993; Cunningham, 1996). In North America the use of commissions has increased significantly in the last decade. Although judges in the US states are usually thought of as being elected, appointment by election is both relatively recent and increasingly less common. Under the original appointment system established after independence most judges were appointed by the Governor or the state legislature. Elections were not introduced until the nineteenth century and had a relatively short heyday. During the last sixty years they have been gradually replaced by commissions, the first of which was adopted in 1940. Since then, 33 states and the district of Columbia have created some form of commission and many of the remaining states seem likely to follow this pattern. The commissions are termed 'Missouri plans' or 'merit plans' and the latter name highlights the key feature of the system, that it is intended to remove politics from the appointment process and replace it by appointment on merit alone.[61]

Similarly, the equivalent Canadian appointment committees have grown in popularity since they were first introduced in the 1980s. The experience of Canada is a useful one because its appointment system before the introduction of committees was very similar to that of England and Wales. Unlike the US, it has no history of appointment by election and has adopted committees in an attempt to provide greater openness and wider participation within a system of executive appointment. The move to the use of committees also coincides with the passing of the Charter of Rights and freedoms in 1982 which led to an expansion of the judges' role in human rights and public policy. This increased activism in turn led to pressure for reform of the appointments process (Marshall, 1995, p. 42). Supporters of a commission in this country have, understandably, identified the Canadian experience as a useful precedent for England and Wales (Fitz-James 1993).

The most recent common law country to switch to a commission is South Africa where the Judicial Service Commission was set up in 1994 under the Interim Constitution. Its rationale was a familiar one; to encourage greater openness, the appointment of a more representative judiciary and the removal of the influence of partisan politics which had dominated the appointments process under the apartheid regime (Kentridge, 1996, p. 252).

Nor are these developments limited to the common law world; a similar trend has occurred in European civil law countries in recent years. Although these countries employ a formalised judicial career structure a growing number have introduced commissions in the form of Higher Judicial Councils to appoint and promote judges. These have been identified as both a consequence and a cause of increasing judicial power (Thomas, 1997). Similar developments have occurred in Eastern Europe since the early 1990s where commissions have been introduced as part of the democractic reforms in order to encourage greater judicial independence.

A common underlying reason behind these developments is the desire to insulate the judicial appointments process from improper political control. Although in recent years the appointments process in England and Wales has been relatively free of the political patronage which has been more common in other countries, there is growing concern that this may change as the power of the judges grows. The Institute for Public Policy Research in its draft written constitution in 1991 suggested that freedom from political interference in the appointment of judges was one of the key features of judicial independence. In order to ensure this freedom in the event of the creation of a written constitution it proposed the creation of a Judicial Services Commission to be responsible for judicial appointments

(IPPR, 1991, p. 19). Although there are no current plans for a adopting a written constitution in England and Wales, the rationale which underpins the proposal applies equally to the provisions of the Human Rights Act since it effectively incorporates a Bill of Rights into domestic law.

This link between judicial activism, judicial independence and the form of judicial appointments process is a recurring theme in the growing body of international treaties and declarations on judicial independence. These documents stress the need to prioritise freedom from executive pressure in the appointments process. The Tokyo Principles specifically recommend the use of an appointments commission to this end.[62] More usually, the treaties do not prescribe one form of appointment or another, but rather all stress that the ideal appointment process is free of exclusive executive or legislative control - a requirement that many have argued is best fulfilled by the use of a commission.

As more commissions are established around the world the variety of models grows. Each system adapts the form and function which suits its own legal and political culture. Consequently, there is no shortage of alternative types of commission for examination in assessing the strengths and weaknesses of the different systems. Although in England and Wales there has been widespread support for a commission of some kind for many years, its membership, powers and functions have not generally been thought through in any detail. The examples drawn on below are by no means definitive but are sufficient to provide some overview of the effects of alternative models.

Role

It should be understood that the use of a commission is not normally a free-standing method of judicial selection but is combined with executive appointment since it is usually a governor, attorney general or minister of justice who carries out the final appointment of the candidates.[63] Not all commissions play the same role in the selection process. A key distinction arises between those commissions which take a proactive part in identifying and recruiting suitable candidates and those which undertake a purely advisory function limited to assessing the quality of candidates who are referred to the commission by the executive. A full nominating commission, such as the South African Judicial Service Commission, plays a determining role in selecting candidates, leaving the executive with, at most, a restricted discretion to choose between candidates, whereas an advisory commission plays no direct role in the selection of the appointees. Even within this distinction there are a wide range of different models of commission. The American Judicature Society (AJS) which promotes and monitors the use of commissions in the US, has suggested that a true nominating commission consists of the following basic elements:

1. The inclusion of both lay and lawyer members to recruit, screen, investigate and evaluate judicial candidates
2. Nomination to the appointing authority of a limited number of candidates, and
3. Appointment by the Governor or other appointing authority.

These broad characteristics are found in many commissions at state level in the US and provincial level in Canada, although throughout both countries there is a wide variety of particular models. In Canada, the extent to which the commissions act in an advisory capacity as opposed to taking a proactive role in recruiting, selecting and nominating candidates differs (Friedland, 1995, p. 243). The Judicial Appointments Advisory Committee (JAAC) in Ontario was the first commission set up in Canada which complied with the American Judicature Society definition. It was created as a pilot project in 1988 and put on a statutory basis in 1994.[64] Despite its name, the JAAC performs the function of a full commission, and replaced the more limited Judicial Council which had been set up in 1968 to advise the executive on the suitability of candidates. The Ontario system is now established as the one which Canadian commentators frequently cite as the most successful example of the use of an appointment committee in Canada and is increasingly being looked to as a model for other provinces.

At the US federal level, judicial appointments are made by the President and confirmed (or not) by the Senate Judiciary Committee. The American Bar Association Nominating Commission, despite its name, fulfils an advisory function only, screening candidates and ranking them according to their suitability. The President is not formally obliged to follow the ABA recommendations, though it would, of course, be politically difficult for a President regularly to ignore them. In Canada at federal level similar appointment committees fulfil an equally limited advisory role. The first Canadian federal judicial appointments advisory committee was established in 1967 in an attempt to reduce the influence of partisan politics in the appointment process. The Canadian Bar Association

National Committee on the Judiciary was given the task of assessing the suitability of candidates for senior appointments. Under this system the Minister of Justice submitted names of candidates to the Committee which assessed the candidates as 'very well qualified', 'well qualified', 'qualified' or 'not qualified' (Friedland, 1995, 28 p. 236). However, concern continued to be expressed about the political nature of the process, and this criticism intensified with the passing of the Charter of Rights and the expansion of the political function of the senior judges (Russell, 1987, p. 130).

In response to these concerns, a new system of national advisory committees based in the provinces and territories was established in 1988 and modified somewhat in the intervening years.[65] The role of the federal committees is to assess candidates whose practices are based in that judicial district. Although the committees have been described by the Minister of Justice as 'the heart of the appointments process' their function is limited.[66] They do not play a proactive role in recruiting candidates and drawing up a shortlist of candidates but rather respond to the names submitted to them by the executive. Their role is to weed out unqualified candidates rather than to identify those who should be appointed. The committee assesses candidates as 'unable to recommend', 'recommended' or 'highly recommended'. The recommendations received by the advisory committees are not the only source of information available in the final appointment process; they are used in collaboration with the views of senior members of the judiciary and bar gathered by the Minister through consultations. Recently, Ministers have agreed only to appoint those who are recommended by the committee although they are under no statutory obligation to do so.

Where a commission fulfils a full nominating function, a determining factor in its role is the extent to which the executive appointing authority has any discretion to choose between different candidates proposed by the commission or to reject the list of candidates provided. In South Africa, a distinction is drawn between the procedure for appointing constitutional judges and ordinary judges of the High Court and Court of Appeal. For the latter, the Judicial Service Commission advises the President of its choice of candidate and he is required to appoint the Commission's choice.[67] However, in relation to the Constitutional Court, the Commission submits a list of nominees which must include three names more than the number of judges to be appointed. The President then makes his selection from this list. He may also reject, with reasons, ptable candidates and require supplemental ones, though this has date, occurred.[68]

In almost all US states where commissions are used, the appointing authority is obliged to choose one of the commission's nominees, though not necessarily the first on the list. Model provisions provided by the American Judicature Society recommend that the commission shall nominate no less than two nor more than five candidates to the appointing authority. In practice, some commissions send as many as seven names but the most common number is three. The JAAC in Ontario similarly provides the Attorney General with a ranked shortlist of at least two recommended candidates with accompanying reasons for its decision. The Attorney General must appoint a candidate on the list although, as in South Africa, he may reject the list and ask for a new one to be drawn up.

Where the executive must select from a list, an important factor is the type and amount of information which the commissions send with the names of the nominees. In the US there is a wide range of different practices. Some send the names with no further material. Others add some or all of the following: the nominee's C.V., a written questionnaire completed by the nominee, bar survey performance evaluation results, a written evaluation by the commission, its investigative file, a letter of recommendation and the number of votes received by each nominee.

Another important factor which determines the extent of a commission's role is whether it is used to recommend candidates for promotion as well as first appointment. In Canada, only initial appointments are sent to the federal committees since it is thought to be inappropriate for them to scrutinise the performance of sitting judges (Friedland, 1995, p. 240). However, in South Africa, the Judicial Service Commission is used to promote judges to the higher ranks. Moreover, such serving judges are interviewed in public in the same way as candidates for first appointments, yet this does not appear to have given rise to any particular problems in relation to judicial independence.

Membership and tenure

It is often claimed that the make-up of a commission is a determining factor in its effectiveness. Questions concerning who the members are, how long they serve and, equally important, who appoints them are relevant because they have a bearing on the degree of independence and accountability of the commission. Just as the independence of judges is affected by their appointment and tenure arrangements, so too is that of the people who appoint the judges.

One of the recurring arguments against the establishment of a commission in England and Wales has been that it would reduce democratic accountability by removing the responsibility for selection from a member of the elected government. In response to such concerns, commissions have developed two methods for maintaining a link with the democratic process. The first maintains a direct connection by including elected politicians on the commission, the second method is indirect, by giving politicians the power to appoint the commissioners. In addition to these mechanisms of electoral accountability, the membership of the commission can be assessed in terms of its social accountability. Since a common reason for establishing a commission is to provide a means of widening participation in the judicial selection process, the background of the members is an important variable in assessing a commission's accountability.

The make-up of the commissions is partly dependent on their size which differs significantly from 23 members in South Africa down to as few as five in many US states (American Judicature Society, 1995). In South Africa, concern has been expressed that the size of the Judicial Service Commission makes it cumbersome, particularly in view of the fact that it meets en banc and all candidates are interviewed by the entire body. But the advantage of a large commission, and indeed, the reason for the size of the Judicial Service Commission, is that it is possible to incorporate a very wide range of representatives in the selection process. It includes lawyers, lay persons, an academic, judges and politicians from both national and regional legislatures. Similarly, the nine member Israeli commission also includes representatives from the legislature as well as judges lawyers and lay persons. Smaller commissions, in contrast, tend to include only some of these groups. In the US, some states, particularly those which adopted the system in the early years such as California, use a commission made up exclusively of judges and lawyers. But most of the more recently established commissions do seek to include some lay representation. There is concern that without lay representation the commission risks being transformed into another form of closed institution. As one Canadian commentator has noted: 'the purpose of the advisory committee is to dismantle the old boys network, not to replace it with a private lawyers' club'.[69] A common US model in practice consists of three lawyers, three non-lawyers and one judge who has a casting vote. In continental Europe the commissions are generally composed of judges, lawyers, lay persons and politicians although judges play a more dominant role than they do in North America (Thomas, 1997).

While lay representation is normal around the world, the proportion of lay members differs. Almost all of the 24 members of the South African Judicial Service Commission are lawyers, either in practice or by training, whereas in Ontario, the JAAC has a majority lay membership of 7 on the committee of 13. Unfortunately, there is very little research evidence as to the relationship between the different groups and the relative influence they exercise. In general, it appears that lawyers and judges tend to exercise disproportion control and sometimes regard the lay members as something of an irritant. In the US, two surveys carried out by the American Bar Association in 1973 and 1989 revealed expressions of tension between lawyers and lay members: 'While this animosity is not necessarily surprising... or even necessarily detrimental, it repeatedly surfaces as a matter of concern amongst commissioners' (Henschen et al., 1990, p. 333). In South Africa and Canada relations between the committee members appear to be generally more harmonious with an emphasis on achieving a consensus and the inclusive involvement of all members, although this is only anecdotal evidence and has not yet been tested by more rigorous research.

The way in which commissioners are appointed differs depending on who they are. Judge members are usually appointed by a Chief Justice or a council of judges. Lawyer members are usually appointed by their professional governing body although in a large minority of the US commission the lawyers are also appointed by the Governor (American Judicature Society, 1995). Lay members are almost always appointed by the executive and politicians will generally be chosen by the legislature.

Because a minister is almost always responsible to a greater or lesser extent for appointing at least some members of the committee, the tenure arrangements are important in determining the potential for executive influence over the decisions of its appointees. The ideal tenure system from the point of view of independence would be long, non-renewable contracts. In fact, the opposite pattern is generally employed. Most commission members hold office for between one and six years, and many can seek to have their membership renewed. Model provisions produced by the AJS provide for fixed tenures of four or six years with a maximum of two appointments. In the Canadian federal committees, the

Ontario JAAC and the South African Judicial Service Commission, renewable terms are allowed while in the US a handful of commissions have members appointed at the 'Governor's pleasure'. On the face of it, these arrangement would appear to represent the worst of both worlds. The presence of renewable terms of office has the potential to reduce the independence of commission members, while long periods of service run the risk of entrenched patterns of selection and the establishment of political factions amongst the members. Again, there is a dearth of empirical evidence from which to judge whether these dangers have materialised in practice.

Since one of the main justifications for creating a commission is to improve the representativeness of those appointed to the bench, the background of the members themselves is clearly a relevant factor in achieving this goal. In most countries which use commissions, there is some overt attempt to ensure representativeness amongst the members. The AJS model provisions, for example, propose that: 'all appointing authorities shall make reasonable efforts to ensure that the commission substantially reflects the gender, ethnic and racial diversity of the jurisdiction' (American Judicature Society, 1994). This provision has been adopted by most of the more recently established commissions. The two American Bar Association surveys which examined their make-up both came to the broad, and not particularly surprising conclusion that the commissioners were well-educated, generally middle-aged and overwhelmingly white (Ashman and Alfini, 1973; Henschen et al., 1990). Although men were still in the majority in the second survey, there was a significant change in the proportion of women between the two studies, rising from 10 per cent in 1973 to 25 per cent in 1989 (Henschen et al., 1990, p. 330).

In the Canadian federal system there is an attempt to ensure a representative range of members in that the Minister of Justice is required to seek to select committee members who reflect the geographical, gender, language and cultural factors in the province. Similarly, in Ontario the lawyers associations and the Attorney General are required by statute to consider the need for demographic representativeness amongst the members of the JAAC.

The process of selecting candidates

The common goals of all commissions can be summarised as being to select candidates on merit whilst promoting a more representative judiciary through processes which are fair and non-discriminatory and are sufficiently open that they are seen to be so. The practical arrangements for achieving this aim differ from commission to commission. In particular, the way in which candidates are recruited, the selection criteria which are applied, the information which is gathered on candidates and the methods of assessment employed all vary widely.

A commission, like any other appointment method, can only appoint or recommend good candidates if they apply so that the initial recruitment stage is a very important part of the process. This is particularly true in the context of the attempts to attract candidates from non-traditional backgrounds who may not automatically consider themselves as likely candidates unless their applications are actively sought out. Many commissions favour the use of advertisements as the most open and inclusive means of attracting a wide range of candidates. In Ontario, the JAAC advertises vacancies once informed by the Attorney General that one has arisen or is anticipated. Advertisements are similarly used in the Canadian federal system, having been first employed in the late 1980s. An applicant wishing to be considered can at any stage apply to the Commissioner for Federal Affairs who is the civil servant with overall responsibility for judicial appointments. Applications are received by the Commissioner who then submits to the relevant federal committee the names of those who are technically eligible for appointment.

Under the AJS model provisions when a vacancy occurs, or it is known that one will occur on a specific date, the chair of the commission advertises the post and solicits the submission of qualified candidates through the media. Some commissions require nominations rather than applications in person. The South African Judicial Service Commission is required to announce vacancies publicly and seek nomination from a range of interested organisations listed by statute.[70] Individuals are at liberty to nominate themselves and some have apparently done so, though thus far without success.

Once candidates have applied to a commission there is a wide variety in the way in which they are assessed and the selection made. The AJS model provisions do not specify in detail how commissions should go about obtaining references, shortlisting, interviewing and assessing candidates, but instead require them to make whatever rules and procedures best aid the appointment of the most qualified candidate. The minimum level of assessment would appear to be a review of the curriculum vitae of candidates. In the 1993 survey of commissions conducted by the American Bar Association, all those commissions which responded claimed to carry out a review of a candidate's biographical information. Almost all conducted a review of questionnaires completed by the candidates and most solicited written recommendations about candidates although only three states declared that they had access to judicial performance evaluation produced by the local bar association. Some criticisms were expressed by commission members that there was insufficient training and guidelines for evaluating candidates and not enough time or information with which to evaluate them (American Bar Association, 1993).

A particularly controversial question concerns the use of interviews. These form a central feature of the selection procedures of many commissions. According to the American Bar Association survey, all US commissions carry out interviews (American Bar Association, 1993, p. 10). In the Canadian federal system, the use of interviews by the committees is encouraged although these are not mandatory and none is public. In contrast, in Ontario interviews are compulsory. A candidate is asked for interview by the JAAC if three members of the commission short-list them. In South Africa, all short-listed candidates are interviewed and these take place in public. This aspect of the process aroused considerable criticism when first proposed. Initial opposition by the Bar Council meant that some early interviews were conducted in private which in turn provoked criticism from those who supported greater openness and objected to the decision to exclude television cameras and radio broadcasting during interviews (Mureinik, 1996). However, despite this controversial beginning, the use of public interviews appears now to be widely regarded as a very successful aspect of the South African selection process. Although the candidates themselves clearly do not relish the experience, they generally support the system and it does not, as was originally feared, appear to have deterred qualified candidates from applying. One member of the Constitutional Court, Mr Justice Langa, summarised the position in the following way during his interview before the Judicial Service Commission:

Speaking as a person who is sitting on this seat now, I must say I would have preferred not to have been interviewed at all, but I realise that the interviewing process is useful and I think it is essential and correct and I am fully in support of open hearings.

Part of the explanation for the popularity of the South African public interviews is the restrained way in which they have been conducted. Each interview lasts for approximately 45 minutes and there is no attempt to catch candidates off-guard. If any controversial allegation is to be put to the candidates they will be given advance notice of it. The stated aim is to promote the positive rather than the negative aspects of the candidates' qualities so that although the questions are sometimes demanding they are not aggressive or personalised in the way that has been witnessed in the past in the US Senate confirmation hearings where candidates have been cross-examined about all aspects of their lives over a period of hours or even days.

Consultations and confidentiality

A particularly controversial issue in the selection procedure concerns the use of confidential consultations with senior judges and lawyers who have knowledge of the candidate's work. Since the consultation process has been the subject of sustained criticism in England and Wales an important question is whether the change to a commission would mean that they could be dispensed with. The experience of commissions in this area is mixed. Some continue to rely heavily on such consultations. In Ontario, the JAAC carries out what are termed 'discreet inquiries' of senior members of the bench and bar which appear to be indistinguishable from the consultation process in England and Wales. It seems clear from the committee's most recent report that these inquiries are considered particularly useful. Although the report clearly states the committee's concern about the lack of openness of this aspect of the process, it concludes that much valuable information is obtained through this channel. During the early days of the new system the committee found that some who were approached were reluctant to provide frank opinions. However, once the committee was well established and the complete confidentiality of the process was assured, the flow of information resumed.

Similarly, just over half the US commissions carry out consultations with members of the bench and bar (American Bar Association, 1993). Almost all adopt rules relating to confidentiality and most states have determined that communications between the commission and third parties are confidential. This is generally held to be justified on the grounds that it is necessary to encourage candour (Comisky and Patterson, 1987, p. 17). However, one of the strongest concern expressed by commission members to the 1993 American Bar Association survey was, in fact, the lack of confidentiality. One respondent to the ABA survey gave a forceful criticism of this:

> Press access to *all* input has eliminated any candor from the bar, sitting judiciary state attorney, public defender and concerned public. We get b.s. (sic) from all quarters and must make decisions often unaware of the true abilities of an applicant (American Bar Association, 1993, p. 65).

In South Africa, the Judicial Service Commission has no formal consultation stage in its procedure but individual members do contact judges and lawyers to seek information about a candidate when they are unfamiliar with his or her work and reputation.

In all these systems consultations form only one aspect of the procedure. In Ontario, for example, the 'discreet inquiries' are supplemented by references supplied by the candidate. These referees are sent a letter setting out the criteria for appointment and are then contacted by telephone to discuss the candidate's suitability. What is not known is what relative weight is given to these consultations throughout the different commissions.

The nature of the procedures employed depends to a great extent on the size of the operation. In most systems which employ a commission the number of judges appointed each year is far smaller than that of England and Wales. For example, between 1988 and 1992 the JAAC in Ontario appointed a total of 67 judges, 26 per cent of the 260 Provincial Division judges in Ontario. At one stage during this period the committee felt it necessary to divide into two panels in order to manage the workload. In contrast, in England and Wales approximately 600 judges are appointed in any one year. If a committee of thirteen members cannot easily manage an average of less than twenty appointments a year, the practicalities of the working arrangements for an equivalent system in England and Wales will need careful consideration. The greater size of the workload may mean that a significant amount of the work may need to be delegated to civil servants leaving the commission itself to fulfil a more overseeing function. Alternatively, a much larger commission would need to be created which then divided into subcommittees to assess applications and carry out interviews.

The possible effects of a commission

In 1991 the Law Society carried out a comparative review of appointments systems in Australia, Canada, New Zealand, the US and all European Union countries. It identified four principles which underpin the different systems as competence, independence, accountability and representativeness (Skordaki, 1991). It concluded that those countries which employ elections emphasise accountability and representativeness at the cost of a degree of independence whereas those in which judges are appointed by the executive emphasise competence and independence at the cost of some accountability and representativeness. Supporters of commissions argue that they combine the best features of the alternatives systems in that they increase representativeness and accountability through the creation of a more open and responsive system whilst securing judicial independence by reducing the political involvement of the executive in the process.

The global expansion in the use of commissions means that there should now be sufficient comparative evidence on which to assess this claim. However, despite a relatively large literature on the subject of judicial commissions there is a surprising paucity of empirical data on their effects. This is perhaps to be expected in areas such as South Africa, Canada and Continental Europe where commissions have been in use for a relatively short period of time, but it is more surprising in the US which has a long history of appointing judges by commission. It is notable that most of the American commentaries on judicial selection are premised on a general preference for one system or another rather than providing an attempt at assessing objectively the empirical findings on the subject (see, for example, Krivosha, 1990). As one recent review of the literature put it: 'The debate over judicial selection is so filled with value judgements and unsupported claims that it is hard to identify what is known from what is not' (Champagne and Haydel, 1993, p. 14). Moreover, the US empirical research which does exist tends, for obvious reasons, to compare commissions with the electoral method which they usually replace rather than executive appointment. This obviously reduces its relevance for English purposes. What follows, therefore, is a preliminary attempt to draw together some of the findings on the use of commissions in order to reach some general conclusions about their effects on the type of judge appointed in terms of competence and representativeness as well as the process itself - whether it promotes more or less judicial independence, accountability and openness.

Competence

It is commonly argued that the way in which judges are appointed is a determining factor in the type of judiciary which is found in any particular country: 'The quality of the judiciary and its composition is largely dependent upon the method of judicial appointment' (Sheetreet, 1987, p. 766). Such a statement has a strong ring of common sense, but it is surprisingly difficult to support empirically. Even when comparing the most fundamentally different methods of appointment - the electoral and executive systems - it is not evident that the judiciaries which the two systems produce are significantly different. One recent review of the US systems of appointment concluded that: 'despite feelings of distaste, it is hard to point to anything in the American evidence which suggests that election has had any profound effects upon the American judiciary' (Palmer, 1993, p. 52). One of the main justifications in the US for adopting a commission over an electoral system is that the use of informed lay people, lawyers and judges would improve the legal skill and intellectual calibre of the bench. However, there does not appear to be any strong evidence to support this contention. Rather, the research seems to suggest that the appointment process makes little difference to the competence of the judges appointed:

> There is no evidence to support the proposition that any one of these systems produces a 'better judge' than do the others. Academic background and prior judicial experience tend to be approximately the same for judges selected under each system (Volcansek and Lafon, 1988, p. 139).

Similarly, another recent review of the appointment system concluded that: 'empirical work suggests that the method of selection has little if any overall effect on the quality of judges' (Webster, 1995). Some commentators have suggested that the use of a commission may actually detract from appointment on merit:

> Contrary to reformist hopes that the attorneys would provide and support professional criteria for selection, the attorneys are motivated to select judges whose social and economic views are most likely to coincide with those of the litigants they represent in court (Glick, 1978, p. 520).

However, there seems to be no more empirical evidence to support this claim than the former.

In Canada, many commentators have argued that the establishment of the JAAC has improved the quality of the bench in Ontario (Friedland, 1995, p. 246) but again this claim is based on a general perception rather than firm empirical data. One reason for this problem is the lack of any rigorous systems for assessing standards of competence in the judiciary. The JAAC is itself conscious of this problem and has recommended that performance appraisal be introduced in order to provide a means of assessing the quality of its appointments. The results of such monitoring would be useful in helping to identify the current standards of competence within the Ontario judiciary, although it would have a limited value for comparative purposes since no equivalent data was gathered under the previous appointments system.

Representativeness

The difficulty in reaching any firm conclusions as to the relative competence of the judiciary appointed under different systems is equally apparent when comparing their representativeness. Many commentators have argued that changing the appointments system will automatically affect the make-up of the bench, but there is no clear consensus to support this in the existing research. In the US there is a wide range of opinions about the effect of the different systems in this respect. Some American commentators suggest that the particular appointment method has no effect on the make-up of the bench; some conclude that women and minority groups do better under a system of exclusive executive appointment and others suggest that commissions provide a better representative balance (Webster, 1995). Those who suggest that commissions make a difference to the type of judges appointed, or at least have the potential to do so, argue that an important variable is the make-up of the commission itself. They claim that ensuring a representative balance of commission members is the way to encourage greater representativeness amongst the judiciary (Ashman and Alfini, 1973). However, although there is widespread support for ensuring that membership of the commissions is broadly representative of the community they serve, there is similarly little evidence to suggest that this variable has a significant effect on the background of the judges appointed. Research carried out in 1990 on the make-up of different US state judiciaries appointed by different types of commissions challenged the view that a more representative membership on commissions increased representation of women and ethnic minorities on the bench. It found that these groups were equally under-represented across different appointment jurisdictions (Alozie, 1990, p. 321). The author concluded, in relation to appointments amongst members of ethnic minorities, that the more important variable in determining the representativeness of the judiciary was the proportion of lawyers from ethnic minorities in the jurisdiction as a whole.

Such research findings on the relationship between appointment processes and the make-up of the judiciary have led to the recognition that the composition of a commission is only one variable amongst many which may affect who is ultimately appointed (Henschen et al., 1990, p. 329). However, there is little empirical evidence which seeks to isolate this one variable in order to determine the nature and extent of its effect. The most that can be said from the US evidence, therefore, is that the make-up of the commissions probably has some effect on the make-up of the bench, but how much and in what way is not yet known. Indeed, since more representative commissions are themselves a relatively new phenomenon, it may be some years before there is sufficient data on their judicial appointment patterns for this evidence to emerge. Moreover, part of the explanation for the inconsistency in the conclusions about the effects of the US commissions on the make-up of the bench is that generalisations are hard to make because of the wide variations in the models of commission employed, making it difficult to compare like with like. However, the very fact that there can be such a range of views suggests that the overall effect is not very great one way or the other. It is likely that if the use of commissions had produced a very significant change in the make-up of the bench there would be less scope for such a diverse range of opinions about their effects.

The picture in Canada is somewhat different. There is some evidence that both at federal and provincial levels the representation of women on the bench has significantly increased during the relatively short period in which they have been used, although it is not clear to what extent this change is directly the result of the establishment of committees. Overall, between 1989 and 1994 there was a rise in the number of female applications for federal appointments from 12 per cent to 26 per cent (Friedland, 1995, p. 242). Evidence from the JAAC in Ontario also suggests that active recruitment drives by a commission can increase the numbers of qualified candidates from non-traditional backgrounds who put themselves forward (Friedland, 1995, p. 246). In 1990, the committee undertook an 'outreach' programme whereby it contacted associations representing women and black lawyers asking them to encourage outstanding lawyers within their association to consider applying to the bench. At the same time the Attorney General also wrote to 1,200 eligible women lawyers similarly asking them to consider applying. These efforts resulting in a significant increase in applications from non-traditional backgrounds and the subsequent increase in appointments from those groups (Judicial Appointments Advisory Committee, 1992, pp. 3-4). Between 1989 and 1992, 41 per cent of judges appointed by the JAAC were women (Addison, 1996, p. 16). In late 1991 when the committee selected an unusually large numbers of nominees because of a sudden requirement for more judges in the criminal courts, half those appointed were women. There was some, though less, of an increase in the numbers of minority judges appointed.

The creation of the Judicial Service Commission in South Africa also brought about a significant change in the type of judges appointed. Between 1994 and 1997 the numbers of black judges on the bench rose from 0.5 per cent to 10 per cent. The judges of the Constitutional Court, most of whom have been appointed by the Commission, consist of seven whites and four blacks of whom nine are men and two are women. However, the fact that creation of the commission was one aspect of the transition from apartheid to full democracy makes it hard to assess to what extent the change was attributable to the new appointment system or to the new political system generally.

In most continental European countries the make-up of the judiciary is less of an issue than in common law countries because the judges are much more representative of society. Nevertheless, the growing use of commissions there has also been associated with an increase in the appointment to the bench of women, minorities and those from non-traditional educational background. One suggestion is that this change may be attributable to the involvement of lower-ranking judges in the appointments system who more actively support the appointments of such groups (Thomas, 1997).

Taken together, the collective experience of those countries which have established commissions does suggest that their use can increase the representativeness of the bench although such an effect is not automatic nor necessarily very marked. An important variable would appear to be the extent to which the commission engages in active attempts to recruit under-represented groups. Such efforts seem to have a significant effect on the type of judges appointed. Supporters of executive appointment might argue, however, that the same results could have been achieved if undertaken by a government department as, indeed, the Lord Chancellor's Department has begun to do. The question remains as to whether significant changes in the make-up of the judges appointed requires a more profound change of institutional culture than can be brought about within an existing system which historically exercised different priorities. It may be that the creation of a commission is less of a structural and more of a cultural prerequisite for the necessary change of approach required to appoint judges from different backgrounds.

Judicial independence

The aim of reducing partisan political patronage in the appointment process is a central one behind the adoption of commissions in many countries. This has been particularly true in those US states where they have replaced an electoral system. The extent to which commissions have succeeded in removing politics from the system is a matter of dispute. Their critics claim that under commissions the selection process is no less politically influenced than under elections but simply more closed and secretive:

> The Missouri Plan has produced a selection system that is much less visible than judicial elections. Yet the insulation seems only to obscure, not remove, many important partisan features and influences in judicial selection (Glick, 1978, p. 519).

Such commentators claim that the Governor's appointees on the commission are there to promote his partisan goals (Roll, 1990, p. 865; Glick, 1978, p. 521). Others have argued that the Governor still exercises a direct partisan influence when choosing between the different candidates provided by the commission. Over half the respondents to the American Bar Foundation survey of commissions in 1993 claimed that political considerations played a role in the appointment decision of the Governor, though they denied that such concerns affected the deliberations of the commissions (Martin, 1993, p. 2). Few supporters of commissions in the US would claim that they completely remove the influence of party politics from the appointment process, but they do argue that its role is significantly reduced. From a comparative perspective, the US experience in this regard may be unhelpful because of the very particular context in which judicial selection operates. Partisan politics plays a much more dominant role at all levels of public life in the US than in England and Wales so that the degree of political activity around judicial appointments should perhaps be seen as a reflection of this more general difference rather than a particular feature of the appointment process. However, one useful lesson which may be drawn from the US experience is that the pre-existing political conditions often continue despite a change in the appointments system (Glick, 1978, p. 539). It appears that where commissions are set up in states where there has traditionally been a high level of local political activity in relation to the judiciary, the commissions are generally politicised, and vice versa. The creation of a new appointments system would appear to have surprisingly little effect on the role of partisan politics. This is an important finding for English purposes since it suggests that the existing culture, in which political patronage plays very little, if any, role in the appointment process, is likely to continue under a commission and that the fears that a commission would politicise the process are not justified.

In Canada, the main criticism of the degree of political involvement in the appointments system is heard at the federal level. The continuing presence of political patronage in federal appointments has been attributed to the limited advisory role of the committees which leaves the system still strongly dominated by the executive (Russell and Ziegel, 1991, p. 4). In contrast, there are much fewer complaints about politicisation at the provincial level. In relation to the work of the JAAC in Ontario, there appears to be a strong consensus that the introduction of the committee has reduced political patronage in the system. Similarly, in South Africa, most commentators appear to agree that the commission is a genuinely independent body which has been effective in limiting the role of patronage in the appointments process. Equally, the creation of Higher Councils in continental Europe has been identified as responsible for increasing the external independence of the judiciary by decreasing the traditional powers of the executive in the appointments process. Though to some extent this has been replaced by a growing political involvement of the legislature in those countries, such as Italy, where the appointment of the commission members is in its hands (Thomas, 1997, p. 17).

Whilst a commission clearly does not offer a blanket protection from the influence of partisan politics, the experiences of commissions around the world does suggest that they can serve to minimise the extent to which judicial appointments are linked to political patronage. Moreover, the achievement of the commissions in this regard may be better than it appears. It should be remembered that commissions have been established at a time when the political role of the judges has increased significantly so that the incentive for governments to seek to maintain political control of the process has generally been much greater than in the past. The global trend might therefore have been expected to be an increase in political influence in the appointments processes. The fact that this has not generally occurred suggests that the commissions have been effective in keeping this pressure for politicisation in check.

A distinction should, however, be drawn between the degree of partisan political influence in the appointments process and the extent of its political significance. Whilst the former may be reduced by the use of a commission the latter may be increased. It has been suggested that the use of commissions in continental Europe, for example, has increased the political significance of the judiciary in general and the appointments process in particular as a result of the greater openness to public scrutiny and debate (Thomas, 1997). This form of politicisation can be regarded as a positive development in the context of increasing judicial activism. As the political role of the judges increases, it is appropriate that the process by which they are selected should be subject to more open public scrutiny. The record of commissions in relation to openness is therefore a particularly important variable in assessing their effectiveness.

Openness

Commissions can express openness in two ways: through the provision of information to candidates relating to their individual applications and to the public in relation to the commission's procedures. In regard to the first limb, commissions generally apply more openness in their dealings with candidates than executive appointment systems. Some commissions, such as the Ontario JAAC have established formal systems for informing candidates of the outcome of their applications at different stages of the process. It is very rare to hear candidates considered by commissions complain of having been kept in the dark for months or years about the progress of their application as has often been the case in England and Wales. However, there is not total openness in the process. Most commissions rely to some extent on confidential references and opinions from third parties as to the suitability of candidates. Lord Irvine has suggested that the introduction of a commission in England and Wales would not affect the current consultation process:

> I do not regard the system of soundings as unsatisfactory, nor if there were to be a judicial appointments commission would a system of soundings cease. The system of soundings is absolutely crucial...An appointments commission is not a substitute for soundings.[71]

However, where commissions do use such soundings they differ in the extent to which this information is acquired formally or informally and the weight which such material is given as against other information such as a candidate's written application and performance at interview. In general, most commissions seek to keep confidential information to a minimum and to ensure that it plays only a limited role in the selection process. The criticisms of secrecy which are commonly heard from candidates under an executive system do not appear to be voiced by those considered by commissions.

The record of openness regarding the interaction of the commissions with the public is equally good. In particular, those commissions which are established under statute have clear obligations in this regard. The selection criteria and procedures are often set out in the establishing statue and it is common for the commission to be required to publish an annual report. In practice, many commissions hold their organisational meetings in public although decision-making usually takes place privately. In general, it is common for commissions to operate a culture of openness and actively seek to inform the public about their work as a means of securing support for the system. The JAAC in Ontario, for example, invites public comments on its performance and in its 1995 annual report stated that it was actively seeking means of disseminating the work of the commission to interested members of the public.

Whether or not these mechanisms of openness are intrinsic to commissions is open to question. Many of the above procedures employed by commissions have been adopted in recent years by the Lord Chancellor's Department. However, supporters of commissions argue that the creation of a new body is required in order to institutionalise a culture of openness as an entrenched feature of the system. Ideally, an appointments system should operate from the premise that all its proceedings should be open and publicised unless it is proved to be absolutely necessary for some aspect to be kept confidential. This approach to official decision-making where openness is the default option has never been the basis for British government as a whole and it is therefore perhaps unrealistic to expect one section of a department to adopt a practice which runs counter to the collective political culture. Similar arguments can be made regarding the related question of accountability.

Accountability

The strongest objection which is made to commissions by the judiciary is that they reduce accountability since their members have no direct responsibility to Parliament. This claim is only partially accurate as in most cases the ultimate choice remains that of a politically accountable minister. Moreover, where the commission includes politicians an element of direct accountability is maintained. Nevertheless, it is correct to say that the individual accountability of the minister who can be said to carry full personal responsibility for the decision is weakened under a commission system. Whether or not this matters depends partly on how effective such accountability is in practice and whether commissions provide alternative means of accountability. This issue is particularly acute in the US, where the use of elections had provided direct accountability for the judges. But in England and Wales and other common law countries such as Canada and South Africa, the relevance of this loss is reduced by the limited extent to which ministerial accountability could be said to have had any real significance. As we have seen, by convention parliamentary scrutiny of judicial appointments has been minimal. In fact, it can be argued that the creation of a commission may actually improve the degree of parliamentary scrutiny. It is entirely appropriate for commission members to be under a duty to appear before a parliamentary committee when called to explain their work, just as the members of the newly independent Judicial Studies Board can now be held directly to account to MPs and Peers.[72] It may well be that Parliament would be less hesitant in questioning commission members than the Lord Chancellor.

While throughout the political system as a whole parliamentary accountability has waned, the role of the media has increased. It is this new method of public scrutiny which may provide a more effective means of enforcing accountability in the appointments process. Commissions, as products of their time, may respond to this challenge more effectively that the existing government departments. One feature of the culture of openness noted in many commissions is a greater willingness to engage with the media than has been traditional in government departments. Again, the comparison with the independent status of the Judicial Studies Board is pertinent. The Board has its own responsibility for dealing directly with the media and does not have to seek the approval of a minister before doing so. The engagement of a wider range of groups outside government may increase the likelihood that active engagement will be encouraged within a commission.

Finally, the use of a commission can be said to increase accountability by the mere fact of its more diverse make-up. If a commission is broadly representative of society at large its choices can be seen to be responsive to the perspectives of the community. Just as the judiciary itself can claim to increase its accountability through a more representative make-up, so too can the appointments process improve its social accountability in this way. A representative commission which operates more inclusive, open and public processes is very likely to be regarded as a more accountable system than the executive system which it replaces. The effect of this may be most apparent in the final test of the effectiveness of a commission - the extent to which it commands public support.

Although the limited research findings may suggest that there is only a weak correlation between the make-up of the commission and the representativeness of its appointments this does not detract from the value of a diverse make-up for purposes of accountability. Just as the representativeness of the judiciary itself is desirable on the grounds of accountability whether or not it improves its decision-making, so public confidence and credibility of the commission requires that its members are not all drawn from the same narrow background and this issue is increasingly recognised in those countries which use commissions.

Public confidence

Much of the evidence reviewed thus far has concluded that some of the claims made for commissions regarding the changes which they bring to the type of judges appointed are hard to substantiate. However, in one area at least a clear consensus on their effect is apparent. The evidence from the US, Canada and South Africa all indicates that public confidence in commissions is generally very high and that they are widely perceived as being a superior method of appointment. Commissions are commonly regarded as fairer either than elections or exclusive executive appointment and where they are used the appointments process appears to attract less criticism. A common conclusion in both the US and Canada is the hope that the provincial system might serve as a model for the less satisfactory, more politicised, federal process (Russell and Ziegel, 1991, pp. 31-32). The extent of support for the use of commissions is best evidenced by the fact that no country, state or province which has changed its appointment system in recent years has adopted any other method and none which has adopted a commission has abandoned it.[73]

Summary

As the number of judges appointed each year has grown, the internal pressures on the appointments system have led to the creation of a far greater degree of formalisation and professionalisation than has ever existed before. At the same time, external pressure in the form of criticism of the secretive and self-perpetuating nature of the system has brought about a series of reforms designed to improve its fairness and openness. On coming to office in 1997, Lord Irvine emphasised his intention of continuing the process begun by Lord Mackay by instituting a further modernisation programme. The question remains as to whether or not these piecemeal reforms can address the more fundamental pressure for change in both the type of judges selected and the way they are appointed which has arisen as a result of the growth in judicial activism.

As the debate about the future of the judicial appointments process develops, the issues involved are becoming more complex. The old certainties which traditionally underpinned the system are weakening and new dilemmas are arising. Even the fundamental question of what sort of judge we wish to appoint is less clear. While it is still almost universally accepted that merit alone should be the criterion for appointment, the consensus about what constitutes merit has broken down in response to the changing tasks which the judges are required to perform. Similarly, while there is widespread agreement that a more representative bench is needed, there is a strong difference of opinion about what is required to achieve such a change. Similar confusion exists over the role of politics in judicial appointments. While there is general support for the proposition that politics must be kept out of the system, there is also a growing recognition that the political values and opinions of policy-making judges may be as relevant as those of elected politicians. A particularly acute difficulty is emerging over the relationship between accountability and judicial independence. Most commentators prioritise the need for an increase in the accountability of the appointments process without articulating the implications for judicial independence which this involves.

A growing lobby sees the answer to many of these dilemmas in the creation of a judicial appointments commission. The experience of some of those countries which use commissions provides support for this proposal since they appear to have been generally successful and widely popular. The use of a commission has advantages and disadvantages. It may weaken formal constitutional accountability but increase openness, scrutiny and social accountability. It will not necessarily be completely free of any form of politics, but it has the potential to insulate the judicial appointments process from direct executive control. The evidence suggests that, on balance, a commission has much to recommend it but it is not a universal panacea nor will it transform the judiciary overnight. This will reassure the judges, and dismay those with more radical visions.

Whether or not a commission is chosen as the best means of addressing the problems currently faced by the appointments system, there is little doubt that further change will be required to meet these challenges. Creating a modern appointments system demands the reconciliation of a number of different, and potential conflicting requirements. In the past, the judiciary was required to be professionally highly competent and strongly independent. Today, in addition to these attributes, it must be both more representative and more accountable. These are demanding aims, but also ones which, if achieved, will produce a system which can command the public confidence which is the essential prerequisite for a process responsible for appointing a body which affects the life of more individuals than ever before and which will increasingly decide public policy matters of the greatest social importance.

Notes

[1] Home Affairs Select Committee, *The Work of the Lord Chancellor's Department, Minutes of evidence.* 13 October 1997, para. 71.

[2] Vol. I para. 10.

[3] *Ibid.* para. 146.

[4] Foreword to Shetreet, 1976.

[5] Bridge, 1978, p. 21, para. 5.14.

[6] Lord Chancellor's Department press release, 9 October 1997. This figure includes appointments to tribunals and stipendiary magistrates but excludes lay magistrates.

[7] Vol. I para. 121.

[8] S. 82. See Shetreet, 1985, p. 626.

[9] Vol. II para 285.

[10] *Ibid.*

[11] *Ibid.* para 459.

[12] Vol. I para. 128.

[13] Law Society, 1991, *Judicial Appointments,* quoted in Stevens, 1993, p. 179.

[14] Vol. II para. 294.

[15] Speech to the Minority Lawyers Conference, 29 November 1997.

[16] Vol. I para. 46.

[17] Speech to the Minority Lawyers Conference, 29 November 1997.

[18] Vol II para. 263.

[19] Vol I para. 67.

[20] *Ibid.* para. 5.

[21] *Judicial Appointments - the Lord Chancellor's Policies and Procedures,* 1986.

[22] Vol. I para. 9.

[23] *Ibid.* para. 15.

[24] Vol. II para. 82.

[25] Quoted in Kentridge, 1996, p. 240.

[26] *The Canberra Times,* 11 March 1998.

[27] See *The Guardian,* 18 July 1998 and *The Sun, 6 August 1998.*

[28] Speech to the Centre for Policy Studies, *The Times,* 25 February 1998.

[29] Hodder, 1974, p. 85 quoted in Palmer, 1993, p. 32.

[30] Figures provided by the Lord Chancellor's Department, March 1998

[31] *The Economist,* 15 December 1956, p. 946.

[32] The provisions of the Judicial Pensions and Retirement Act 1993 took effect on 31 March 1995.

[33] Memorandum of Evidence by the Lord Chancellor's Department to the Home Affairs Select Committee 1996, p. 162, annex 13.

[34] The benefit of a non-contributory pension offsets this loss to some extent and is a strong incentive for successful barristers to take a cut in income when appointed to the bench.

[35] S. 174(2).

[36] Vol II para. 2.3.3.

[37] Griffith pointed out this constitutional confusion in his evidence to the Committee, Vol II p. 261 appendix 30.

[38] Vol II para. 2.3.3.

[39] Judicial Service Commission, (1994) *Guidelines for Questioning Candidates for Nomination to the Constitutional Court* s. 7.

[40] *Ibid.*.

[41] Figures provided by the Lord Chancellor's Department, March 1998.

[42] Vol I para. 79.

[43] Speech to the Minority Lawyers Conference, 29 November 1997.

[44] Sir Frederick Lawton, *Solicitors' Journal,* vol. 44, 1990, p. 1254.

[45] Speech to the Minority Lawyers Conference, 29 November 1997.

[46] NACRO *Criminal Justice Digest* No. 93, July 1997.

[47] Vol. I paras. 81- 82.

[48] Many of these are former barristers who have qualified as solicitors and who have been given exemptions from the advocacy training requirements.

[49] Vol. II para. 68.

[50] *Law Society Gazette,* 27 February 1991.

[51] Vol. II para 280.

[52] *Ibid.* para 185.

[53] Home Affairs Select Committee, *The Work of the Lord Chancellor's Department, Minutes of Evidence,* 13 October 1997, para. 69.

[54] See Sheetreet, 1987 p. 776 for a discussion of the concept of 'fair reflection'.

[55] Vol. II para. 2.3.3.

[56] Department of Health Statistical Bulletin 1996/6 and 1996/18.

[57] Vol. I para. 3.

[58] *Ibid.* paras. 143-146.

[59] The proposals for establishing such a body have a long pedigree, having been put forward as early as 1918 (see the *Report on the Committee on the Machinery of Government* chaired by Lord Haldane. Quoted in JUSTICE, 1992, p. 27).

[60] Lord Chancellor's Department press release, 9 October 1997.

[61] Missouri was one of the first states to establish a commission.

[62] See Shetreet, 1987, pp. 769 - 772.

[63] Exceptions include Israel where judges are appointed by a committee of nine made up of three judges, two lawyers, two members of Parliament and two ministers (Shetreet, 1984, p. 992).

[64] See Judicial Appointments Advisory Committee (1990) *Interim Report,* Ontario; Judicial Appointments Advisory Committee (1992) *Recommendations and Final Report,* Ontario; Courts of Justice Statute Law Amendment Act 1993.

[65] For a full description of the system as established see Department of Justice (1988) *A New Judicial Appointments Process,* Ottawa.

[66] See Rock, 1996, p. 2.

[67] Judicial Service Commission Act 1994.

[68] The Constitution of the Republic of South Africa 1996, 174(4).

[69] Quoted in Marshall, 1995, p. 40.

[70] Judicial Service Commission Act 1994, schedule 1.

[71] Home Affairs Select Committee, *The Work of the Lord Chancellor's Department. Minutes of Evidence*, 13 October 1997, para. 59.

[72] Under the Judicial Studies Board *Memorandum of Understanding* it is stated that the Chairman and Secretary of the Board will normally attend before the Home Affairs Select Committee in place of the Lord Chancellor if the subject under scrutiny is the operations of the Judicial Studies Board (Report 1991-1995, p. 37, para. 7.7).

[73] Although there have been efforts in Colorado and Arizona in recent years to move away from the merit system (see Champagne and Haydel, n. 14, p. 14.)

5 Training

Thirty years ago formal training for judges did not exist. Its introduction has been one of the most significant and clearly defined markers of change in the judiciary. Most of the reforms described thus far have been incremental and introduced with the support of the judges. In contrast, the establishment of a training structure in the form of the Judicial Studies Board in 1979 was a sharp break with tradition and one which was carried out in the face of strong judicial objections.

Until relatively recently, the belief amongst judges that training was unnecessary and that it posed a threat to judicial independence, was strongly held throughout the common law world.[1] Yet despite these objections there has been a global explosion of activity in the field of judicial training in the last decade (Sallman, 1993). As in so many areas of judicial reform, this development was pioneered in the US in the 1960s, to be followed by Canada in the 1970s, New Zealand in the 1980s and most recently, Australia and South Africa. One of the most notable features of this global process has been the speed with which judges have come to accept, and even welcome, training once introduced. This conversion to the cause has been particularly marked in England and Wales. Despite the strength of resistance to training from many judges before its introduction, the Judicial Studies Board quickly established itself as a permanent feature of the judicial system and its work now enjoys widespread support amongst the judges. Though there may be disagreements over the content or emphasis of the training, there are almost no objections in principle to its existence. Indeed, there is strong support for the current expansion of training which is being undertaken.

There is little doubt that the introduction of training has been a success story in the history of judicial reform. When compared with the position before 1979 the change has been radical. Nevertheless, despite gradual expansion, judicial training has to date remained a relatively informal, amateur and low-key process. This too is changing. Whereas training was once seen as a supplemental process grafted onto the existing system it is increasingly regarded as an intrinsic feature of new developments in the legal process. Examples of this shift can be found in relation to Lord Woolf's recommendations for reforming the civil justice system and in the provisions of the Human Rights Act. Both these new developments, when introduced, were premised on the explicit assumption that training would be required before the changes could be implemented. One consequence of this more central role for judicial training in the legal process has been to encourage a greater degree of professionalisation. The structure, resources and approach of the Judicial Studies Board is being formalised in order to respond to its enhanced position and to meet the increasing demands being made of its services.

The aim of this chapter is to analyse the process by which training has come to occupy such a central place in the judicial system. Throughout these developments, as in all the areas of the judiciary reviewed in this study, the relationship between judicial independence and accountability can be seen to be a strong factor influencing the nature of the process of change.

Overcoming judicial opposition to training

Although there was no formal system of training before 1979, it is a mistake to suggest that judicial training did not exist. Traditionally, the process by which new judges learnt their skills and old judges improved them was through informal contact with peers, and this is still an important method of judicial education today. The move to a formal system of training was not initially an easy one for the judges. The first training sessions on sentencing matters were started by Lord Parker, then Lord Chief Justice, in 1963 but it was not until the 1970s that the first proposals for establishing a training structure began to emerge. In 1972, JUSTICE produced a report on the judiciary which included the radical proposal that the judges should undertake an initial training course of between three and six months. Three years later an interdepartmental working party headed by Lord Justice Bridge was set up to investigate and make recommendations on the subject. Its report acknowledged the strength of opposition to the proposal to introduce training, described by one judge as 'nothing more than a public relations gimmick'.[2]

A number of specific objections to the Bridge proposals were raised by judges. First, it was argued that the nature of the judicial appointments process made training unnecessary. Before appointment to the bench, it was claimed, a judge had demonstrated his skills in court as an advocate over many years. A new judge was not a novice who required lessons but a highly experienced practitioner.[3] Lord Hailsham, for example, argued that the capacity to be a judge was acquired in the course of the practice of law and could not be taught. He described his response to proposals for specialist training in terms of: 'a degree of indifference verging on contempt' (Lord Hailsham, 1983, p. 50).

In addition, it was argued that the skills of a judge were fundamentally 'unteachable' being somehow innate and intangible:

> I would attach very little value to any formal training for judicial office. I do not see how you can effectually train a man to be a judge...The judicial quality is something that the man has or has not got; and whatever training may do to improve the native quality, it cannot graft a judicial temperament on to barren stock (Sir Robert Megarry, 1973, p. 81.)

A particularly strong critic of the idea of training was Lord Devlin. In 1976 he went so far as to argue that training would be positively damaging:

> Once you start training [a judge] in anything...he loses the essential character of the English judge. He no longer speaks and reacts to the ordinary man, he sits on the bench as what would never be more or better than a half trained expert.[4]

In some cases this approach amounted almost to a pride in being untrained as if the best judges came from the bar to the bench untainted by any influence which would detract from their innate judicial qualities. The ability to learn 'on the job' was considered a particular marker of judicial skill. Lord Parker, Lord Chief Justice from 1958 to 1971 claimed with apparent pride, that the first summing-up in a criminal case that he ever heard was the first one he delivered himself.[5] This cult of the untrained judge held that innate skill and years of court room experience combine to produce an effortless transition from advocate to adjudicator. In Australia, where judicial training has only recently been established, the debates which have accompanied its introduction have a familiar ring. Chief Justice Mason, in his opening address to the Inaugural Judicial Orientation

Programme in 1994, criticised the myth perpetuated in Australian legal culture that judicial know-how could be absorbed by a process of osmosis which left barristers sufficiently experienced by dint of being an advocate to conduct any type of trial.[6] It was precisely this belief which underpinned the early claims by judges that training was unnecessary in England and Wales.

In addition to these practical objections to training, the Bridge working party had to address the more fundamental criticism that its introduction posed a threat to judicial independence. There were two aspects to this claim. On the one hand it was suggested that training might provide a back-door route to executive control of the judiciary.[7] On the other, the judiciary might be seen to be less impartial if training brought pressure to bear on the judges to modify their behaviour in favour of one section of society's interests over another (Armytage, 1996, p. 28). The Bridge report recognised the importance of judicial independence but suggested that the dangers posed by training had been exaggerated. It argued that informed judges were more capable of being independent than those who were not and that structured safeguards could be provided for judicial independence. The answer to these objections, the practical and the principled, was found in the creation of a training system which was controlled by the judiciary and in which the training was provided by judges.

The importance of judicial control

The Bridge working party had originally recommended that the Judicial Studies Board should be headed by a salaried Director of Studies and that it should have an institutional base in a university, thus envisaging that although the training should be provided by other judges the Board need not be run by the judiciary. These proposals were rejected on the grounds that the judges would not find the introduction of training acceptable if the Board was directed by an outsider on their behalf (Partington, 1994, p. 323). Instead it was decided that the training system should be entirely judge-controlled and this structure continues today. The chairman of the Board is always a sitting Lord Justice and with the exception of two or three academics and the Lord Chancellor's Permanent Secretary, the Board of 15 members is made up of judges and magistrates.

As well as retaining structural control of the process, the training itself has, to date, almost all been provided by the judges. In the early days of the Judicial Studies Board this system was essential as a means of persuading judges that the training offered would be relevant and of practical value and so countering the objections that it was unnecessary. In 1995, the Chairman of the Judicial Studies Board, Lord Justice Henry, argued that training needed to be carried out by judges to be credible to other judges: 'When it comes to the difficulties of conducting trials, if you have not been there and done it, you cannot know'.[8]

The provision of training by other judges, who had themselves been through the transition from advocate to adjudicator, allowed the judiciary to dispense with the collective myth that the change of role was an inherently unproblematic one which required no formal assistance. This change was influenced by the experience of judges in the US. There, the fact that the two jobs did not constitute a seamless career path and that new skills needed to be learnt when a practitioner moved to the bench had been recognised openly for many years:

> Lawyers don't become good judges by the wave of a magic wand. Not even the best lawyers. To reappear behind the bench as a skilled jurist is a tricky manoeuvre. Going from adversary to adjudicatory means changing one's attitude, learning and using new skills, and in some cases, severing old ties. In many jurisdictions judges must learn their new roles by the seat of their pants.[9]

The key to the success of the Judicial Studies Board in winning judicial confidence therefore lay in the structural arrangements which played an essential role in reassuring the judges that training was not dangerous and that it had a useful function to fulfil.

The belief in the fundamental importance of judicial control is still a strongly held one. In 1996, the Lord Chief Justice, Lord Bingham, giving the annual lecture of the Judicial Studies Board, stressed that the principle of judicial independence required that training should remain under the control of the judges (1996, p. 11). Similarly, in 1995 Lord Mackay, when Lord Chancellor, emphasised that he gave his wholehearted support to the work of the Judicial Studies Board in the knowledge that it would maintain judicial independence by continuing to be run 'by judges for judges'.[10] This phrase has been so successful in generating judicial support for training that it has become something of a mantra for judges not just in England and Wales but throughout those countries which have introduced training (Armytage, 1996, p. 38).

Judicial confidence

Once the Judicial Studies Board had been established under its judge-controlled structure and the fears of the judiciary were assuaged, its role began to expand relatively quickly. The Board's original remit was limited to sentencing but by 1985 the judicial mood had changed sufficiently to allow for the original Board to be restructured with much wider terms of reference to include civil and family matters.

By 1994, the work of the Judicial Studies Board had come to be widely regarded as worthwhile by judges. Professor Martin Partington, a former member of the Judicial Studies Board, noted the extent of this change: 'Twenty years ago, a majority of judges would have denied there was any need for judicial training. Today, only a minority would share that view' (Partington, 1994, p. 322). In 1979, as a concession to judicial sensibilities, the phrase 'judicial training' had been dropped from the title of the new body in favour of the more neutral and academic title Judicial Studies Board.[11] By 1996, the Lord Chief Justice, Lord Bingham, commented that training programmes no longer needed to be disguised as 'judicial studies' to make them acceptable (1996, p. 11).

In recent years the Judicial Studies Board has stressed that the demand for increased training comes not only from outside the judiciary but also from the bench itself, particularly from amongst younger judges.[12] This is so despite the fact that trainee Assistant Recorders are paid half their usual sitting fee during training (itself a significant reduction in earnings for most part-time judges). The ultimate change in attitude to training amongst judges was recently foreshadowed by Judge Christopher Pitcher, former Director of Studies of the Judicial Studies Board, who argued that judges should now come to see training as a right rather than a duty: 'something to which judges are entitled to and should insist upon' (Pitcher, 1998, p. 19). The vision of judges demanding training as their due is so far removed from the original spirit with which the establishment of the Judicial Studies Board was received that it is difficult to imagine how the likes of Lord Devlin would have responded to such a suggestion.

One reason for the support generated by the Judicial Studies Board is that the quality of the courses is generally considered to be high and they are increasingly seen as an opportunity to exchange ideas and knowledge with other judges in a relatively relaxed environment. But the full explanation for the change in approach of the judges to training is rooted in the changing structure of the judiciary and the increasingly demanding task which the judges are required to fulfil.

The need for training

Until relatively recently the fact that the judiciary was a small, stable, tight-knit group with a strong collective culture allowed advice and information to be passed on to new judges from those with more experience relatively easily. However, since the 1970s a number of structural changes have taken place which have meant that this informal system can no longer function as the only means of teaching new judges their job.

The expansion in the numbers of judges

Many of the factors which were responsible for the establishment of judicial training in England and Wales can be identified to a lesser or greater extent in all common law countries which have introduced it. A key variable has been the expansion in the numbers of judges. Not all countries which have introduced training have experienced the extensive expansion experienced by the judiciary in England and Wales. But the general increase in the amount of business handled by courts and the numbers of judges required to deal with it is a universal trend in liberal democracies. A particular feature of this expansion in England and Wales which is not evident in other countries is the greatly increased number of part-time judges resulting from the restructuring of the courts in the Courts Act 1971. The effect of the creation of the post of Recorder and Assistant Recorder, combined with the continuing increase in court workloads, has been that the judiciary is over ten times larger than it was in 1970. However, this expansion is not evenly spread throughout the judiciary, but is disproportionately evident in the lower ranks. In 1971 the ratio of High Court judges and above to those in the lower ranks was 1:2 whereas it is now 1:20. The increasing proportion of part-time judges also affects the stability of the judiciary. After a few years in the post a proportion of Assistant Recorder and Recorders are appointed to the Circuit bench or High Court. Others who are not offered a full-time post will leave the bench to return to practice full-time or may no longer be asked to sit by the Lord Chancellor's Department. The result is that there is a relatively high turn-over of judges in the lower ranks. This change in the ratio and turnover of new part-time judges to experienced full-time judges has inevitably undermined the system of informal instruction from the senior to the lower ranks. Ensuring consistent standards of skills and knowledge in a more frequently changing body of over 1000 part-time judges cannot be done through the same informal process which was appropriate for 200 predominantly full-time judges.

The effects of these structural changes on the training process have been further accentuated by the growing pressure to appoint judges from a broader social background. The increasing numbers of solicitors, women and members of ethnic minorities on the bench has begun to change its make-up. But almost all this change has come about in the lower ranks. The upper ranks of the bench are still predominantly occupied by those with more stereotypical judicial backgrounds. The effect of this uneven distribution is that there is a growing division in the make-up of the different tiers.

The consequence of this demographic change is that new judges now come to the bench with a wider range of experiences, skills and career patterns. These may be very different from those judges occupying the senior ranks first appointed ten or twenty years ago. This greater diversity in the experiences of new judges has begun to be addressed by the Judicial Studies Board. In 1997, it set out its support for the introduction of a degree of self-selection by judges in the training they undertake so that individuals could tailor their training needs to their different skills and knowledge.

The result of these changes is that quantitatively, through expansion, and qualitatively, through increased heterogeneity, the bench has begun to lose the characteristics generally associated with a club and has gradually acquired those of a profession. The move to a more formalised training process is one of the inevitable consequences of this transformation.

Specialisation and diversification

In addition to these changes to the size and make-up of the judiciary there has also been a growth in the complexity of the jobs that judges are expected to perform. One reason why judges may increasingly come to see training as a right rather than a duty is the difficulty of doing their jobs without it. Since training was first introduced, the speed at which the law, both substantive and procedural, has developed has accelerated at such a pace that a conscientious judge cannot hope to keep up with these changes without assistance. New statutory provisions such as the Criminal Justice Act 1991 and the Children Act 1989 have required considerable input from the Judicial Studies Board in order to ensure that the legislation was applied accurately and consistently. In the case of the Children Act this included a 'road show' which took training on the new Act around the country.

In addition, the increase in the complexity of new legislation is matched by increasing expectations that judges should have a developed understanding of the social phenomena which are the background to these new laws. An example being the growing awareness of child abuse and its role in the court process. In recent years the Judicial Studies Board has organised two-day seminars devoted to the issue of child abuse for those judges who hear family and criminal cases. Judges hearing cases involving children in these areas now need to understand detailed and complex legislative provisions while at the same time applying a sophisticated understanding of the social and psychological context in which these operate.

This growth in the need for specialised knowledge has made it increasingly difficult for judges to acquire and retain expertise in a wide range of areas. Traditionally there has been a great faith in the all-round judge who could adapt his or her skills to different fields of law. But the pressure towards specialisation has meant that this culture has weakened considerably in recent years. Circuit judges are now occasionally appointed exclusively to carry out civil work and there is growing support for this approach. One of the few substantive recommendations of the Home Affairs Select Committee on judicial appointments in 1996 was that this practice of specialisation should be extended in order to ensure that those candidates with exclusively civil practices would not be deterred from applying.[13] Lord Woolf, in his report on the civil justice system, similarly supported a move to greater specialisation (Woolf, 1995). These changes are partly a reflection of the fact that the Bar, from which the bench is still largely drawn, is itself increasingly specialist. As the size and complexity of each area of law has grown the days when most barristers could hope to master a wide range of different areas of the law are passing.

In tension with this trend towards specialisation is a growth in the diversification of the tasks judges are expected to perform. The judicial function has always encompassed a wide range of different roles from dispute settlement to rule determination to the enunciation of public standards of behaviour. These tasks require very different skills:

> Some are more technical, such as authentication; some involve a sensitivity to the interests of the parties while others require greater attention to the public interest; some require more expertise in appropriate social or political policy (Bell, 1983, p. 1767).

In addition to these functions, the Woolf reforms and the Human Rights Act mean that judges will now be expected to learn new sets of skills. At the heart of the Woolf reforms is the recommendation that the judiciary adopt the role of case managers. Lord Woolf has made it clear that this reform will involve a change of judicial culture which will require the acquisition of new skills through extensive judicial training. The Judicial Studies Board has responded by providing a full programme of training on the new tasks facing judges under the reformed system.[14] Similarly, the Human Rights Act will require the judiciary to develop a new approach to statutory interpretation and adjudication (Hunt, 1998, p. 7). During the passage of the Bill the Government stressed that the training for the Human Rights Act would be prioritised since the new Act would require that 'minds are opened, altered and attuned'.[15] As with the civil justice reforms, the Judicial Studies Board has embarked upon an extensive training programme to provide the training necessary for this change of approach. The consequence of these reforms is that judges will need to be trained to fulfil the roles of legal specialists, broad-brush policy-makers and administrators.

These different skills are not, however, necessarily all performed by the same judges. In particular, a general distinction between the tasks of the upper and lower ranks can be identified. The expanding constitutional role carried out by the senior judges is in sharp contrast to the largely social service role of the judiciary carried out by the lower ranks. The job of part-time judges sitting for approximately twenty days a year is primarily that of dispute resolution. They are not expected to contribute to the development of the law, counterbalance the power of the executive or determine the ultimate boundaries of human rights.

Most judicial training has, to date, been provided for the lower ranks. One reason for this is that the upper ranks are still sufficiently small and homogeneous to ensure coherence and consistency through the more traditional informal methods of peer support. In addition, the imposition of consistency which is perhaps the primary aim of judicial training, is not necessarily a strong requirement amongst senior judges. When judges are fulfilling a constitutional or law-making role the presence of differences between the individual judges can be seen as a necessary reflection of a high degree of independence of thought. The expression of dissension in the judgments of hard cases is a legitimate and healthy reflection of this independence. As judges increasingly decide issues of public policy where there is little in the way of legal doctrine to guide their decisions, this divergence between the training needs of the upper and lower ranks may become even sharper. In the US it is accepted that constitutional judges must bring with them an individual world view when deciding important matters which affect public policy (Thompson, 1986, p. 831). The role of training in ironing out individual differences in approach therefore has much less relevance at the upper ranks.

The combined effect of these changes has been that the judiciary, in common with many others around the world, has been faced with the need to ensure consistency and competence amongst a far greater number of increasingly heterogeneous judges applying more complex law and exercising a wider range of judicial functions which demand different levels and types of training.

The growth of public scrutiny

In addition to these internal changes brought about by expansion and structural change, the judiciary has become subject to growing external pressure to introduce formal training programmes as a result of the increase in public scrutiny of its work. Thirty years ago, in common with most judiciaries, English judges enjoyed a higher degree of public confidence than they do today. Since then, media criticism of judicial performance has gradually increased. The introduction of training has provided the judiciary with a means of responding to that criticism, and of being seen to do so.

This increase in public criticism of the judiciary is one manifestation of a wider growth in the external scrutiny which has affected all professional groups in recent years. Since the 1960s, continuing education has been widely introduced in the professions as a means of responding to this public criticism by demonstrating a willingness to maintain standards of competence amongst members and to respond to changing social conditions (Armytage, 1995). This process is particularly apparent in the legal professions. In recent years the quantity and subject-matter of continuing education has increased significantly and the current trend is toward further expansion of compulsory training.[16] Judicial training therefore needs to be understood in the context of a more widespread process of professionalisation which has taken place throughout public and professional life in response to criticism of poor standards of competence and low levels of accountability.

The combined effect of these changes has been to undermine the viability of the unstructured system by which judges traditionally learnt their jobs. The expectation that judges could be left to pick up judicial skills and new legal material as they went along with only the informal assistance of colleagues, has become less and less sustainable over the last thirty years.

Expansion and professionalisation

Despite the advances made by the Judicial Studies Board since it was established, the quantity of training undertaken by each judge is still relatively small. Newly appointed Crown Court judges attend a compulsory residential induction course lasting four days after which they shadow the work of an experienced judge for approximately ten days. In civil matters the judges are invited back to three day continuation courses every three years and in criminal matters every three to four years.[17]

Although this amount of training sounds very limited, it needs to be understood in the context of part-time appointments. On average an Assistant Recorder will sit for 100 days in five years. He or she will undergo ten days training during this period with the effect that ten per cent of his or her time is spent training. In any other profession this ratio of training to productive work would probably be regarded as excessive. Nevertheless the pressure to increase the amount of training is growing. The Royal Commission on Criminal Justice in 1993 recommended that continuation seminars in Crime should be offered every three years in line with the Civil Committee. The Judicial Studies Board accepted that recommendation in principle and has plans to introduce this change as resources permit.[18] There have also been proposals that training should be available before appointment. JUSTICE, for example, has recommended that training should become a prerequisite of judicial appointment so that before becoming eligible for judicial appointment a barrister or solicitor should have attended a judicial training course.[19] There are currently no plans to expand training in this way, but the Judicial Studies Board is undertaking an expansion programme of the present system. The Board's aims for the future are: 'To provide, and *to expand and improve where necessary* the facilities for the training and instruction of full-time and part-time judges' (emphasis added).[20] In pursuance of this goal, the Board is increasing the frequency of continuation seminars, aiming for a total of five days training per judge per year. This would match training levels in the US, currently the leading provider of judicial training in the common law world (Armytage, 1996, p. 13).

As well as an increase in the frequency and quantity of training sessions offered, there have been a number of developments which have expanded the type of training provided. In 1991, the Ethnic Minorities Advisory Committee was established to offer advice and training on matters of race. Although there was initially some resistance to its training sessions from amongst the judges, its activities have expanded in recent years and it is now a firmly established aspect of the training process. Gender issues have also increased in importance and the Board is considering integrating equal treatment training with training on ethnic minority issues.[21] This pattern reflects a trend that has been occurring in many other judicial training programmes around the world. In Australia, for example, there has recently been a period of 'intense self-reflection' regarded the problem of gender bias in the judicial system and the prospects for tackling it through judicial training (Armytage, 1995). In addition, in response to a proposal from the Royal Commission on Criminal Justice that issues of gender should be addressed, the Judicial Studies Board established the Human Awareness Working Group. As well as considering gender issues, this group has looked at how training could be adapted to ensure the fair treatment of unrepresented parties, witnesses and jurors, victims and their families, children, and those with disabilities.[22] This broad approach to the scope of training was also supported by JUSTICE in its 1992 report on the judiciary. It proposed that judges should be trained in those qualities required for being a 'good judge' in the broadest sense (1992, pp. 24-25).

Reforms to the legal system

In all the above areas the Judicial Studies Board is responding to external changes in society which affect the legal system and the judges' jobs. But the future of training will also involve a more proactive role for the Board through its role in the implementation of reforms to the legal system. Increasingly, as proposals for change are put forward, it is now expected that training will be provided before reforms are put in place. Proposals for greater case management in the criminal courts made by the Royal Commission on Criminal Justice in 1993 emphasised that training was a prerequisite to change:

> ...our recommendations will require a more informed and decisive control of trials by judges and their training and performance in this enhanced role must be regarded as essential matters.[23]

The same intrinsic role for training has been developed in the two major reforms of the 1990s - the Woolf reforms to the civil justice system and the Human Rights Act. Because both reforms required extensive training the timetable for their implementation was dependent on the completion of the necessary training. The involvement of the Judicial Studies Board in the planning process for the introduction of changes to the legal system will inevitably enhance the role of the judiciary in the development of policy in these areas. The formal aims of the Judicial Studies Board now include the task of advising governments of the likely training requirements for judges of any proposed changes to the civil or criminal law and the Board has stated that it now expects the government to include it in the planning of new initiatives at an early stage.[24]

One effect of this new enhanced role for the Judicial Studies Board in legal reforms has been to speed up the process of professionalisation. In particular, the added burden placed on the Board has undermined the principle that training be carried out primarily by judges. Until recently almost all training had been provided by judge tutors who carry out the work on an unpaid basis mostly in their spare time. By 1995 this arrangement which relied on the goodwill and commitment of a small group of judges was described by the Chairman of the Board as: 'not a satisfactory professional basis on which to proceed'.[25] The scale of the Woolf reforms and the Human Rights Act has been such that the Judicial Studies Board could not have provided sufficient numbers of judges to carry out these extra training programmes. Moreover, even if the manpower had been available, the judges would not have had the necessary skills to undertake the training. Both reforms required that judges learn new skills which, by definition, other judges do not generally have. Case management and the interpretation of a Human Rights Act have not been traditional judicial tasks. This training has therefore had to be carried out largely by specialist practitioners and academics on a more professional basis.

Restructuring the Judicial Studies Board

The effect of this professionalisation in the provision of training has meant that the relatively amateur structural arrangements for managing the Judicial Studies Board have had to be reformed. This change has been taking place gradually over the years. One former member of the board described the process in the following way: 'Quietly, with few resources and without amendment to the statute book, an increasingly complex machinery has been established' (Partington, 1992, p. 336).

In 1995, this process of formalisation was taken a step further when the Judicial Studies Board was given a greater structural independence from the Lord Chancellor's Department by being granted the right to set and bid for its own budget. In June 1996 a Memorandum of Understanding was drawn up between the Lord Chancellor's Department and the Judicial Studies Board giving formal recognition to its autonomous status. The main reason behind this change was the growing concern at the Judicial Studies Board that more resources were needed than were being provided. To date the funds allocated to training have increased slowly but steadily. The total budget of the Judicial Studies Board for 1996/7 was just over £3 million compared with £1.8 million in 1992/3.[26] Despite these increases the Board began to express concern about the limitations of its budget during the 1990s. In 1995, it stressed that the remit of the Judicial Studies Board was to serve the needs of over 60,000 judges, magistrates and tribunal members and that if it interpreted this task broadly it would be quite disproportionate to the resources available.[27] The Board emphasised that it had: 'both the need and the demand for more judicial training than can presently be delivered'.[28]

Having been created by executive order, the Judicial Studies Board had no independent existence from the Lord Chancellor's Department. Its level of funding had therefore been a matter for internal negotiations within the Lord Chancellor's Department which limited the extent to which it could bid for extra resources with reference to its obligations to carry out statutorily defined duties (Partington, 1994, p. 319). Although the Board has acknowledged that it has always received the funds it requested it attributed this to the fact that: 'the board's requests have been tempered by a realistic understanding of what has been practicable'.[29] It was clearly not in a position to argue forcefully for greater funding in the way that an independent statutory body could do.[30] The new power to establish and manage its own budget thereby allows it greater independence to bid for resources.[31]

This change has taken place at a time when the scale of the resources required has risen very significantly to accommodate the Woolf reforms and the Human Rights Act. The training requirements of the Human Rights Act alone has been estimated by the Government at £5 million. This level of funding is therefore very different from the relatively small sums required in the early years of the Board's work. This growth underpins the need for a more formalised system to determine and justify the budget needed. To support this new system there has been a professionalisation of the management structure. In 1995, the Board obtained the Lord Chancellor's agreement to the secondment of two circuit judges as joint Directors of Studies, each giving half their time to the job.[32] This arrangement was replaced by a full-time director of studies in 1997, also a circuit judge. In recognition of this increasingly professional management organisation and the fact that the Board had become directly publicly accountable for its use of public funds, the Board's triennial reports were replaced in 1997 by an annual report covering its achievements against its performance targets and its future activities. In addition, the Board now produces a three year strategy plan.

The effect of these changes has been to create a more independent Board controlled by the judiciary but with more training provided by others in order to meet the expanding demand. The Chairman, Lord Justice Henry, explained the changes as follows:

> While there may be some regret about the passing of less formal arrangements, I am convinced that the judiciary can only carry out its duties effectively with high quality training professionally managed and professionally delivered.[33]

The increasing use of outsider trainers suggests that the original claim that judges would only find the training credible if provided by judges is no longer felt necessary by the judiciary. Provided the training is relevant and of a high quality it would seem that the judges do not now need to be trained exclusively by other judges in order to be persuaded of its worth or that it does not threaten judicial independence.

Judicial independence

The review of the development of judicial training demonstrates that from a standing start against a background of hostility the Judicial Studies Board has won widespread support amongst judges. It is transforming itself from an amateur sideline into a professionalised service which is intrinsic to the judicial process. The key to this success has been the acceptance that the demands of judicial independence require that the training process remains in the control of the judges. Because this formula has been so successful in practice, there has been very little incentive to examine the claim that training might pose a threat to judicial independence. But as the role of the training process expands, influencing more of the judges' work and requiring more public resources, the relationship between training and judicial independence requires some scrutiny.

Whether or not training can be said to threaten judicial independence depends both on the definition of the principle and the nature of the training. The nature of the relationship between training and judicial independence comes back, once again, to the distinction between collective and individual independence. Lord Justice Henry, the Chairman of the Judicial Studies Board, has claimed that the need to retain overall judicial control amounted to a 'constitutional imperative'.[34] This implies the application of a broad definition of judicial independence as a collective principle; that the judiciary, as an institution, should be free from outside interference. This requirement is clearly fulfilled by the current arrangements. However, if a narrower definition of judicial independence is adopted, as a means to the end of party impartiality, then the critical question is not who controls the training but whether it interferes with the judges' impartiality. The focus is shifted from the structural arrangements for providing the training to its content and whether it amounts to an improper influence. By its very nature, training is intended to influence the practices of judges in their day to day work and training which does not affect a judge's performance in any way is not effective. But the question of whether or not this influence is proper or improper depends crucially on what aspect of the judges' performance it affects. Provided that training influences the *way* in which the judges carry out their tasks rather than the particular decisions themselves, there can be no objection to it on the grounds of judicial independence.

Lord Bingham argued in 1996 that if training was controlled by the executive it would become possible for the state to instruct judges how they should decide cases (1996, p. 12). This straightforward statement requires some qualification. Lord Bingham would acknowledge the right of the state quite legitimately to interfere in the collective decision-making of the judges, for example in setting minimum and maximum sentencing levels or statutory frameworks such as in the Criminal Justice Act 1991. There should, therefore, be nothing objectionable about the judges being instructed through training as to how to apply this framework consistently and coherently. But if the purpose of the training was to dictate how judges should exercise their discretion in individual cases, this would clearly be an improper interference and so a breach of judicial independence. Whether or not certain judges are trained to deal sensitively with, for example, issues of race and gender, or handle conflict in court, or ensure a balanced presentation of the prosecution and defence cases does not impinge on judicial independence properly defined.

In only one respect can it be said that training is intended to affect the result rather than the process and this relates to training on the existing law. The purpose of such training, whether in relation to sentencing or the substantive law is to reduce the number of successful appeals from judges' decisions which are based on an inaccurate application of the law. Since few would suggest that judicial independence should encompass the right to apply the substance of the law incorrectly, this exception should also not be seen as posing any threat since it does not undermine a judge's impartiality but merely improves his or her accuracy in applying the law. In all other areas of training the focus is on the process not the end result of the judges' work.

As well as distinguishing between proper and improper influences, it is necessary to examine more closely the question of the source of influence. By ensuring that training has been run by judges the judiciary implicitly adopts a definition of judicial independence as limited to freedom from outside interference. But the judges themselves recognise that judicial independence can be threatened internally by improper influence from other judges. Therefore the control of training by judges does not, per se, remove the danger that it might undermine judicial independence. Although there has never been any suggestion that senior judges, through the training process, might exercise some crude influence on the impartiality of other judges (whether of their own volition or the behest of the executive) it is possible to argue that this danger does exist in a more subtle and indirect form. Training can be seen as part of the wider formalisation process. Judicial training is intended to encourage conformity by reducing the differences in approach between individual judges. The ethos behind training is that members of the public are entitled to expect a degree of consistency in the standards of legal knowledge, courtesy, patience, speed, and efficiency from any judge they appear before. The introduction of model directions in the 'Bench Books' provided to judges by the Judicial Studies Board is a good example of this process. They are intended to encourage judges to conform to predetermined and approved wording when directing the jury on particular aspects of the law or procedure.

This development is rightly regarded as a positive one which has the potential to increase standards of competence. But there may also be a cost to be paid for this benefit. Encouraging consistency in decision-making is likely to erode the culture of autonomy and individualism which has traditionally been a strong feature of the judiciary. It is a system which has relied on the exercise of a wide measure of discretion, the result of which has been the development of a culture of individualism: 'The judge is encouraged to be very much his own intellectual creature conditioned by his own limited training and specialised methods of reasoning' (Dhavan, 1985, p. 172). This is partly the result of a simple practical fact that the day to day work of the judges has traditionally been solitary and relatively isolated, requiring the judges to be largely self-sufficient. But this individualism is also valued because of its link with the principle of judicial independence. The freedom of the judges to carry out their decision-making without interference only becomes an issue in practice if the judges are individually willing to reach controversial or unpopular decisions. There is very little danger of interference in judges' decision-making in a judiciary which seeks to avoid judgments which challenge the authorities or populist opinion. In order for the situation to arise in which individual judges are likely to reach decisions which attract opposition the judiciary as a whole must have a culture which values independence of thought.

This independence of thought has been acknowledged both by the judges and their critics. John Griffith recognised that the judges are not 'all of one piece' and that a strong individualistic strain runs through their decisions:

The judges seldom give the impression of strong silent men wedded only to a sanctified impartiality. They frequently appear - and speak - as men with weighty, even passionate views of the nature of society and the content of law... (Griffith, 1997, p. 284).

Griffith considered the influence of the judges' personal convictions in their decision-making as a source of uncertainty and so potentially dangerous. Lord Diplock, by contrast, believed that the bold and imaginative attitude of the judiciary in the latter part of the 19th century was responsible for producing a great generation of judges.[35] Even the extreme individualism of Lord Denning was regarded by the judges (at least until the latter part of his office) as an appropriate expression of judicial autonomy. There is little doubt that the expansion of judicial review in recent years would not have occurred without this culture of individualism which has allowed senior judges to push boundaries and reshape the law.

Training may threaten this culture of individualism because it marks the transference of responsibility for competence and performance from the individual to the group (Armytage, 1995). If there is any danger in this process to judicial independence it is that this move to collective responsibility curbs individualism by encouraging conformity in the judges' approaches to the decision-making process. The line between consistency and standardisation can be a fine one and if one slips into the other it is possible that training might indirectly come to undermine the independence of thought that is the bedrock upon which judicial independence rests.

This indirect and subtle risk is not one which has concerned the judges. They have identified the risk to judicial independence as exclusively concerned with the question of external interference. The Chairman of the Judicial Studies Board, Lord Justice Henry has stated that the principle that training must be 'by judges for judges' is an integral part of judicial independence: 'If it is not run by judges it will be run by others who will inevitably use it for their own ends'.[36] Maintaining control of the training process has, for the judiciary, provided the means to avert this risk. But if there is a risk that consistency is promoted at the cost of individualism then the source of control is irrelevant. Most commentators would say that the trade-off is worth making and that some erosion of individualism is a price worth paying for the imposition of minimum standards of behaviour and levels of consistency. But it is nevertheless important to acknowledge that this trade-off is being made and that it is one which is not necessarily protected by ensuring that the process remains under the control of the judges.

One senior judge has acknowledged that training represents: 'a positive and beneficial contraction of the accepted boundaries of judicial independence' (Sedley, 1997, p. 314). This change recognises that judicial independence does not require that judges are free from all influence. The principle exists to protect judges from improper interference, whether from external sources or from other judges, which would affect the impartiality of their decision-making. While training ensures that decision-making is carried out efficiently, fairly and within the statutory bounds of the judges' discretion it will amount to a beneficial form of influence whether controlled and carried out by judges or outsiders. If there is a price to be paid in this change of emphasis through the reduction of individualism, there are also indirect benefits to be gained through the increase in judicial accountability which training offers.

Accountability

Constitutionally, the Lord Chancellor remains answerable to Parliament for the work of the Judicial Studies Board. However, the development of the Board's autonomous status has given rise to the need for an increase in its direct accountability. The duty to produce a three year strategy plan and an annual report are examples of this change. In addition, MPs and Peers are now encouraged by the Lord Chancellor to deal directly with the Judicial Studies Board on matters which are its responsibility and the Chairman may be asked by the Lord Chancellor to attend Select Committee hearings if the subject concerns operational matters.[37] These mechanisms ensure that the Judicial Studies Board conforms to the formal requirements of accountability expected of a public body. But this political process is not the only, or even necessarily the most important, form of accountability. There are other means by which the training process can contribute to judicial accountability which are only just starting to be recognised in England and Wales.

In countries with a longer history of training, such as the US, it is widely appreciated that introducing continuing education for judges is one way in which the judiciary can demonstrate that it is responsive to public criticism of poor judicial performance (Armytage, 1996). The development of training which takes account of changing social conditions and attitudes such as around such issues as race, gender, disability, child abuse and the rights of victims can constitute an important form of social, or soft, accountability. By being seen to respond to concerns about the behaviour and attitudes of judges in court the judiciary can claim to be accountable to the public it serves. The effect of this form of accountability should, in turn, enhance public confidence in the judiciary. Since public confidence is the bedrock of judicial independence, it can be seen that increasing training can serve indirectly to reinforce judicial independence. This connection has been identified as a cause of the growing support for training amongst judges in Australia:

> It is now recognised within the judiciary that judges should participate in continuing education because this is, among other reasons, an appropriate means to increase accountability which, in turn, consolidates judicial independence in a democratic society (Armytage, 1996, p. 12).

The effectiveness of this process is, however, entirely dependent upon a degree of public awareness of the existence of judicial training. To date, in England and Wales the judiciary has demonstrated very limited consciousness of the need to publicise the work of the Judicial Studies Board to a wider audience and so the potential for demonstrating accountability and enhancing public confidence has not yet been realised.

One reason for this reticence may be the realisation that by increasing public awareness of judicial training the judiciary would also be required to take more account of the views of a wider audience. The nature of training, the way it is delivered and the priorities it adopts will all be subject to scrutiny and criticism. The danger of promoting training as a means of enhancing accountability is that the form of training may come to be shaped more by public perceptions than sound educational needs. Livingstone Armytage has claimed that it is the demands of accountability which explains the mandatory nature of most judicial training around the world. He argues that compulsory continuing education is undesirable both in terms of educational effectiveness and the principle of judicial independence:

> Mandatory judicial education has much more to do with demonstrating a concern for the pursuit of competence rather than implementing an effective means of attaining it (Armytage, 1995).

Nevertheless, Armytage argues that the requirements of accountability may legitimately supersede those of education. He suggests, for example, that whether or not judicial training has any meaningful effect in areas such as race and gender the mere fact that judges attend continuing education programmes on these subjects contributes to the requirements of accountability. But again, in England and Wales the public remains largely ignorant of the fact that judges are attending such programmes. Therefore this opportunity to promote the accountability of the judiciary and so strengthen judicial independence has not yet been fully recognised. The Judicial Studies Board has, however, come to recognise the importance of training judges to counter inaccurate media representation:

> We must give judges the skills to recognise and deal with diversity, and to project their good work in a world whose ideas are increasingly driven by tendentious media and which is happy to adopt a view of judges at least forty years out of date.[38]

The next step which must be taken is to appreciate that public awareness of the commitment of judges to training is in itself a means of countering that inaccurate image and so to reinforce the accountability of the judiciary. One effect of the increased independence of the Judicial Studies Board is that it is now responsible for its own relations with the media. This change provides it with the opportunity to publicise its work more thoroughly and widely.

Summary

The introduction of training thirty years ago was an innovative gamble which has paid off. The Judicial Studies Board has won widespread support from judges at all levels who now accept, and are even beginning to demand, its services. Few commentators in the 1970s would have predicted the central role which training now occupies in the judicial process. The key to this success has been the maintenance of control of the training process by the judges as a means of protecting judicial independence. The argument that training poses a threat to judicial independence through the introduction of external interference is an example of the 'trumping' power of the principle of judicial independence which has as much to do with protecting the judges from critical scrutiny as the need to maintain impartiality.[39]

The introduction and expansion of training represents the clearest example of the modernising trend within the judiciary. The early amateurism of the Judicial Studies Board is being replaced by a more formal and professionalised approach in order to equip it to respond to the growing demands for training. The increased independence of the Judicial Studies Board will allow it to expand the provision of training and so to offer the judges a means to maintain and improve standards and counter public criticism of its performance. As the public demands better service and is more willing to complain if it does not get it, training provides the opportunity of ensuring the consistent quality on which public confidence rests. It has the potential to demonstrate accountability and so enhance public confidence, thus in turn, reinforcing judicial independence.

Confidence in the Judicial Studies Board is generally high amongst those who know of its work. However, few outside the judiciary are aware of the role it plays. The greatest weakness of the judiciary to date in this area has been its failure proactively to publicise its achievements. This reticence on the part of the judges is partly an example of a general phenomenon, that the judges have not yet learnt to 'sell' themselves and their achievements. One of the greatest challenges currently facing the judiciary is to expose their processes to full public view. The price of such engagement is that they will face criticism of the training process and will be required to engage in a wider debate about the role and nature of training. But this cost will be outweighed by the benefits which will accrue to public confidence by the knowledge that judges are committed to maintaining and improving standards of performance through training. In the 1970s, the judges argued that the public image of the judiciary would be impaired if the public were told that a judge was required to undergo a period of training on appointment.[40] If that were ever true, today it is far more likely that public confidence in the judiciary is undermined by the erroneous belief that judges are still untrained amateurs.

Notes

[1] In 1997, the Chief Justice of South Africa, Ismail Mahomed, addressed the first training session in South Africa with the comment that forty years ago the suggestion of training judges would have been 'heretical' (Mahomed CJ, 1997, p. 1).

[2] Bridge, 1978, p. 7, para. 3.2.

[3] In the words of Professor Zander: '...the assumption is that by the time a person is appointed as a judge he has knocked around the system for so long that he can be expected to know enough about it to function effectively' (Zander, 1989).

[4] Address to the annual meeting of the Howard League for Penal Reform in 1976. Quoted in Zander, 1989, pp. 123. See also, Devlin, 1979, pp. 34-38.

[5] Quoted in Pannick, 1988, pp. 223-4.

[6] *The Role of the Judge,* unpublished paper quoted in Armytage, 1996, p. 18.

[7] See the Bridge report, para, 1.6.

[8] Judicial Studies Board, *Report 1991-1995,* p. 5, para, 2.8, and 2.11.

[9] DW Catlin, founding head of the Michigan Judicial Institute, commenting in 1977. Quoted in Armytage, 1996, p. 13.

[10] Speech to the Anglo-American Judicial Education Seminar in Cambridge, 26 July 1995.

[11] See Ashworth, 1995, p. 52.

[12] Report of the Judicial Studies Board, 1991-1995, p. 5, para. 2.12.

[13] Vol. I para. 163.

[14] Report of the Judicial Studies Board, 1995-7, p. 7.

[15] In a speech at the London School of Economics, 4 February 1998.

[16] In July 1997 the Lord Chancellor's Advisory Committee on Legal Education and Conduct produced its second report on continuing education for solicitors and barristers which recommended significant extension of current arrangements.

[17] The Bridge report had originally proposed that judges should undertake an initial three to four week training course on appointment. This was widely regarded as excessive and was later reduced.

[18] As per the recommendations of the Royal Commission on Criminal Justice (see 1991-1995 report, p.14, para. 4.14).

[19] It proposed that it would, ideally, be an extended residential course and that the course would phase out the need for the position of Assistant Recorder. See JUSTICE, 1992, p. 24.

[20] Report of the Judicial Studies Board, 1991-1995, p.1, para. 1.2.

[21] Report of the Judicial Studies Board, 1995-1997, p. 26, para. 7.17.

[22] Report of the Judicial Studies Board, 1991-1995, p. 8, para. 2.23.

[23] The Report of the Royal Commission on Criminal Justice, ch. 8, para. 82.

[24] Report of the Judicial Studies Board, 1995-1997, p. 6.

[25] Report of the Judicial Studies Board, 1991-1995, p.6, para. 2.13.

[26] This compares with an average of 1.2 million dollars spend by the National Judicial Institute in Canada and 18 million dollars by the US federal judicial centre.

[27] Report of the Judicial Studies Board, 1991-1995, p. 3, para. 2.2.

[28] *Ibid.* p. 3, para. 2.1.

[29] *Ibid.* p. 3, para. 2.2.

[30] Support for increased expenditure on training has come from the Royal Commission on Criminal Justice which argued that significant additional investment in judicial training would undoubtedly be cost-effective for the criminal justice process as a whole by reducing the number of mistakes which must be put right on appeal.

[31] The Board accepted the recommendations of the Clayton report carried out on its behalf that in future it would need to provide more detail, more argument and more evidence in support of its funding requests (see Report of the Judicial Studies Board, 1991-1995, p. 6, para. 2.14).

[32] The two appointees were His Honour Judge Pitchers and His Honour Judge Sumner.

[33] Report of the Judicial Studies Board, 1995-1997, p. 3, para 2.1.

[34] *Ibid.* p. 5, para. 2.10.

[35] Quoted in Griffith, 1991, p. 257.

[36] Report of the Judicial Studies Board, 1995-1997, p. 4, para. 2.4.

[37] *Ibid.* p. 27, para 7.6.

[38] *Ibid.* p. 7.

[39] It is hardly surprising if, as a body, the judges wish to protect themselves from such critical review. Harlow has commented that judicial independence: 'has served the judges well in protecting them from outside scrutiny' (1986, p. 199).

[40] Bridge, 1978, p. 2, Para. 1.6.

6 Scrutiny

The development of more open, accountable, and professionalised processes has been central to the changes to the appointments process and judicial training reviewed thus far. These same trends are equally apparent in the way in which judges' performance is scrutinised, but here the developments are at a much earlier stage. The informal and closed mechanisms which once dominated the appointment and training of judges are still very much in evidence in the arrangements for monitoring and improving judicial performance. With the exception of the growth of media criticism, the work of the judges has remained almost completely free from external scrutiny.

As the size and influence of the judiciary has grown, this lack of an ongoing process for setting, monitoring and maintaining standards of performance has become more controversial. To date, questions around judicial conduct have focused almost exclusively on the relatively narrow problem of removing individual judges whose work is affected by personal scandal, gross incompetence, senility or illness, and doing so without undermining the principle of judicial independence. The more general requirement of ensuring consistency and adequacy in judicial performance and maintaining minimum standards of judicial conduct have only just begun to be regarded as necessary and relevant concerns.

The increasing pressure for accountability which underpins so many of the developments in the judiciary reviewed thus far, lies at the root of the growing demands for improved mechanisms of scrutiny. Because judges cannot be held directly accountable to the electorate, other means of assessing and, where necessary, censuring judicial performance increase in importance. The fact that full-time judges are effectively appointed until retirement means that poor performance can continue for many years unless it is identified and remedied. The resignation of Mr Justice Harman from the High Court bench in February 1998, after many years of criticism from lawyers and litigants about his conduct, is a case in point. The inability of the system to address such inadequate performance in that, and other similar cases, has served to draw attention to the failings of the informal system of self-regulation.

Since dismissal is only an option in the most rare and excessive cases of judicial misconduct or incapacity, alternative systems of evaluating performance and identifying and correcting failings are essential. As other areas of public and professional life have developed structured systems of performance appraisal, complaints processes and disciplinary machinery, the insulation of the judges from such formal scrutiny is increasingly anachronistic. These changes have left the judiciary standing out as one of the last areas of public service in which decision-makers remain immune from any formal systems of scrutiny. The contrast between the judiciary and other spheres of public and professional life in this regard is highlighted by changes in other judiciaries. Just as the developments in training and judicial appointments can be traced in many different countries around the world, so the introduction of more formal mechanisms of scrutiny is a global phenomenon. The contrast between the judiciary in England and Wales and those jurisdictions which employ more open and accountable performance appraisal, complaints systems and disciplinary machinery is growing sharper and adding to the pressure for change. Moreover, the arguments often advanced by judges that such developments undermine judicial independence are growing weaker as the experience of other judiciaries has shown that fear to be unfounded. Against this background, this chapter considers current and possible future developments in the methods for identifying poor judicial performance, censuring it and seeking to improve it.

Public debate and the media

Traditionally, debate about the judiciary outside the confines of the legal world has been very limited and what little there has been has usually been rhetorical and imprecise (Dhavan, 1985, p. 166). Whilst qualitatively little may have changed in the last decade, quantitatively there has been a significant increase in public awareness of the work of judges through the growth in critical media coverage, particularly in the area of sentencing. In response to this development, the judiciary has itself begun, slowly, to participate in the public debate on the judicial system and the work of the judges. This process is therefore two-way, with the media serving as the 'transmission belt' by which the public is informed of the judges' decisions and the judges are informed of public reaction to these (Lee, 1988, p. 207).

There are a number of reasons for the growth of media interest in the judiciary. The common factor which underlies them is the gradual erosion of unquestioning public respect for the judges which once inhibited public criticism and debate.

Public confidence and scrutiny

In 1936 Lord Chief Justice Hewart remarked that: 'His Majesty's judges are satisfied with the almost universal admiration in which they are held'. Nearly fifty years later Lord Taylor, then Lord Chief Justice, commented that such unqualified praise sounded 'breath-takingly arrogant and complacent' (Lord Taylor, 1992, p. 5) Nevertheless, he went on to claim that judges were generally more deserving of public confidence than ever before. At one level, many commentators would agree with Lord Taylor that the standards of the judiciary are high. The intellectual capability of the judiciary is widely well regarded (Pannick, 1988, p. 205; Zander, 1989, p. 107; JUSTICE, 1992, p. 14). In 1993, judges in criminal cases received a very favourable assessment from jurors in over 3000 cases reviewed by the Crown Court Study conducted for the Royal Commission on Criminal Justice. They were asked how good the judge had been at keeping proceedings under control, keeping a fair balance between the defence and prosecution and explaining things to the jury. Over 99% of the jurors questioned thought that the judge had performed these tasks 'very well' or 'fairly well' (Zander and Henderson, 1993, p. 221). In addition, the corruption scandals which have undermined many other jurisdictions in which judges are more closely linked to the party political system have not, to date, been a problem in England. Brian Abel-Smith and Robert Stevens wrote in 1968: 'There is probably no country in the world where the integrity of lawyers and judges is higher' (1968, p. 9). In the last thirty years since they wrote, the reputation of lawyers may be less secure, but the judiciary is still widely regarded as untainted by corruption. At the height of concern about standards in public life in 1996, Lord Kenett commented in debate in the House of Lords: 'We do not - thank God - have sleaze, as the current mix of corruption and mendacity has come to be called, in the judiciary'.[1] Nor is there is any reason to suggest that this feature of the judiciary will change. The security of tenure and financial stability which judges enjoy as well as the culture of the bench all mitigate against such a development. The judiciary is therefore likely to continue to command public respect in this regard.

This conclusion does not, however, guarantee that the judges will continue to enjoy widespread public confidence. Freedom from corruption cannot alone secure such support. In recent years the level of confidence in the judiciary has undoubtedly fallen. In 1993, John Griffith claimed that by the end of the 1980s the reputation of the senior judiciary was lower than at any time this century (1993, p. 190). Whilst some judges might question the extent of this loss of confidence, very few would dispute it altogether.

A number of underlying causes can be identified for this change. The high-profile miscarriages of justice cases which arose in the late 1980s and early 1990s such as the Guildford Four, Birmingham Six, and Maguire cases undermined faith in the criminal justice process generally and the judiciary specifically. To some extent the criticisms which the judges attracted were misplaced since the responsibility for those errors was primarily that of the police and occurred before the cases came to trial. Nevertheless, the judiciary was widely perceived as having contributed to the injustices, if only by its perceived reluctance to correct the errors once they had come to light.

Although the strength of public feeling generated by such cases was high, their long-term adverse effect is likely to be limited as they fade from public memory. In contrast, the continuing expansion of judicial activism is likely to bring about a more permanent change in the public view of the judges. The relationship between activism, scrutiny and public confidence is, historically, relatively clear. The judicial restraint which marked the period from the 1880s to the 1960s which removed the judges from controversy also immunised them from public criticism. During the 1950s, when public confidence in the judiciary was very high, scrutiny was at its lowest. Increased activism from the late 1950s onwards brought increased criticism and in turn greater scrutiny (Abel-Smith and Stevens, 1967, p. 299).

In the years after the Human Rights Act comes into force, as the judiciary increasingly comes to be asked to fulfil the role of the third branch of government, it is likely that there will be a greater tendency for it to be judged in the same way as the other political institutions. If so, the criticisms which politicians face on a daily basis will be experienced by the senior judges as they reach decisions in relation to more controversial social issues. Moreover, it is precisely in such areas that public confidence is already weakest. The most common criticism which is currently voiced about the judges is that they fail to understand and reflect current societal values. The 1996 British Crime Survey found that four out of five respondents believed judges to be: 'out of touch with what ordinary people think' (Mayhew and Percy, 1996).

To some extent these expressions of reduced public confidence may be less of a reflection of dissatisfaction with the judiciary specifically than with public institutions generally. The trend away from deference to authority figures is a common feature of all liberal democracies in recent years. In New Zealand, the Minister of Justice commented in 1995 that the increasing public criticism of judges' decisions was a reflection of a greater willingness to question existing processes and institutions generally:

> Increasingly the traditional institutions have ceased to engender respect simply because of their venerability. Rather, people are today making their own assessment of the performance of standing institutions, often by reference to criteria that reflect today's standards and judgements rather than any unquestioning acceptance of an institution just because it has always functioned in a particular way (East, 1995, p. 2).

It may not be possible to identify the extent to which poor performance on the part of judges can be held to blame for the loss of confidence, or whether this development is rather the consequence of the reaction against institutions of authority generally and the social elitism of the judges particularly. But either way it is clear that there has been a change in the public attitude to the judiciary and the clearest manifestation of this has been the changing relationship between the judiciary and the media.

The growth of media criticism

Until relatively recently, media criticism of the judiciary was strictly limited. In theory, journalists and others who criticise judges run the risk of being found to be in contempt of court for 'scandalising the judiciary'. Although this form of contempt had fallen out of use by the late 19th century, it was reactivated in 1900 in the case of *Gray*.[2] Mr Gray was the editor of a paper which had published an article personally criticising the 'conceit and empty-headedness' of Mr Justice Darling in seeking to limit the press from publishing indecent evidence given at a trial for obscene libel over which he was presiding. In the court's judgment the definition of the contempt was drawn widely to cover: 'any act done or writing published calculated to bring a Court or a judge of the Court into contempt or to lower his authority'. However, having re-established the courts' power to curb press criticism of the judiciary, in practice, the judges rarely felt the need to use it and the last use of this form of contempt of court was in 1931. Although the Phillmore Committee on Contempt of Court in 1974 argued that contempt of the judiciary should be maintained, since the 1980s the courts have suggested that only in the most serious case would contempt proceedings be brought (see Pannick, 1988, p. 115).

For most of this century, the mutually supportive relationship between the media and the judiciary rendered the contempt of 'scandalising the judiciary' all but obsolete. In the years after the War the judges generally regarded the press as a benign channel for informing the public of the work of the courts. Lord Denning was particularly supportive of the role of the court reporter in monitoring the performance of the judges (1954). As late as 1970 it was possible for a retired circuit judge to write that the public held the judiciary in almost universal admiration, and to quote from journalists and newspaper editors to support this claim (Henry, 1970, p. 53). By the mid 1970s however, some commentators were starting to claim that the absence of critical press coverage served to diminish the quality of justice administered in the courts (Shetreet, 1976, pp. 194-196). This mood gradually came to influence the approach of the press in its coverage of the judiciary. In 1988 David Pannick argued that the presence of the contempt power still acted as an unjustifiable inhibition on journalists (1988, p. 115). If so, the inhibition has been relatively ineffective, since the degree of media criticism has risen very considerably during the last ten years, apparently unconstrained by the contempt rules. By the 1990s the extent of this criticism had given rise to an unprecedented tension in the relationship between the media and the judges. In 1994, the former Permanent Secretary to the Lord Chancellor's Department, Sir Derek Oulton, wrote that:

> one of the most dramatic changes that has taken place over the past thirty years or so has been the increasing freedom felt by newspapers, in particular, to attack judges with a vigour...that was formerly quite unknown.[3]

Many commentators have described this development as a necessary and healthy consequence of the judges' expanding role: 'As judges move more actively into political areas, they cannot expect to be treated as above criticism' (Holland and Stevens, 1997, p. 699). Some senior judges have also expressed support for the public scrutiny of their work:

> Rightly the public views the conduct of all arms of government - and the judiciary is one, with intense scepticism. A sceptical and ever watchful public opinion is the best guarantee of the quality of our democratic processes (Lord Steyn, 1997, p. 84).

Such expressions of support by judges for scrutiny by the media are usually qualified. A common argument is that whilst media criticism is acceptable and even desirable in principle, the degree of criticism which the judiciary faces in practice, is often excessive, unjustified and inaccurate. Lord Donaldson, for example, commented in 1995 that: 'criticism of individual decisions is the right of everyone although informed criticism is preferable'.[4] He went on to argue that there had been an increase in uninformed criticism, particularly in the area of sentencing. Similarly, Lord Taylor, when Lord Chief Justice, acknowledged that it was: 'salutary for judges to have some feed-back as to the impact of their decisions and as to public opinion'. But he too claimed that: 'too often, especially in regard to sentences, press comment is based on an incomplete or slanted version of the facts...' (1992, p. 6). In 1997, Sir Stephen Sedley commented that there was an epidemic of: 'sustained public critique of the judiciary which descends at times from argument to abuse' (1997, p. 312). He went so far as to suggest that this development constituted a potential threat to judicial independence. Similar arguments have been heard from judges in other jurisdictions. The Chief Justice of Australia commented that: 'Media scrutiny is healthy...but at times public comment upon the work of the courts demonstrate ignorance of the meaning of the independence of the judiciary (Doyle CJ, 1997, p. 39).

If the belief amongst judges that the current level of criticism amount to a threat to judicial independence spreads, it is possible to imagine that the courts might seek to check what they regard as an abuse of the power of the media. There are a number of means at its disposal to do this. The first, and least satisfactory, is to reactivate the power of contempt. If, however, the courts sought to reassert control on media coverage in this way they might well face a legal challenge to their actions once the European Convention on Human Rights is incorporated into domestic law. A precedent for this is found in Canada in relation to the Charter of Rights. There, the contempt power had been used relatively freely. In 1985, a young student was jailed for contempt for 10 days for describing a trial as 'a mockery of justice'. In addition, a journalist was fined $250 for commenting in an article on capital punishment that the judge had decided the time and place of the convicted man's 'murder' (Nejelski, 1995, p. 52). In 1987 the issue of the scope of the contempt power came before the Supreme Court in the case of *Kopyto* in which a lawyer had described the police and the courts as: 'sticking so close together you'd think they were put together with Krazy glue'. The court held that although contempt of court proceedings were not a violation of the 'due process' provisions of the Charter, contempt should only be used if it was clear that there was a serious risk that the administration of justice would be interfered with and its use to prevent the 'scandalising' of the judiciary should be curbed.[5] In 1992, the Canadian Judicial Council held that: 'generally speaking, judges must henceforth be prepared to endure almost any form of out of court criticism'. This change of approach may suggest that any attempt to resuscitate the power to restrict criticism of the judiciary in England and Wales after incorporation would fail.

Contempt powers are not, however, the only means at the judges' disposal of limiting media criticism. Judges, while protected from civil actions themselves, are quite entitled to issue proceedings for defamation. In 1993, Lord Taylor, then Lord Chief Justice, in a letter to the Times accused the newspaper of libel in suggesting that he had ignored the provisions of the Criminal Justice Act 1991 in increasing a sentence on appeal: 'I do not ignore Acts of Parliament. To suggest the contrary is not only wrong but a gross libel'.[6] The Times published a retraction and apology in response. Although such incidents are still very rare, it is possible to imagine that if judges increasingly feel beleaguered they may more commonly seek to defend their reputations through this means.

An alternative method which is open to judges to protect themselves against the growth of media criticism is to counter it through an active public relations campaign rather than seeking to stifle it altogether. In 1993, Lord Mackay, when Lord Chancellor, was sufficiently concerned about the poor media coverage being attracted by the judiciary that he advised the judges to issue press releases before controversial decisions in order to pre-empt adverse comments.[7] This suggestion was notable because it was one of the first times that the senior judiciary has acknowledged publicly that the judges themselves need to play a part in influencing the nature of the publicity that they receive. Lord Mackay's approach represented the beginnings of a new judicial willingness to engage proactively in the generation of media coverage rather than to remain the passive recipients of criticism.

Judicial participation in public debate

Lord Mackay was a key figure in changing the attitude of the judges to public debate. It was his understanding of the benefits to the judiciary of participation which led to the abolition of the so-called Kilmuir rules which had largely kept the judges out of public debate since 1955. The rules were actually no more than guidelines set out by the then Lord Chancellor, Lord Kilmuir, which stated that:

> so long as a judge keeps silent, his reputation for impartiality remains unassailable; but every utterance he makes in public, except in the course of the actual performance of his judicial duties, must necessarily bring him within the focus of criticism.

This approach linked silence with impartiality so that during the thirty years in which the rules were in force, public participation outside the court was regarded as a potential threat to judicial independence. By the 1980s the connection between judicial independence and judicial participation in public debate was increasingly questioned. An Australian commentator summarised the arguments against the traditional position:

> If the maintenance of judicial independence and ultimately the separation of powers depends solely on silence, lack of controversy and a refusal to enter public debate, then we are entitled to ask what it is, exactly, that we are seeking to preserve and whether it is worth preserving (Brown, 1986, p. 348).

A common criticism of the rules was that they promoted a highly selective use of the principle of judicial independence which allowed judicial intervention when it suited the judges but stifled democratic debate. In response to these concerns, one of the first acts of Lord Mackay on taking office in 1989 was to announce that he no longer regarded the Kilmuir guidelines as effective. He stated that it was more appropriate for each judge to reach his or her own assessment of what to say in public. While this decision attracted widespread support on the grounds of principle, it was also no doubt driven by considerations of political expediency. By the late 1980s, senior judges were increasingly recognising that rules restricting their participation in debate hampered the judges from influencing public understanding of their function. The need for proactive engagement with the media was particularly relevant for Lord Mackay himself in the light of his proposals for reform of the legal profession. These radical changes were highly controversial and required a full public relations exercise to achieve even the modest degree of acceptance which the Lord Chancellor eventually won.

The tone set by Lord Mackay in the 1990s gave a lead to the rest of the judiciary. A number of judges began to give interviews to the press and participated in documentaries. In 1992, for example, a group of high court judges participated in a television documentary about their work. This new era of openness was reinforced by the appointment of Lord Taylor as Lord Chief Justice in 1992. His approach was demonstrated in a number of press interviews which he gave shortly after taking office. In one, asked how he intended to restore confidence in the judiciary he replied simply: 'by being more open'.[8] One of his first public appearances as Lord Chief Justice was to give the Dimbleby lecture for 1992 which he agreed should be televised. His talk was titled, *The Judiciary in the 1990s,* a forward-looking review of the role of the judge in contemporary Britain in which openness was a strong theme. He recognised the fact that the judiciary was now: 'scrutinised and criticised not just by the cognoscenti but by all and sundry' and he expressed his support for the abolition of the Kilmuir rules:

> I think it right that the judges' voices should be heard when our justice system is debated. Senior judges responsible for judicial administration should be prepared to state their policies and, on general topics, to answer criticism (1992, p. 6).

Putting this rhetoric into practice, Lord Taylor presented a public profile which was unlike any Lord Chief Justice before him. In 1994, he gave the Tom Sargeant memorial lecture at the organisation JUSTICE and engaged in questions and answers from the floor. He appeared twice before the Royal Commission on Criminal Justice, the second time at his request to clarify an earlier point. He also attended and chaired a number of conferences in the post-Royal Commission debates.

Such actions undoubtedly represented a real change in the approach of the judges to participation in public debate. Even a staunch critic of the judges such as John Griffith has acknowledged that there has been a positive shift in the way judges now respond to criticism:

> This responsiveness contrasts strongly with the former tradition. They could so easily have withdrawn behind barriers of self-regarding rectitude, and it is wholly to their credit that they have not done so (1997, p. 329).

The unwritten rules regarding the boundaries of acceptable judicial engagement now clearly determine that it is entirely legitimate for judges to participate in debate on topics related to the law and the legal system. In contrast, there is a clear injunction against public discussion about individual cases in which they are or have recently been involved. In between these two positions there is a wide grey area. It is generally expected that a judge would not engage in public debate on controversial areas such as abortion[9] but the exact line between what is and is not acceptable is not always easy to define and judges have sometimes contributed to debates in the House of Lords on controversial matters outside the law and legal system (Stevens, 1993, pp. 174-175).

Despite uncertainty at the boundaries, the extent of public engagement is clearly much wider than that which existed before 1989. However, the current climate should not be seen as unprecedented. The tradition of judicial silence determined by the Kilmuir rules was a relatively recent and short-lived development, lasting only thirty years. In earlier times there had been a strong tradition of judges engaging in public debates on matters of justice. For example, the senior judges took an active part in the debates on the proposals to establish a Court of Criminal Appeal which took place between 1845 and 1907. Many judges commented at length about the proposals for change in Parliament, before a Royal Commission and in the press (Pattenden, 1996). They expressed their views freely on the nature of justice and the role of the criminal justice process in a way which is very familiar in the current climate of judicial 'glasnost'. Interestingly, this period of judicial participation was also a time of strong press criticism, much closer to the situation today than thirty years ago. Press attacks were so aggressive that there were calls in Parliament for the government to take action against the offending newspapers (Shetreet, 1976, pp. 182-183).

Although the current relationship between the judges and the media may in some respects suggest a resurrection of the arrangements of an earlier age, there are also striking differences which indicate the development of a quite new relationship. The role of the press in the 18th and early 19th century could not be more different from the media today. When judges engaged in public debate in the past they were communicating with a small section of influential members of the public which was literate and educated. They were not required to engage with the majority of the people in order to retain public confidence in their work. Today, the judges are just beginning to recognise that their success in retaining and gaining public confidence depends on their ability to utilise the mass media. John Doyle, the Chief Justice of Australia, has recognised the benefits which can accrue to the judiciary by taking a proactive role in promoting understanding of its work:

> To put it bluntly, it is not enough to do what we can to help the media improve the quality of the information that it provides to the public. The judiciary should have its own programme for informing the public about its work... the courts can also dispel misconceptions that they consider are harmful to the institution of the judiciary (1997, p. 43).

This proposal demonstrates an awareness that judges must be prepared to undertake an ongoing public relations exercise. He went on to argue that the basis for earlier judicial reticence was: 'a mixture of sound professional reason, a mistrust of the forces of competition and a false sense of professional dignity' (1997, p. 45). In the past, the work of the judges touched the lives of a relatively small number of people. As judicial activism increases, their decisions will be recognised as affecting a far wider audience. That audience will need to be persuaded that the judges are both competent and responsive. In Canada, the advent of the Charter of Rights in 1982 resulted in greater judicial participation in the media (Baar, 1991, pp. 64-65) and it is very likely that judicial participation in public debate through the media will similarly increase in England and Wales in the years after the Human Rights Act comes into force.

Although judges now accept, in principle, that they cannot assume unquestioning public support but rather that they must generate it, they have not yet translated this understanding into a coherent media policy. While judges are now individually free to make public comments, the judiciary as a body has barely begun to develop the tools which professional users of the press, television and radio require, let alone those appropriate for the new electronic media such as the Internet. The judiciary does not yet employ press officers to work on its behalf and ensure the co-ordination of media coverage so as to promote the most advantageous presentation of its work nor does judicial training yet include the skills necessary to equip the judges individually for dealing with the media. One effect of this passivity is that many of the positive reforms identified in this study are barely known about outside the judiciary. The out-dated view which many people hold of the judges can therefore partly be attributed to the judges' failure to educate the public about the changes it is promoting. In contrast, the judiciaries of many other countries have already recognised the importance of such activity. Media training programmes for judges are currently being developed in the US by the American Judicature Society. Elsewhere, press releases are an established feature of life for many judiciaries. For example, in Australia, the Institute of Judicial Administration issued press releases in 1992 to announce publicly its sponsorship of Australian judges attending training in Canada on gender equality, thus promoting the image of the Australian judiciary as a body committed to developing judicial awareness in this area.[10]

Judges in England and Wales have recently begun to understand that their failure to engage proactively has been partly responsible for their poor press. Lord Taylor suggested in 1992 that lack of confidence in the judiciary was due to misconceptions: 'for which the judges themselves have in part been responsible through self-imposed isolation'. In 1997 Lord Nolan acknowledged the need for a more proactive approach:

> much of the responsibility for poor publicity which judges often receive lies with the judges themselves. The legal profession in general and the judges in particular have always been bad at cultivating the art of public relations...but in recent years judges have increasingly come to recognise the need to anticipate reaction to controversial decisions and to cater for it in their judgment - or even, in extreme cases by holding a press conference (1997, p. 70).

The need to develop such self publicity is particularly acute in the field of sentencing where judges' decisions regularly attract media attention. A review of such coverage would suggest that the judges were failing to respond to public opinion, with sentences being criticised for being excessively lenient or for being too harsh or for taking into account inappropriate considerations. However, the 1996 British Crime Survey showed that criticism of the judges was largely based on misinformation about sentencing practice. The public widely believed that sentences were lighter than they actually were. When given the circumstances of real cases and asked their opinion about the appropriate sentence, the survey respondents were no more punitive than the judges and actually shared very similar views about correct sentencing levels. Similarly, jurors who completed questionnaires for the 1992 Royal Commission on Criminal Justice Crown Court Study demonstrated a wide level of satisfaction with the sentence imposed. 64% of juror respondents thought that the sentence handed down was what they expected based on the evidence or that they had had no expectations of sentence. The remaining third were equally divided between those who thought the decision too lenient and too harsh which suggests that judges are broadly in the middle of the range of different views on sentencing (Zander and Henderson, 1993, p. 223). This evidence indicates that the judges are right to claim that much of the criticism on sentencing is misinformed. Lord Nolan has commented that: 'if the judiciary was really as ignorant and insensitive as they are often portrayed, the criminal justice system would collapse (1997, p. 70). This misinformation is likely to be reinforced by the effects of distorted media coverage and could, to some extent at least, be corrected by a more vigorous use of the media by the judiciary.

In areas such as sentencing, the function of the media as a transmission belt between the judges and the public is most apparent. As sentencers, judges are expected, to some degree, to reflect public opinion. To do this judges need a channel through which they can gauge what the public thinks, and to some extent the media provide this. Newspaper editorials, letters from the public and popular television and radio programmes in which the public express their opinions tell judges something about popular views. However, the extent to which judges should be influenced by media representation of public opinion is debatable. Lord Bingham has stressed the need to ignore populist passion in public debate:

> Judges should take care not to be blown hither and thither by every wind of political or penal fashion. And in determining sentence in any given case the judge should close his or her ears to public and media clamour concerning that case. [11]

A sentencing judge is also expected to weigh up short term and long term public opinion and distinguish between a genuine underlying public groundswell of opinion and a transitory moral scare (Sedley, 1997,

p. 322). However, the task of determining where 'genuine' public opinion lies is not an easy one. The media does not provide the judges with effective tools for differentiating between a passing knee-jerk reaction and deep-seated community values. Its role as a transmission belt between the judges and the public is a limited one. It provides a very partial view of public opinion to the judiciary while supplying the public with equally limited information about the judiciary. The range of cases made known to the public through the media is neither a representative nor systematic review of the judge's work. Cases are selected by the media on the basis of their capacity to sell papers and airtime. The coverage exposes some judges unfairly while equally failing to spotlight others whose conduct ought to be scrutinised. Poor performance by a judge is revealed only if it happens to come to the attention of a journalist and is sufficiently shocking or unusual to attract public attention. Sexual scandals, however trivial, are likely to fall into this category whereas routine rudeness, incompetence or insensitivity which might have a far more profound affect on the standard of justice, may well be neglected. The media cannot, therefore, be relied upon as a systematic means of reviewing judicial performance. The images which it presents are likely to be partial, anecdotal and inexact. The advantages which the media present as a means of increasing accountability are quantitative. As a channel of mass communication it draws the public at large into a debate which might otherwise be left to lawyers and the cognoscenti as it was in the 18th century. But its qualitative limitations mean that it cannot act as a substitute for alternative mechanisms of external scrutiny, in particular academic research, which has the potential to provide the rigorous and in-depth scrutiny lacking in media coverage.

Academic research

Despite its potential role in auditing the performance of the judiciary, the body of academic research on the judiciary in England and Wales is extremely small compared to many other counties, in particular the US. One explanation for this is that the judiciary as a topic of research has fallen into a disciplinary gap between law and politics. In the US, the strong policy-making role of the Supreme Court and the widespread use of elections for appointing judges have meant that the political function of the courts could never be obscured. In contrast, in England and Wales, law and politics have traditionally been treated as separate spheres (Harlow, 1986).

The advent of socio-legal studies and the general flowering of inter-disciplinary work in recent years have helped to break down these barriers to some extent. But political scientists are still wary of carrying their ideas into the legal system while academic lawyers remain reluctant to apply unfamiliar political concepts, such as accountability, to the judiciary. Although lawyers now increasingly apply the methodologies of the social sciences to the study of legal processes, the culture of empirically based legal research which enjoys a long tradition in the US is still in its infancy in the UK.

This account of the disciplinary divide between law and politics may provide some explanation as to why academics have been reluctant to subject the judiciary to rigorous scrutiny. But an equally important factor in the dearth of academic research has been the lack of judicial co-operation in its production. To date, judges have generally been unwilling to engage in research which might shed light on the way they work. In 1968, Brian Abel-Smith and Robert Stevens commented that: 'the judges are seemingly protected not only from political criticism but from scholarly enquiries....' (1968, p. 173). This picture had changed very little by the 1980s:

> The relative insulation of the English judiciary from the type of research directed at other areas of the political process is unhealthy, has inhibited informed debate and has obscured the basic similarity of political and judicial decision-making (Harlow, 1986, p. 183).

The unwillingness on the part of judges to be interviewed for research has presented a particular hindrance to the development of academic research because interview data provide a key tool in shedding light upon the way in which powerful groups operate (Crewe, 1974, p. 43). Alan Paterson's 1981 study of the Law Lords is the only example, to date, of a study based on a systematic series of interviews with senior judges.[12] Many other projects have sought and failed to secure judicial co-operation.[13] Some have been abandoned after the judges' agreement to participation was withdrawn during the research.[14] One study on race and sentencing in the Crown Court originally secured the agreement of the judges to participate. However, the interviews had to be abandoned after the judges were apparently instructed by 'the powers that be' not to co-operate with this aspect of the research (Hood, 1992, p. 37). A small number of studies have proceeded with judicial participation,[15] but the overall record is poor, particularly when compared with the position in the US where over 100 studies on appellate judges have been completed which have involved interviews or questionnaires.[16] In Canada, too, a number of studies have been based on extensive interviews with judges of all ranks (see, for example, Friedland, 1995; Greene, 1990).

This lack of co-operation has been attributed to a: 'prevailing climate of hostility to critical appraisal' (Harlow, 1986, p. 191). To some degree this reluctance on the part of the judiciary to participate in research is understandable. All subjects of academic research have valid reasons for fearing that their weaknesses will be exposed or their views misrepresented. Co-operation in research results from the belief that there is more to gain than lose and that refusal is inappropriate. To date, the judiciary have been insulated from any pressure to participate since it has been considered legitimate for the judges to refuse to co-operate in research on the grounds that it might undermine judicial independence. The prevailing attitude amongst judges is still generally that such research has little to offer the judiciary, that it may be damaging and that it is not required of them to co-operate. The English judiciary has not seen academic research as a means of disseminating knowledge about the legal system in the way that the US judge and legal scholar, Jerome Frank highlighted as long ago as 1949:

> I am unable to conceive that...in a democracy it can ever be unwise to acquaint the public with the truth about the workings of any branch of government. ...The best way to bring about the elimination of those shortcomings of our judicial system which are capable of being eliminated is to have all our citizens informed as to how that system now functions (1949, pp. 2-3).

While it is unlikely that in the near future English judges will come to view research as a democratic necessity, the traditional dismissive approach is becoming less and less sustainable. As the power of the judiciary in England and Wales grows the need to secure public support by encouraging well informed research is likely to be increasingly recognised by judges. Similarly, the argument that the demands of accountability require a degree of co-operation in reputable research projects is likely to grow more persuasive as the influence and cost of the judiciary increases. If this change occurs, the production of rigorous and reliable research will play a more important part in contributing to the increasing scrutiny of the judiciary. It cannot, however, be a substitute for ongoing mechanisms for assessing all aspects of judicial performance and conduct. Just as the media has its own interests to pursue in scrutinising the judiciary, so too academic research is driven by the particular interests of researchers and their funders rather than the needs of the justice process. Whilst these may overlap and sometimes coincide, they are not identical. For this reason, academic research cannot alone be relied upon for monitoring and maintaining standards in the judiciary. For this task, internal systems are also needed.

Performance appraisal

The introduction of a structured system of performance appraisal for monitoring the work of the judges and promoting good practice is still some way off. Traditionally, the judiciary has relied upon an informal system for encouraging good performance and discouraging bad through the application of peer pressure. The effectiveness of this mechanism as a means of enforcing collective standards should not be under-estimated and in the past, it achieved a relatively high degree of conformity and consistency amongst the judges (Shetreet, 1984, p. 1008). Such informal mechanisms of performance appraisal work particularly well in a small, highly cohesive and homogeneous group where common standards are clear and deviation from these attracts the disapprobation of one's peers. Until relatively recently the judiciary displayed the classic characteristics of an informally self-regulating body. This is still largely true of the upper ranks of the judiciary which continue to function as a relatively tight-knit group. The judges of the High Court and above share broadly homogeneous backgrounds and experiences and they operate in a small professional and social community which is based largely in London. The Court of Appeal, for example, has been described by one former Lord Justice as 'the best working man's club in England'. This club-like environment may allow the senior judges to maintain a strong informal network for promoting common standards. Moreover, variation in approach is more acceptable at the upper end of the judiciary where innovation and flexibility are necessary qualities for those whose tasks involve the development of the law and the review of policy-making.

However, outside this elite corps of less than 150 judges, the growth in the size of the judiciary, the rising numbers of part-time judges and the increasing heterogeneity of their background have all weakened the capacity of such informal processes to operate effectively. The majority of judges no longer belongs to a small club with a strong collective culture and shared values in which most members are known to each other. They are one of nearly 3,000 men and women fulfilling a wide variety of different jobs around the country. Ensuring that this number of full and part-time members of the judiciary with different types of knowledge and experiences are performing to a consistent standard cannot be achieved solely through informal mechanisms.

In addition, as the structural and cultural conditions which supported an informal system have been eroded, the external expectations of judicial performance have changed. Traditionally, the guiding approach of the judiciary was that judges were masters in their own courts and should be granted a wide scope to run them as they saw fit. Only if a judge stepped beyond these broad boundaries did the informal control mechanisms come into play. Lawyers widely accepted this approach and the idiosyncrasies of individual judges were well known and generally tolerated. Although this ethos still exists to some degree, there is a growing expectation both amongst lawyers and litigants that judges should demonstrate a commitment to a basic level of consistency in their performances. As judges come increasingly to be regarded as public servants rather than figures of unquestioning authority, these expectations are likely to increase. In addition, the absence of formal processes for monitoring and promoting this consistency amongst full-time judges has come to stand out in contrast to other fields of public service where performance appraisal is regarded as an integral feature of working life. Framework documents, performance agreements and corporate plans borrowed from the private sector are all common expressions of the new forms of accountability which have been introduced into the public sector (Oliver and Drewry, 1996, p. 136). It is now widely perceived that the public has the right to know what standards of performance are being set, whether they are being met and what action is being taken to improve performance where they are not. To do this requires a method of appraisal which allows those providing a service and those managing them to receive systematic feed-back on their performance.

The combined effect of these internal and external factors has been gradually to increase the pressure for the introduction of formal monitoring systems in the judiciary. In 1992, JUSTICE, in its review of the judiciary highlighted the lack of methods for appraising judicial performance: 'Unless judges know where they are going wrong they cannot improve what they do' (JUSTICE, 1992, p. 14). In particular, the absence of performance appraisal in judicial training has attracted attention since this is a standard feature of most other equivalent training programmes. As judicial training has expanded and become increasingly professional, the fact that judges receive no feed-back on their performance during training is more noticeable. One of the most successful features of the training programme for the criminal process has been the use of mock trials in which judges are faced with a variety of difficult scenarios which might arise at trial. Many judges who have attended this course have stressed its usefulness, particularly for those with little experience in criminal cases, and yet it is hard to see how it can be a fully effective teaching tool if judges who participate are not assessed on how well they handle such situations. In 1993, the Royal Commission on Criminal Justice drew attention to the absence of monitoring during training and the report proposed that an effective formal system of performance appraisal should be instituted.[17]

As well as criticising the absence of monitoring during training, the Royal Commission also concluded that there were not satisfactory monitoring arrangements in place during the judges' routine work to ensure that standards were maintained, and it expressed surprise that full-time judges seldom, if ever, observed trials conducted by their colleagues. The Commission proposed that presiding and resident judges should attend trials to assess the performance of judges in their courts. In 1995, Lord Woolf, in his report on the civil system, similarly recommended that there should be a general extension of monitoring.[18] He argued that appraisal would allow judges to be given constructive comments on their work which would help to promote consistency between one judge and another in management decisions.

The absence of performance appraisal for full-time judges is also more notable since it has been introduced for part-time judges and for tribunal chairpersons. The induction programme for Assistant Recorders requires a period of sitting in with an experienced Circuit judge who is required to report back to the Lord Chancellor on the trainee's suitability to sit. In 1996, Lord Mackay, when Lord Chancellor, announced that the role of pupil-master judge was to be extended to allow for an element of in-court observation to provide further advice and assistance to newly appointed Assistant Recorders.[19] In January 1998, Lord Irvine continued this approach with the announcement that a mentoring scheme would be set up in which senior members of the judiciary would advise and guide their more junior colleagues.[20] This trend has been supported by those judges who have been appointed to the Circuit bench after having sat on tribunals where they have had experience of performance appraisal:

> Judges have one great disadvantage: we have no opportunity of seeing how colleagues perform in court and it is difficult to assess our own performance or the impression we make on those who use our own courts.[21]

The absence of formal performance appraisal in England and Wales is in stark contrast to its use in other jurisdictions, in particular in other European countries. In France, judges are subject to 'évaluation', a system of appraisal introduced in 1992. This is carried out by senior judges every two years and involves an appraisal of the judge's work and his or her future training needs (Septe and Campbell, 1995). Nor is appraisal limited to the career judiciaries of civil law systems. In the US it is an intrinsic feature of the judicial system at state level. Originally introduced in the 1970s as a tool to assist the public in assessing the quality of candidates in elections, evaluation programmes were based on assessments by members of the bar which were then collated and made publicly available to voters. In the last twenty years its use has spread to most states whatever selection method they use as a means of providing feedback to the judges in order to improve performance. In Canada, moves to introduce systems based on the US models have been made in Nova Scotia, Ontario and Manitoba (Friedland, 1995, pp.161-163). Until 1997, the strong opposition of Lord Mackay to its introduction blocked the serious consideration of any similar developments in England and Wales. However, the appointment of Lord Irvine indicated that the Lord Chancellor's Department was more willing to consider the potential for change. In 1997, Lord Irvine announced that he would be reviewing, in the long-term, the scope for improving arrangements for performance appraisal of the part-time judiciary with the aim of improving the assessments which contribute to his decisions on full-time office. In 1998, as part of this new approach, the Lord Chancellor's Department began to examine the possibilities of establishing performance benchmarks as a means of setting standards. However, even these relatively modest steps in the direction of a more systematic performance appraisal mechanism are likely to meet with strong judicial resistance.

Judicial opposition to performance appraisal

The response of the judiciary to proposals for instituting performance appraisal has mirrored its reaction to the proposal for introducing training during the 1970s; that it is unnecessary and that it threatens judicial independence.[22]

Various arguments have been put forward to support the claim that performance appraisal is not needed. It is claimed that, in contrast to the Continental judicial career system, the appointment of judges in England and Wales occurs at a later stage in their career by when they have already been exposed to a sufficient degree of scrutiny and appraisal (Septe and Campbell, 1995). This argument rests on the assumption that the responsibilities and qualities of an advocate are the same as those of a judge. This is an assumption which has been questioned often enough both by judges and those who appear before them to need no further refutation.

A stronger argument against the need for performance appraisal is that the work of the judges takes place: 'in the searchlight of public opinion' (Lord Steyn, 1997, p. 85). The public nature of the courts means that individuals and the media have more access to judges' work than to that of most other decision-makers. Unlike ministers or civil servants, almost all judicial decision-making is carried out in public with reasons given orally and/or in writing which are available for scrutiny. However, there are serious limitations to the claims that the public nature of the court process substitutes for alternative means of scrutiny of judicial performance. Courts and law reports are, in practice, only observed and read by a small proportion of the population. It is only when the media decide to take up a particular case that it reaches a wider audience and can be said to be subject to the scrutiny of the general public. The introduction of routinely televised courts, (still strongly resisted by the judges), might change this to some extent, but unless or until such time as the cameras record the judges' work, the public nature of the court process will remain limited.

The appeal process as a monitoring mechanism

Another argument commonly put forward for saying that performance appraisal is not needed is that the functions of the appeal process provides the necessary means for checking judicial performance. On the face of it, this claim is a persuasive one since the most common type of appeal to the

Court of Appeal (Criminal Division) is against the trial judge's sentencing decision whilst the most common ground of appeal against conviction is that of judicial error (Malleson, 1993). This suggests that in the criminal trial at least, the judge's decision-making is subject to review by a higher court. The threat of being overturned on appeal is one which is taken very seriously by almost all judges, most of whom keep a close watch on the outcome of appeals against their decisions and thus can be assumed to be influenced in their future decision-making by a critical decision from the Court of Appeal. However, the essential weakness in relying on appeal process as a means of monitoring judicial performance is that the functions of the appeal process and a system of performance appraisal are quite different. The purpose of the former is both broader and narrower than the latter. Broader, because the appeal system exists to correct errors of law, fact or procedure from whatever source, not only those emanating from the judge. Narrower, because it does not cover a wide range of judicial behaviour which would be the natural subject of performance appraisal.

Research findings have consistently confirmed what most lawyers who regularly appear before the Court of Appeal know, that where an appeal in a criminal case is based on judicial error the types of error almost always relate to the content of a direction to the jury on law, fact or procedure, usually in the summing-up. The appeal hearing is generally concerned with what was said and done at trial and whether this rendered the conviction unsafe. It is therefore not a good medium for reviewing poor conduct which cannot be easily encapsulated in a written ground of appeal, such as lateness, rudeness, inappropriate body language, lack of control of the court proceedings, interruption of counsel or insensitive treatment of victims, all of which are not easily revealed in the trial transcript (Shetreet, 1976; Malleson, 1993). These failings might not raise a ground for claiming that the conviction was unsafe but they would certainly affect the quality of justice and would typically form the subject matter of a system of performance appraisal.

The appeal process cannot be a substitute for performance appraisal because the two do not share the same goals. The purpose of an appeal is primarily to put right a mistake rather than to ensure that the same mistakes do not reoccur. Historically, the Court of Appeal has been reluctant to exercise a disciplinary or supervisory function, whether of the police, lawyers or the trial judge. Even in the rare case where a judge's misconduct is accepted by the Court of Appeal as a valid ground of appeal, there is no requirement that the matter must be referred to the Lord

Chancellor. No doubt this is sometimes done, but if so, it is an informal process and dependent on the decision of the individual judges who are sitting in the Court of Appeal to hear that case. Although information is collated in the Criminal Appeal Office on judges who are regularly the subject of successful appeals, the Court of Appeal does not exercise any systematic mechanism for providing feedback to the judges themselves as to their appraisal by the Court of Appeal. If the appeal process serves in some way to improve future performance of individual judges or the judiciary as a whole, this is incidental to its main function.

An appeal system cannot modify judges' behaviour in the same way as an appraisal system because it does not impose direct adverse consequences as a result of poor performance in the way that an effective system of performance appraisal can do (Okeeffe, 1986, p. 594). However, it is precisely this pressure to which many judges object on the grounds that it poses a threat to judicial independence.

Judicial independence

In addition to the claim that performance appraisal is unnecessary, it is commonly argued that its introduction exposes the judges to the danger that improper influence will be brought to bear on their decision-making. In 1995, Lord Mackay, then Lord Chancellor, was asked in Parliament whether the Royal Commission's proposals for introducing performance appraisal would be implemented. The Lord Chancellor's Department's written reply stated that:

> The Lord Chancellor attaches the highest importance to the constitutional principle of judicial independence. He has established no procedures for monitoring the competence of the full-time judiciary.[23]

The need to prioritise judicial independence and the view that it is undermined by performance appraisal is a recurring theme in the debate on judicial performance around the world. In Canada, for example, the disproportionate attention paid to judicial independence when compared with judicial performance has been attracting comment for over a decade:

> While the concern for security of tenure has been progressively addressed, until quite recently very little attention has been given to the other side of the coin; ways and means of protecting society from judicial incompetence or arrogance (Russell, 1987, p. 173).

The common response to the problem of judicial independence from those who advocate the introduction of performance appraisal is to emphasise the need to ensure that the system is controlled by the judges themselves and that the results of the assessments are kept confidential. The Royal Commission on Criminal Justice, for example, stressed that the appraisal should be carried out by judges and the findings should be kept within the judiciary: 'in order not to put their independence at risk'.[24] Lord Woolf, in his recommendations for performance appraisal in the civil system similarly emphasised that monitoring should be kept within the control of the judges.[25] This approach to the problem is mirrored in the US where the American Bar Association Guidelines for the Evaluation of Judicial Performance stress that responsibility for performance appraisal must remain with the judiciary (ABA, 1985, p. 2).

Such proposals accept uncritically the claim that performance appraisal represents a threat to judicial independence. Neither the Royal Commission nor the Woolf report explained how or why public knowledge of judicial performance would put judges' independence at risk. In order to assess the relationship between performance appraisal and judicial independence it is necessary to revisit the definitional question examined in chapter three. If judicial independence is defined very widely as freedom, both collective and individual, from all influences then performance appraisal intrinsically threatens it. But if the boundaries of judicial independence are narrowed to exclude only improper influences which affect the party impartiality of the judge in adjudication then the threat would arise only if performance appraisal involved an assessment of the correctness of the judge's decision. It is for this reason that the first rule of any judicial appraisal system is that it focuses on process not outcome. Many of those who support the introduction of performance appraisal in England and Wales have stressed this distinction. JUSTICE, for example, in its recommendations, stated that judges need feedback on: 'the way in which they conduct themselves so as to secure a fair trial'. Appraisal should therefore relate to the conduct of the trial not the correctness of the judges' decisions which is for the appeal courts to review (1992, p. 14). In the US, the criteria for evaluation set out by the American Bar Association Guidelines covers such matters as communication skills, preparation, attentiveness, punctuality and control over proceedings (1985, pp. x-xi).

If judicial independence is defined as the need to ensure freedom to administer the law impartially, that is according to the judicial oath, without 'fear or favour, affection or ill-will', and if performance appraisal is the process for monitoring the way in which judges conduct themselves so as to secure a fair trial, then the two are quite separate. The function of performance appraisal is essentially to ensure good judicial administration and as JUSTICE argued in support of its introduction: 'judicial independence cannot be a justification for substandard justice' (1992, p. 4).

Suggestions that judicial independence would be secured by ensuring that the results of any performance appraisal are kept within the domain of the judiciary are a response to the political sensibilities of the judges rather than a coherent analysis of the relationship between performance appraisal and judicial independence. The connection between the two concepts lies not in the extent of the dissemination of the findings of the appraisal but in its subject matter. Whether or not certain judges are assessed to have dealt sensitively with vulnerable witnesses, or responded effectively to conflict in court should not in any way impinge on judicial independence whoever knows about the results. It may, of course, expose weaknesses in judicial performance which might incur public criticism, but that is the potential consequence of all mechanisms of accountability.

The practicability of separating outcome and process in monitoring while operating an open system using outside appraisers is demonstrated by the citizen court monitoring programmes used in the US. Started in New York State in 1975 by the Fund for Modern Courts, with similar schemes now running in Chicago and Washington, it employs 600 lay volunteers to monitor each court's work once a week for a period of 3-6 months depending on the size of the court being monitored. Any danger that the programme would impinge on judicial independence is avoided because the monitors do not assess the results of the cases but only the way in which the judges handle witnesses, victims, jurors and counsel, as well as the judges' general demeanour. They also consider the nature of the court facilities such as the information available to the public and the physical conditions and spatial arrangements of the court. Their aim is to view the work of the courts from the perspective of outside users and make recommendations for their improvements which would make them more user-friendly and efficient. The monitors' findings are widely disseminated to court administrators, judges, the media, bar associations and civic groups. Their report generally receives substantial media coverage and a full response from the court being monitored. The New York programme is widely regarded as having been very successful in improving the court service. It has lead to improvements in judges' timekeeping and their willingness to explain the reason for delays as well as practical changes such as the increased use of microphones by judges in courts where audibility was poor.[26]

The distinction between process and outcome should be sufficient to assuage fears that the introduction of performance appraisal would undermine judicial independence. Nevertheless, the essential requirements of judicial independence do pose practical problems for the effective enforcement of a programme of evaluation. Monitoring performance is only a worthwhile exercise if there are mechanisms, either structural or cultural, for encouraging good performance and discouraging bad. Structural methods usually take the form of financial reward, dismissal or promotion. For judges, the last two are not realistic options since security of tenure is widely regarded as the most basic prerequisite of judicial independence. Dismissal is only permissible in the most limited circumstances in order to avoid any danger that a judge might feel pressured through fear of losing his or her job to decide a case one way or the other.

Linking pay to performance raises similar difficulties. In order for judges to be free from the danger of improper influence their salaries must be both adequate and secure and for this reason many jurisdictions prohibit salary cuts for judges. Although there is no formal restriction in England and Wales, an attempt to reduce the salaries of judges in 1931 during the Depression was successfully resisted by the judges and would be very unlikely to succeed today.[27] However, a prohibition on salary cuts does not, in theory, rule out the introduction of pay differentials on the basis of performance, provided any reward for productivity was paid strictly as additional pay over and above the ordinary judicial salary and, again, provided the incentive payments related to processual matters rather than decision-making. Nevertheless, although this approach to performance related pay might reduce the danger of undermining judicial independence, it could not remove it altogether. In addition, even if the payments were strictly limited to procedural aspects of a judge's performance, the fear that judges might be influenced in their decision-making by financial incentives might well cast a doubt over their perceived impartiality and the quality of their justice. These limitations therefore probably rule out the use of performance related pay as either practicable or sound in principle.

The main structural enforcement mechanism available for performance appraisal is therefore that of promotion. To date, advancement within the judiciary has, in practice, been dependent on the assessment of a judge's performance by other judges and barristers. The creation of a system of performance appraisal would therefore do little more than replace this existing informal system with a formal process of evaluation. Indeed, it could be argued that the creation of more open and objective appraisal criteria would strengthen rather than weaken judicial independence since there would be less danger that a judge might be denied promotion when it was merited or promoted undeservedly. However, there are limitations to the scope for linking performance appraisal to the promotions system. In those jurisdictions where performance appraisal plays a major role, it tends to be strongly linked to a structured career path which, despite the increasingly formal career structure of the judiciary in England and Wales, does not exist in the continental European sense. For this reason critics of the introduction of performance appraisal in England and Wales stress that the differences between the English and the Continental European system in terms of promotion limit the role which performance appraisal can play (Septe and Campbell, 1995). In addition, because the base of the judicial pyramid is so much larger than the pinnacle, for a large proportion of judges promotion is not a realistic option. For this group, the only reward for improved performance through performance appraisal is the inherent satisfaction of competence which, not surprisingly, causes difficulties in practice in creating effective appraisal systems (Armytage, 1995). Such problems are to some degree inherent in any system of performance appraisal, whether judicial or otherwise. Once individuals are no longer looking for advancement, either because they have reached the peak of their profession or because they have decided not to seek it, performance appraisal is necessarily less effective.

Because the requirements of judicial independence place limitations on the structural mechanisms available to encourage good performance and because of the practical difficulties which limit its effectiveness, there will continue to be a need to rely on informal cultural mechanisms for enforcing standards. But these alone cannot provide the consistency of performance which the public increasingly expects and demands from its public servants. While it is right to point to the differences between the promotions system of continental Europe and England and Wales and to realise that those differences mean that performance appraisal is unlikely to fulfil the same role in both systems it is also the case that there is still plenty of scope for the introduction of mechanisms to encourage the improvement of judicial performance.

As the pressure for the introduction of more formal systems of performance appraisal grows, the objections of practicality and principle outlined above are likely to be strongly argued by the judges, as they have been in Canada and other countries where similar proposals have been introduced (Friedland, 1995, p. 157). However, the experience of the US suggests that as in the area of training, once performance appraisal is introduced the judiciary becomes quickly reconciled to it and moreover, that it comes to be widely regarded as a useful tool. For good judges, the ability to demonstrate their competence, and for this to be formally recognised in an open and structured process, often represents an improvement on the traditional subjective and closed systems. In addition, the fact that performance appraisal provides some means of exposing the failings of their less competent colleagues is ultimately a positive change. When public confidence in the judiciary was secure it mattered less if a certain amount of poor performance went uncorrected. Today, when the public is more critical of inadequate judges the cost of ignoring the failings of a few individuals is paid by the whole judiciary.

Enforcing standards of judicial conduct

The aim of performance appraisal is to provide judges with feed-back in order to improve the quality of their work. Like the media and the appeal process it represents an important, but limited, method of scrutiny. Performance appraisal offers a long term promise of improved judicial standards, both at an individual and collective level, but it cannot provide an immediate response to instances of poor judicial conduct. Nor can it detect or correct extra-judicial failings which have a bearing on a judge's performance in court. This aspect of judicial performance can only be addressed by a mechanism for receiving complaints about misconduct and, where necessary, taking action against a judge found guilty of such behaviour. To date, however, the judges have enjoyed a remarkable degree of freedom from any such forms of scrutiny, being almost completely unaccountable for anything but the most extreme forms of misconduct.

Legal action for misconduct

Lord Mackay, when Lord Chancellor, stated that: 'judicial independence does not mean that judges are above the law. The rule of law applies to them and their work'.[28] This statement is only true up to a point since in common with many other jurisdictions such as Israel, Canada, the US and New Zealand, judges in England and Wales enjoy a wide measure of immunity from civil and criminal action for acts committed in the course of their duties.[29] The protection which they are granted is extensive, covering not only negligent actions but also including acts committed recklessly or maliciously. The definition of judicial immunity devised by Lord Denning in 1974 still applies: 'No matter that the judge was under some gross error or ignorance, or was actuated by envy, hatred and malice, and all uncharitableness, he is not liable to an action'.[30] The scope of this immunity has been criticised by many observers, recently being described as presuming not so much an independent judiciary but an 'imperial judiciary' (Olowofoyeku, 1993, pp. 194-5). Olowofoyeku and others have argued that the requirements of judicial independence could equally be protected by a qualified immunity in which actions which were reckless or motivated by malice would be subject to review. An alternative approach which was adopted in France in 1972, is to allow vicarious state liability for judges' actions. A judicial agent of the Treasury may be sued for the personal fault of a judge. If the finding is upheld the state may seek reimbursement from the judge, though this has never happened in the few cases which have successfully been brought (McKillop, 1997, p. 129). The abolition of absolute immunity would not, in practice, lead to judges regularly being brought before the courts, but it would be an important statement of principle that judges themselves, as Lord Mackay claims, should not be above the law and would demonstrate that at least in rare cases of serious misconduct the judiciary placed its duty to the public before its own interests.

Dismissal

The protection enjoyed by full-time judges against legal action is paralleled by their job security. It is often said that the judiciary enjoys a degree of security of tenure 'unique among civil servants' since the removal of a judge is almost impossible. Under the Act of Settlement of 1701 High Court judges and above hold office 'during good behaviour' and can only be dismissed by a motion of both houses of Parliament. The only High Court judge to have been removed was an Irish judge, Sir Jonah Barrington in 1830, for embezzling fees paid into court (see Shetreet, 1976, pp. 143-44). The definition of misbehaviour as limited to such criminal behaviour is now a strong convention and any attempt to institute proceedings for anything less would be very unlikely to succeed. Lower ranking judges are, on paper, less secure since their removal can be effected by the Lord Chancellor alone. He can dismiss a judge up to and including circuit judges on the grounds of 'incapacity and misbehaviour'.[31] In practice, these powers appear to be similarly restricted to conduct which amounts to criminal behaviour, having only been used once in recent times, against a circuit judge caught smuggling whiskey and cigarettes. In cases involving other serious misconduct the threat of action has usually been enough to induce a resignation.

A review of the arrangements regarding tenure in other jurisdictions reveals that security against dismissal is a universal feature of those systems which prioritise judicial independence. In Israel under the Judges' Law a judge can only be removed before retirement age for medical reason or on carefully defined restricted grounds (Shetreet, 1984, p. 900). In New Zealand, The Constitution Act 1986 provides that a judge can only be removed by the Sovereign or Governor General on the address of the House of Representatives. Removal is limited to grounds of misbehaviour or incapacity (Goldfinch, 1993, p. 156). Similar rules exist in Canada, Australia and South Africa. In all these countries, the history of judicial independence has been relatively secure for many years and the extent of the protection appears excessive. However, in the Westminster style system of Malaysia in 1988, the Lord President of the Supreme Court was removed from office along with several other judges. They were found guilty of misbehaviour by a tribunal appointed by the Prime Minister after expressing concern about the Government's criticism of the courts (McGarvie, 1991, pp. 15-20). Such an incident is a reminder of why security of tenure has been regarded as a cornerstone of judicial independence.

However, despite its status, the principle of security of tenure is not absolute. In 1959, a retirement age of 75 was introduced; reduced to 70 in 1993.[32] The interpretation of the tenure rule which allowed judges to sit until death or illness removed them was clearly an excessive interpretation of the requirements of judicial independence and one which has caused real problems in individual cases of judges sitting beyond the period when they were physically or mentally fit to do so. The provisions of the 1959 Judicial Pensions Act were considered controversial at the time, and yet no one would now suggest that this change has impinged upon judicial independence in practice. By 1993 the claim that judicial independence was incompatible with a retirement age was barely raised in the light of the further reduction of the retirement age. The decision attracted more criticism on the grounds that it wasted talent and limited the time judges had to amass a suitable pension rather than on any grounds of principle. Indeed arguably, the introduction of a retirement age has actually served to reinforce judicial independence since it has reduced the necessity for the Lord Chancellor or Parliament to remove a judge on the grounds of incapacity.

More problematic has been the extensive increase in the use of part-time and temporary appointments. Since 1993, judges may sit on an ad hoc basic at the request of the Lord Chancellor from the age of 70 until 75. In addition, a significant proportion of work in the lower court is now carried out by Recorders and Assistant Recorders, while there is also now widespread use of circuit judges or QCs sitting as deputies in the High Court. In 1994, it was estimated that the number of deputies sitting at any one time was approximately two thirds of the number of High Court judges (Sir Francis Purchas, 1994, pp. 1308-1309). All these part-time and temporary judges can effectively be dismissed at any time by the Lord Chancellor without reasons simply by not being asked to sit again or, in the case of Recorders, not being promoted to the full-time bench. In some jurisdictions the dangers inherent in these arrangements are recognised and the use of part-time or temporary judges is forbidden or severely restricted. The Australian Declaration of Principles of Judicial Independence, for example, states that the appointment of acting judges, whether retired or not, is only acceptable if made with the approval of the judicial head of the court in which the judge is appointed and only in special circumstances which render it necessary.

Concerns have been expressed about the arrangements in England and Wales. The system of employment after retirement have been described by JUSTICE as constituting a 'casual approach' to the independence of the judiciary:

> In our view, this arbitrary power of extension should be in the hands neither of other members of the judiciary or the government.... We

believe the present discretionary system to offer the possibility of abuse (JUSTICE, 1992, p. 19).

Whilst it can be argued that in the case of Assistant Recorders and Recorders the danger of the executive and the judges coming into conflict in a way which might threaten judicial independence is slight, the same cannot be said for deputy High Court judges and retired judges, who may be involved in decision-making in which the Government has a clear vested interest. The fact that the continuing employment of those acting as senior judges should be at the whim of the executive is hard to reconcile with the strong role attributed to security of tenure in the rhetoric of judicial independence. The contrast between their protection and that of permanent appointees is very striking. Although there has been no evidence of abuse of the power of dismissal, the current arrangements suggest that for one group the protection is too little, for the other it is too great. One possible solution to the problem is the use of non-renewable fixed term contracts, as proposed by JUSTICE. It suggested in 1992 that the *ad hoc* system of deputies be replaced by fixed term appointments of four to five years. This would allow the Lord Chancellor a measure of flexibility in the deployment of personpower to match supply with demand whilst improving the degree of security for temporary judges (1992, p. 21). The report argued that term appointments would bring to the bench lawyers who: 'do not wish to commit their lives to judging but who could be expected, during a four or five year term, to make a significant contribution'(pp. 21-22). In some jurisdictions, fixed term appointments are the norm and they are generally allowed for in the jurisprudence on judicial independence provided they are for a substantial period and are not renewable.

The ideal arrangement is one which provides all judges with equal protection from dismissal for political motives but which ensures that those whose conduct is flawed can be adequately dealt with. Since in practice, the demands of judicial independence mean that the grounds of dismissal for judges are likely to remain far more limited than for other public servants, being restricted to criminal behaviour or incapacity, the need for an alternative means of dealing with misconduct of a judge which falls short of such extreme failings is an essential feature of the scrutiny system.

Current complaints and disciplinary procedures

Members of the public and the legal profession who use the courts must be able to complain when a judge's conduct falls short of acceptable standards. They are entitled to know that their complaints will be taken seriously and investigated and that if found to be justified, the fault will be acknowledged, the system will make amends if possible, and an attempt will be made to deter the judge in question (and the judiciary generally) from committing similar breaches of conduct in the future.

The system in England and Wales cannot be said to fulfil these requirements. To date, it has operated a limited form of self-regulation: 'The unfortunate reality is that in England judicial performance very much depends on judicial self-restraint and self-control' (Pannick, 1988, p. 76). The demands of judicial independence have been held to require that criticism of a judge's conduct be strictly restrained. The convention that a judge's conduct cannot be discussed in Parliament except on a substantive motion for removal limits the extent to which the legislature can fulfil any form of disciplinary role. Although there have been instances in which judges have been criticised in Parliament, despite the convention, these have been sporadic and cannot be said to constitute a reliable channel for regulating judicial conduct (Shetreet, 1976). In 1973, the Speaker of the House of Commons ruled that MPs were permitted to suggest in Parliament that a judge had made a mistake and reasons for that contention could be given. However, it was held to be unacceptable for any charge of a 'personal nature' to be raised or for a suggestion that a judge should be dismissed to be made except on a formal motion. In 1980 when one MP described Lord Diplock as being a 'Tory judge' he was duly reprimanded by the speaker.

Outside Parliament, a wider convention dictates that members of the legislature and the executive should avoid making direct criticisms of judicial decisions. The extent to which the limits of ministerial comment on individual cases is still restricted was demonstrated in 1995 when Michael Howard, then Home Secretary, commented on a decision against him in the Divisional Court. The case had been brought by five IRA prisoners sentenced to life imprisonment in 1976. They challenged the decision of the Home Secretary not to send their case to the Parole Board for review until the expiry of the tariff period. The court held that since the Board would take at least six months to review the papers this action effectively lengthened the period of detention and was therefore unreasonable. After the decision, Michael Howard commented that:

> The last time this particular judge found against me, which was on a case which would have lead to the release of a large number of illegal immigrants, the Court of Appeal unanimously decided that he was wrong.[33]

The response from the judiciary to this statement was sharp. One senior judge suggested that it was a 'complete breach of convention'. Since Michael Howard's statement was, at one level, no more than a statement of fact, the boundaries within which ministers are expected to act in discussing the decisions of judges are clearly still very tightly drawn. Other jurisdictions similarly impose strict controls on ministers' rights to comment on judicial decision-making. In New Zealand, the Cabinet Office Manual states that ministers should at all times: 'avoid any comment which could be construed as being intended to influence the Court in subsequent cases'.[34] The effect of these rules designed to protect judicial independence in its narrow sense of the party impartiality of judicial decision-making has been to restrict complaints from politicians and officials about the quality of judges' work in all its aspects. Although this restraint has weakened somewhat in recent years as the greater willingness of the media to criticise judges testifies, the effect of the convention is that the task of supervising the conduct of judges is generally regarded as an internal matter for the judiciary alone.

The first principle upon which the present system for controlling judicial conduct rests is that the definition of what is acceptable and unacceptable is for the individual to determine, with support and advice from his or her peers. Only where this judicial self-control fails, does responsibility for discipline then fall to the Lord Chancellor as head of the judiciary. By convention, he receives and investigates complaints about misconduct. However, the Lord Chancellor's formal powers over other judges are very limited. His powers to discipline judges are not statutory and it is left to his discretion to determine what process should be used in a case of alleged misconduct. The inadequacy of the present arrangements were highlighted in 1989 when a Circuit judge, James Pickles, was threatened with dismissal proceedings over public comments which he made about a trial over which he had presided. Judge Pickles refused to attend a hearing which the Lord Chancellor had arranged to consider the matter and threatened judicial review of the process on the grounds that the Lord Chancellor was 'complainant, prosecutor, judge and jury' in the case (Pickles, 1992, pp. 165-169).[35] Whatever the merits of that particular case, the failings of the dismissal procedure in terms of due process were clearly highlighted.

Under the Courts Act 1971 there is no action less draconian than dismissal which the Lord Chancellor can invoke in response to poor judicial conduct. By convention, he may admonish a judge whose behaviour has been criticised and may issue a public rebuke. In practice, it is very rare for a reprimand to be publicised. Moreover, the complainant may not even be informed that any action has been taken. Lord Hailsham, when Lord Chancellor, explained that when he received a complaint about a judge's conduct he showed the complaint to the judge in a number of cases, though he seldom told the complainant that he had done so.[36]

Whilst it should not be surprising that it is extremely rare for the Lord Chancellor to exercise his powers of dismissal since it is very unusual for judicial behaviour to fall so low as to warrant such action, the fact that it is so rare for judges to be disciplined is a cause for concern. It is hard to believe that amongst a bench consisting of nearly 3,000 judges, poor conduct of a less serious nature is not a routine occurrence. The fact that such failings rarely provoke any official response does not indicate that they do not happen, rather that they are presently going unacknowledged and uncorrected. It is in this area that the system is weakest - in its failure to deal adequately with those majority of failings which fall short of the 'capital punishment' of removal, yet which cause a sense of injustice and alienation on the part of the public (Russell, 1996, p. 8). For these cases the judiciary has, to date, relied upon the informal control of peer pressure as the principle means of ensuring compliance (Shetreet, 1976, p. 279). Sir Robert Megarry, writing in 1973 praised the informal disciplinary system and highlighted, in delicate language, its effectiveness:

> Other and more subtle forces, and not least, association with the Bar and the influence of the Inns of Court, do much to sustain the judge in England on the difficulties of his office (Megarry, 1973, p. 100).

However, the professional and social environment in which judges and barristers operated in the 1970s has changed. The strong sense of 'bar etiquette' which Shimon Shetreet identified in 1976 as a controlling force does not exert the same influence today. Twenty years ago, according to the judges and barristers whom Shetreet interviewed, the factors responsible for the success of this informal system were; 'the old boys network'; 'public school ethics' and; 'the gentlemen's code of conduct' (Shetreet, 1976, p. 254). These social forces are far less influential today. The process by which the bench has evolved from being a small and homogeneous club to an increasingly heterogeneous profession has been even more marked at the bar. Its expansion in size and geographical spread and the increasing diversity of the social and educational background of barristers has weakened many of the mechanisms by which the bar and the bench traditionally maintained their common values.

In addition to the cultural changes which have been brought about by the expansion and diversification of the bench and the bar, the increase in the volume of work handled by the courts has contributed to the pressure for the creation of a more formal complaints and disciplinary system. As the number of cases before the courts has grown, so too has the number of complaints about judicial conduct. This does not necessarily reflect any reduction in standards, but rather a change in scale which inevitably undermines the viability of the informal system of scrutiny and increases the pressure for the creation of new processes.

These internal changes, both cultural and structural, have been paralleled by external developments which have increased the stress on the existing informal arrangements. The absence of an open or formal complaints and disciplinary system increasingly stands in contrast to the developments in other areas of public life. Formal grievance mechanisms set out in Citizens' Charters and access to Ombudsmen are now an inherent feature of government. The Court Charter is intended to set standards for many aspects of the court system and to encourage members of the public to consider themselves as consumers of the legal system with rights to expect a minimum level of service and to complain if they do not receive it. The development of independent disciplinary and complaints procedures in the professions, including both branches of the legal profession, also stands out in marked contrast to the arrangements for the judiciary. In 1996 the Law Society established the Office of Supervision of Solicitors including lay members, in response to criticism of its failures in dealing with the rising numbers of complaints against solicitors. Similarly, in 1997, the bar set up a formal complaints machinery headed by an independent lay complaints commissioner. Regardless of whether or not these bodies prove themselves to be effective in responding to complaints, their very existence is an indication of the extent to which formalised complaints and disciplinary processes are now an established feature of professional life.

The combined effect of these internal and external pressures on the judiciary is to increase demand for more formalised and open procedures by which to set minimum standards, investigate complaints and provide corrective action when a judge's conduct is found to have been at fault. The most common proposal put forward for achieving these goals is the establishment of some form of judicial commission.

The use of a judicial conduct commission

By the 1980s, calls for the establishment of a formal complaints and disciplinary system were being voiced by academics and senior members of the legal profession.[37] The creation of a quasi-judicial tribunal of judges and peers with responsibility for judicial conduct was supported by Lord Hailsham, when Lord Chancellor, but apparently resisted by other members of the judiciary (see Rozenberg, 1994, p. 115). In 1992, JUSTICE proposed that a judicial standards committee should be set up as part of a judicial commission which would be responsible both for drawing up written standards of judicial conduct and for investigating poor performance. JUSTICE explained that its concern was not with serious cases of misconduct which it concluded were 'virtually unknown' but with behaviour 'falling short of ideal' which the current informal arrangements did not address adequately (JUSTICE, 1992, p. 14). In the same year, a similar recommendation was made by Lord Williams, then Chairman of the Bar Council. The creation of such a body moved a step closer in 1995, when the Labour party supported the proposal to establish a Judicial Appointments and Training Commission which would be responsible for investigating complaints about judicial conduct (Labour Party, 1995, p. 14). However, this proposal was not included in the Labour Party's election manifesto and was not pursued when it came to power in 1997. The new Government's decision not to transfer responsibility for appointing judges to a judicial commission meant that the new disciplinary machinery was also abandoned and very little comment was made either by the Government or outside commentators about this aspect of the decision at the time.

Despite the official rejection of a new complaints and disciplinary machinery, the pressure to introduce some form of formalised process, whether in the form of a judicial council, a committee or a full-blown commission, is likely to grow as the influence of the judges increases and public dissatisfaction with the present arrangements intensifies. If and when the Government does decide to proceed with this reform, it will have no shortage of different examples of complaints and disciplinary machinery in other jurisdictions to examine in the search for an appropriate model for England and Wales. The US, in particular, operates a wide variety of different systems. At federal level, circuit chief judges and judicial councils have statutory powers to investigate complaints (Barr and Willing, 1993). The first state judicial conduct commission was adopted by California in 1960 and since then every state has established some form of commission (Miller, 1991, p. 16). Canada, too, has both a Federal Council and a number of provincial and territorial level bodies. The Federal Council was set up in 1971, its purpose being: 'to bring about greater efficiency and uniformity in judicial services and to improve their quality' (Friedland, 1995, p. 87). Its disciplinary function was the main reason for its establishment in the view of many of those who played a role in its creation. In Australia, the Judicial Commission of New South Wales was created by statute in 1986 and given responsibility for both judicial education and the examination of complaints against state judges (McLelland, 1990).

The common experience of those countries which have established formal complaints and disciplinary machinery is that the new systems reveal a previously undetected level of dissatisfaction with the conduct of judges. As knowledge of the system spreads, the number of complaints rises. In Canada, in the early years of the Federal Council's work it received very few complaints - less than ten per year filed against specific judges. This figure rose steadily to 164 in 1993-4 (Friedland, 1995, p. 93). The significant rise in the early 1990's has been attributed to a public statement made by the Chief Justice of Canada that: 'if there are judges that are misbehaving or are making sexist or racist comments, I want to know and I want to know who' (Friedland, 1995, p. 94). This declaration provided the necessary reassurance that such complaints would be taken seriously and today approximately 20 per cent of the complaints made are about sex, race or religious bias.

In New South Wales complaints to the Commission rose from 45 in 1995 to 138 in 1998, most being about bias, failure to give a fair hearing or discourtesy.[38] The South African judiciary has undergone a similar experience. Although it does not yet have a formal complaints and disciplinary system, the establishment of the Judicial Service Commission led to a flood of complaints about judicial conduct. Under the 1996 constitution, no judge can be impeached unless the Commission recommends such a course of action to Parliament and this role has given it, by default, the responsibility for investigating complaints about judicial conduct. According to Justice Arthur Chaskalson, the President of the Constitutional Court and a member of the Judicial Service Commission, the complaints received fall short of any misconduct warranting impeachment but nevertheless include legitimate grievances which require proper investigation.[39] This situation has led the Commission to examine ways in which it can establish a stronger infrastructure in order to deal with these complaints.

Powers and membership of judicial conduct commissions

The effectiveness of a commission and the level of public confidence which it commands is closely related to its membership and powers. The same tensions which arise between the demands of judicial independence and accountability with regard to an appointments commission are equally present in relation to a judicial conduct commission. The judiciary has generally opposed the creation of a disciplinary body which includes non-judges on the grounds that this would give outsiders, who may well be appointees of the executive, an improper degree of influence over the judiciary. However, the creation of a commission made up exclusively of judges raises the problems common to all forms of self-regulation. The experience of other self-regulating disciplinary bodies such as the Police Complaints Authority, suggests that such arrangements are fundamentally flawed in that they fail to gain public confidence and attract strong criticism on the grounds that complaints are not investigated rigorously and disciplinary machinery is too rarely exercised.

These arguments have led to a broad consensus outside the judiciary that the inclusion of lay members is a essential for a judicial conduct commission. The Labour Party's 1995 proposal for a Judicial Appointments and Training Commission went further, and did not include any judges at all, proposing that members would be appointed from amongst lawyers, academics and lay persons. Most proposals, however, have suggested a mixed membership. The models recommended by both JUSTICE and Lord Williams envisaged a body made up of lay members, lawyers and judges. This membership mix is commonly found amongst existing judicial conduct commissions. The American Bar Association

Model Rules for Judicial Disciplinary Enforcement, which were adopted in 1994, recommend that a judicial conduct commission should be made up of 12 members in an equal number of lawyers, lay persons and judges. In practice, many commissions have a majority of judges. The Judicial Commission of New South Wales, for example, consists of six judges, one lawyer and one lay person. Where lay persons are included, as in New South Wales, they do not appear to have caused any concern about the erosion of judicial independence. If anything, the real danger is that a small number of lay persons may be relegated to the role of token outsiders and their perspectives dominated by that of the judges. There is no winning formula which can guarantee the right balance between protecting judicial independence and ensuring that the presence of the lay members has some real effect in opening up the closed self-regulatory system to external scrutiny.

Equally problematic is the issue of the commission's powers. The judiciary, again, has emphasised the dangers of undermining judicial independence which arise if a commission is given extensive powers over judges. The current proposals differ in this regard. Some have suggested that a commission should have no formal disciplinary powers, being limited to an advisory role, reporting its findings to the Lord Chancellor (Pannick, 1988, p. 101). JUSTICE, in contrast, proposed that commission members would have the power to advise the judge as to future conduct and/or recommend an apology. First and second written warnings and a recommendation for retraining would be the normal penalties in more serious cases with the ultimate sanction of recommending dismissal to the Lord Chancellor (1992, p. 80).

In practice, the need to protect judicial independence has usually limited the commissions' powers to dismiss a judge. The extent of their role in this regard is generally to recommend dismissal or impeachment to the body constitutionally empowered to remove judges. In the US, for example, the federal judicial councils have the power to recommend the impeachment by Congress of a federal judge. Where commissions have been given these powers, they are very rarely used in practice. In Australia, the Judicial Commission of New South Wales used its full powers for the first time in 1998 when it recommended, by a majority, the impeachment of a state Supreme Court judge, Justice Vince Bruce, on the grounds of incapacity after it investigated an allegation that he had failed to deliver judgments over a number of years due to depressive illness. The decision came close to causing a constitutional crisis after Justice Bruce sought to challenge the recommendation in the Court of Appeal. Because the situation was unprecedented, the legal and academic community was divided over the appropriate proceedings, for example, whether the Commission's decision removed Parliament's duty to examine the allegations itself before voting. In the event, the Upper House voted against dismissal and the crisis was averted leaving a number of procedural and constitutional issues unresolved.

Since such cases which might warrant dismissal are very rare, this aspect of the powers of judicial commissions is perhaps less critical than the question of what powers they have to respond to less serious misconduct. For some commissions, this role is also limited. The Canadian Federal Council has no formal powers to reprimand and in practice the strongest criticism appears to be a statement that a judge's conduct was 'regrettable'. At the time it was set up it was not intended that the Council's powers would be limited to the rare cases of disciplinary proceedings which could lead to dismissal, but in practice it appears that the Council has taken this restricted approach. In other jurisdictions reprimands and warnings are a normal aspect of the commissions powers, although these too are relatively rarely exercised.

In addition to the question of a commission's powers, the procedures which it adopts for investigating and hearing complaints are instrumental in determining its effectiveness and the level of confidence which it commands. JUSTICE proposed that more serious cases would be heard by a tribunal at which the case against the judge would be represented independently of the complainant so that there would be no confrontation between the judge and the person making a complaint. In the US state system the ABA model rules divide the responsibility for investigation from the adjudication process by requiring that commission members who investigate a case do not decide it. The rules also guarantee confidentiality in the investigation stage but provide for open hearings after the point where a formal charge is made. In practice, 27 states provide public hearings and a similar process is adopted in Canada by the Federal Council. It is likely that there would be strong judicial opposition to the use of public hearings in England and Wales. Lord Taylor, when Lord Chief Justice, objected to proposals for such hearings on the grounds that there was no advantage to be gained in 'pillorying the judges in public' (Rozenberg, 1994, p. 118). The position in relation to disciplinary hearings for solicitors and barristers is that they are held in private although the results of any disciplinary action are made public. It is very unlikely that the judiciary would agree to a more public process than that accorded to lawyers, although it is hard to see why the public should be excluded from the hearing of a complaint which has already been investigated and found to warrant a full hearing. It is one thing to protect judges from the publication of baseless allegations, it is another to deny such a central tenet of the rule of law, that justice be seen to be done, when matters of genuine public concern are being considered.

The fear that the creation of judicial conduct commissions encourages vexatious and unmeritorious complaints is commonly made by their critics (Marshall, 1995). Mr Justice McLelland has objected to the establishment of the judicial commission in New South Wales on the grounds that the judges should be protected against harassment, damage to reputation and media coverage which such complaints might bring (McLelland, 1990). Some support for these concerns is derived from the fact that a large percentage of complaints which are received by commissions are found to be not suitable for investigation. A significant proportion of these are simply unmeritorious, but the most common reason for commissions rejecting them is that they go to the merits of the case and should therefore be ventilated through the appeal process (Bar and Willging, 1993).

The distinction between the role of a complaints process and an appeal process is generally not appreciated by complainants. Nor is it always a clear cut one. Inevitably there can be an overlap between a matter which could be the subject of an appeal and which should be investigated by the commission - the expression of bias by a judge being an obvious example. Nevertheless, a significant amount of the commissions' time and effort goes into a screening process to identify those complaints which fall within their remit and have some grounds (Barr and Willing, 1993). Despite the fact that many complaints satisfy neither criterion, the experience of those countries which have adopted some form of conduct commission suggests that once this sifting process has been carried out there remains a significant number of genuine and legitimate grievances against poor judicial conduct which might well not have been identified and investigated before the establishment of the commission. Complainants will only come forward if they have reason to believe that the matter will be taken seriously and this requires a system which is both open and independent.

The evidence from around the world suggests that if there is a weakness in the system of judicial conduct commissions it is not that they threaten judicial independence but rather the opposite, that they tend to adopt an unduly restrained approach to their powers and do not necessarily demonstrate that they are sufficiently willing to investigate those more routine allegations of poor performance, which currently have no mechanism for review. For example, in the Canadian Federal Council only eight cases in total since it was created in 1971 have proceeded to a full investigation of the complaint. Even those commissions which are regarded as adopting a vigorous approach to the task of investigating allegations of poor judicial conduct are sensitive to the requirements of judicial independence and exercise their disciplinary powers with restraint.

But if the judiciary has little to fear from the creation of a commission it has much to gain. The creation of a formal system for investigating complaints not only benefits the public and lawyers who have cause for complaint against a judge, but also ensures that complaints will be investigated fairly by applying acceptable standards of due process and so protecting judges from arbitrary censure of the kind complained of by Judge Pickles. In addition, by creating a system which can command public confidence the judiciary will bolster the foundation on which their independence rests. Where genuine grievances are left unheard the support for judges is undermined. In the long run it is this lack of responsiveness which poses the greatest threat to judicial independence. Those who argue for the continuation of a high degree of insulation from complaints and disciplinary proceedings sometimes justify their position on the grounds that the imposition of any form of sanction against a judge in office will count as a 'black mark' against his or her name and will undermine the confidence of litigants and practitioners in his or her competence (McLelland, 1990, p. 393). This artificial maintenance of an image of infallibility and complete protection from the pressures of public office can no longer be reconciled with an acceptable level of accountability. Judges are not such a 'fragile bastion' as to require their removal from such legitimate scrutiny. However disagreeable it may be to the judges, it is a price which must be paid for the maintenance of public support.

Codes of conduct

In addition to the development of formal structures for investigating complaints about judicial conduct, many judiciaries now have codes of conduct which set out acceptable boundaries of behaviour both in and out of court. In England and Wales, judicial rules of conduct are unwritten conventions which are learnt through experience and the informal network of information exchange. In common with all other public officials judges are required to act with civility and perform their duties diligently (Marshall, 1995, p. 67). But in addition, they are obliged to observe higher standards of conduct because of the need to be impartial and to be seen to be so (Miller, 1991, p. 17). This requirement affects the judges' personal and professional associations and their financial arrangements. Thirty years ago, such rules of conduct, both judicial and extra-judicial, were relatively unproblematic. A broad consensus held that outside court judges needed to be scrupulous in avoiding anything which might give rise to the taint of corruption and that the easiest way to achieve this was to live lives which were as far as possible removed from party politics, commerce or social controversy:

> Plainly [a judge] must not visit disorderly houses or striptease shows or entertainment of that kind. There was a High Court judge towards the end of the last century who was found in a brothel, but at least he had the grace or foresight to be found dead (Henry, 1970, p. 109).

Although today death might seem a slightly extreme penalty for a judge who was found to have visited a prostitute, judges are still expected to be free of the threat of blackmail and to act within the law. However, even these relatively uncontroversial requirements are now more problematic since it is no longer considered either possible or desirable for judges to live hermetically sealed lives. The requirement that judges be free from the risk of blackmail is therefore also now countered by the demands of non-discrimination and personal freedom. Previously the danger of blackmail was a reason given for the exclusion of gay judges from appointment.[40] But this policy has been reversed by Lord Irvine:

> I'm strongly of the view that it must be made absolutely clear that sexual orientation of itself, or living in a gay relationship, shouldn't be a bar to appointment to the bench and I have to say, though I won't say more on this, that this has not always been so (Lord Irvine, 1996, p. 20).

The words 'of itself' suggests that sexual orientation might constitute a bar to appointment depending on the manner and context in which it manifested itself. Thus the boundaries of what is acceptable and unacceptable in the area of a judge's sexual orientation and behaviour are increasingly uncertain. This example suggests that as the judiciary seeks to modify its rules both in relation to appointment and conduct in order to respond to changing social circumstances, the definition of misconduct is increasingly open to challenge at the margins.

While the boundaries of extra-judicial behaviour have become more fluid, the rules determining acceptable conduct within court have tightened. Thirty years ago, judges had almost complete freedom in the way they conducted themselves in their courts within the broad confines of ensuring party impartiality. Today, judges' conduct is increasingly subject to scrutiny so that rudeness or behaviour deemed offensive is not tolerated to the same degree. In particular, racist and sexist behaviour is no longer considered acceptable in the way that it once was, and in their interaction with the public, lawyers and court staff, judges are now expected to conform to certain standards of conduct. However, since one person's friendly horseplay is another person's sexual harassment, the boundaries of acceptable and unacceptable behaviour in the courtroom are as uncertain as those relating to extra-judicial activities. In both work and personal spheres, the judges are expected to play by rules which are both more uncertain and yet more constricting than ever before. The result of these changes of expectation is that judges cannot be left to acquire a knowledge of what constitutes appropriate judicial conduct by osmosis from other members of the bench, particularly one which is now so large and increasingly diverse in its membership. As a result of these changes, there are growing demands for the unwritten rules of conduct to be codified. The introduction of a code of conduct and a formal system for enforcing it would not resolve the difficulties about where the boundaries of acceptable and unacceptable behaviour both in and out of court should lie. It would, however, ensure that the debate would be conducted more openly and that whatever was agreed as constituting the rules at any one time would be explicit both for judges and for the public.

Although these changes of expectation in judicial conduct have encouraged the growth in the use of judicial codes of conduct around the world in recent years, they are not a new phenomenon. The first US code was drafted by the American Bar Association in 1924 and last updated in 1990. It has been adopted by almost all the state and the federal judiciaries and has been influential in other parts of the world. In Canada, for example, British Columbia and Quebec have adopted a similar code, while the federal Judicial Council, amid much controversy, is currently drawing up an advisory document entitled 'Principles of Judicial Conduct'.[41] Some of the provisions of the ABA code are very general, for example that judges should carry out their tasks with impartiality and propriety. Others are more specific. The circumstances in which a judge should disqualify himself or herself because a friend or relative is involved in a case are, for example, set out in some detail.

A common prohibition which is found in such codes is against membership of clubs or lodges which might give rise to a suspicion of bias. The ABA code prohibits a judge from holding membership of any organisation that practices: 'invidious discrimination on the basis of race, sex, religion or national origin'.[42] This would clearly have some relevance in England and Wales to the controversial issue of judge freemasons. Membership of the freemasons, and indeed men-only clubs such as the Athenaeum might well fall foul of such a provision. The unprecedented conflict which arose in 1997 between the Home Affairs Select Committee and the judiciary over the disclosure of the names of judges who were freemasons, would probably have been less acute had there already been a code of conduct in existence since it would either prohibit such membership or state that membership should be declared. The absence of any guidelines about the matter meant that the Government was forced to create a new rule that newly appointed judges who are freemasons should be required to declare the fact on a register.[43] The formulation of conduct rules on such an *ad hoc* basis in response to pressure from Parliament and the public is not a coherent means of setting standards in the judiciary, nor one which inspires public confidence in the willingness of the judges to institute an effective system of self-regulation.

The main attraction of a code is that it strengthens accountability. By being required to formulate written rules of conduct, the judiciary must articulate for itself and for the public how it expects a judge to behave. In so doing, more opportunity arises for public debate about that difficult question, so providing feedback for judges on the views of those outside the judiciary. A code has the advantage of flexibility in that it can be updated regularly to take account of changing social values and circumstances. The prohibition on joining discriminating organisations, discussed above, for example, was added to the ABA code in 1990 in response to growing public sensitivity to such matters. Similarly, the 1990 edition revised the provisions concerning the expression of opinion on public affairs to give judges greater freedom to make public comment provided that these do not commit, or appear to commit, a judge to a particular view in respect of issues which may come before him or her. In addition, a code can fulfil an educative function. By providing an open and clear statement about what judges should and should not do the public are kept better informed about the role and function of the judiciary. Thus, by providing a channel through which knowledge is transferred from the public to the judges and vice versa it has the potential to provide the two-way flow of information which is a requirement of mechanisms of soft accountability.

Arguments against the creation of a commission or a code of conduct are essentially based on the desire to shield the judiciary from criticism in order to protect judicial independence (Marshall, 1995). This objection is particularly strong in relation to the use of a mandatory code where breaches constitute a disciplinary offence, such as the ABA code. However, the experience of other countries suggests that, as in the case of a conduct commission, these fears are unfounded. Where codes of conduct, whether mandatory or advisory, have been instituted, the investigation of alleged breaches is rare and disciplinary action tends to be restricted to the most extreme cases of misconduct. Indeed, supporters of more radical accountability have criticised codes of conduct as being a token gesture to greater accountability rather than an effective mechanism for ensuring good conduct amongst judges. Neither extreme is accurate. On their own, codes of conduct cannot have more than a moderate impact on judicial behaviour. Nevertheless, they should be regarded as one useful aspect of a more extensive process by which the judiciary can demonstrate its commitment to developing mechanisms of accountability by which their work can be scrutinised through more open and responsive processes.

Summary

In 1988, David Pannick described the judiciary as an extremely isolated group about which very little was known and which deliberately maintained a very low profile (1988, p. 10-15). Today it is still the case that many people could not name a single judge and even within the confines of the academic community what is known about the work of the judiciary is very limited. However, the era of self-imposed isolation which Pannick described has come to an end. Judges now engage in public debate in a way which would have been unthinkable even ten years ago. The growth of critical media coverage of the judiciary has changed the way that the public view the judges and the judges view the media. Moreover, this process is still in the early stages. The judiciary has only just begun to recognise the potential of the media as a tool for promoting understanding of the judges' work and correcting misconceptions about the role of the judiciary.

But important though these changes are, they do not represent the development of a full and adequate system for scrutinising judicial performance. The goal of the media is ultimately to attract an audience, while that of the judges is to promote their work in a positive light. Both of these are legitimate and appropriate aims but they do not amount to an acceptable substitute for a structured system for appraising judicial performance or responding to poor judicial conduct. Nor can this task be left to the appeal process, which is similarly not designed to provide a systematic, consistent and objective process for monitoring and improving judicial performance. The first steps are being taken to create more systematic processes for scrutinising judicial performance and enforcing standards of conduct. These developments are still, however, embryonic and judges remain almost immune from the consequences of all but the most extreme forms of misconduct or incompetent behaviour.

The judiciary understandably opposes the creation of more formal mechanisms of scrutiny. Few groups willingly expose their members to increased external review, while judges have the added disincentive that they fear the erosion of judicial independence. Many judges do, however, recognise that some change is necessary and that the mechanisms of scrutiny which were appropriate for a small, homogeneous body operating in a deferential society are no longer acceptable for the new judiciary. The tolerance both of lawyers and litigants for poor standards has grown less while the capacity of the judiciary to self-regulate has weakened as it has expanded in size and power. The development of a more extensive system of performance appraisal and the creation of more formal machinery for investigating complaints and disciplining judges found guilty of misconduct is therefore now inevitable. If, rather than waiting to be pushed into instituting the necessary changes, the judiciary adopts a proactive approach and develops these processes under its own initiative, it will have the advantage of being able to construct the mechanisms best suited to the English judiciary.

The experiences of other judiciaries should do much to reassure judges in England and Wales that they have more to gain than to lose from these changes. Those countries which have developed performance appraisal, conduct commissions, codes of conduct and complaints machinery have found that they address a previously unmet need and allow the judiciary to demonstrate its responsiveness to the legitimate demands of the public for consistent standards of performance and protection from misconduct. The willingness of judges collectively and individually to scrutinise their performance and account for their conduct has tended to strengthen rather than weaken public support. Though judges around the world have resisted these changes, in the event of their introduction few have seriously argued that the development of formal and open processes for assessing judicial performance, investigating complaints and disciplining errant judges has undermined judicial independence.

Notes

[1] Hansard, HL.. 5 June 1996 col. 1276.

[2] *R v. Gray* [1900] 2 QB 36.

[3] Sir Derek Oulton, quoted in Lord Bingham, 1996, p. 7.

[4] *The Guardian,* 11 December 1995.

[5] (1987) 39 C.C.C. (3d) (Ont. C.A.) pp. 65-6, (see Friedland, 1995, p. 32.).

[6] *The Times,* 8 May 1993.

[7] See *The Lawyer,* 1 April 1997.

[8] *The Guardian,* 1 June 1992.

[9] See Lord Mostyn, Hansard, HL.. 5 June 1996 col. 1307.

[10] Quoted in Armytage, 1995, n. 21.

[11] Speech to the Police Foundation, 10 July 1997.

[12] Originally carried out for a doctoral thesis.

[13] See Harlow, 1986, for a discussion of the lack of co-operation of the judiciary. John Baldwin and Mike McConville's research on plea bargaining was completed without the co-operation of the judiciary. Doctoral research on the Court of Appeal carried out by the author in 1993-6 was based on interviews with retired judges after the Lord Chief Justice refused access to sitting judges.

[14] Paterson provides a useful summary of such failed research up to 1981 as well as a note of the few successful projects (see Paterson, 1981, p. 217, n. 26).

[15] Shetreet's study of the judiciary in 1976 included material obtained in interview with judges. Baldwin and McConville's study of the jury trial is noteworthy in that it was successful in obtaining the co-operation of the judges in completing written questionnaires (see Baldwin and McConville, 1979). Similar co-operation was obtained by Zander and Henderson for their Crown Court Study commissioned by the Royal Commission on Criminal Justice in 1992. Paul Rock's study of Wood Green Crown Court also managed to secure judicial co-operation.

[16] Marvell, 1978, Bibliography D, quoted in Paterson, 1981, p. 216, n. 26.

[17] Chapter 8, paras 97 and 99.

[18] Lord Woolf, 1995, chapter 11, para 38.

[19] Hansard, HL., 16 October 1996, column WA219.

[20] Hansard, HL., 21 January 1998, column WA556.

[21] Judge Holden, *The Times,* 9 November 1993.

[22] See, for example, Lord Mackay's comments, Hansard, HL., 16 October 1996, column WA221.

[23] Hansard, HC. column WA393.

[24] Chapter 8, para 99.

[25] Chapter 11, para 39. JUSTICE similarly expressed the view that a balance needed to be struck between: 'protecting the public and protecting the constitutional position of the judges' (1992, p. 25).

[26] Information on the court monitoring programmes can be obtained from the American Judicature Society website at http://www.ajs.org.

[27] For example, in New Zealand the salary of a sitting High Court judge cannot be reduced. S. 24 Constitution Act 1986 (see Goldfinch, 1993, p. 157). However, in Manitoba, the Court of Appeal held that governments elected on the basis of manifesto promises to cut public sector spending can reduce judicial salaries without impinging on judicial independence (see Russell, 1996a, p. 24).

[28] Hansard, HL., 11 May 1994, column 1050.

[29] In France a similar immunity in enjoyed but there is vicarious liability in that a minister of the Treasury may be held responsible for a judge's failings and may seek reimbursement from the judge (see McKillop, 1996, p. 26.).

[30] *Sirros v. Moore* [1975] 1 Q.B. 118 at p. 132.

[31] Courts Act 1971 s.17(4).

[32] Judicial Pensions and Retirement Act 1993 s. 26.

[33] Quoted in Rozenberg, 1997, p. 3.

[34] See Goldfinch, 1993, p. 158.

[35] For a review of the Pickles affair, see Rozenberg, 1994, pp. 112-115.

[36] Quoted in Pannick, 1988, p. 93.

[37] See, for example, Pannick, 1988 and Beckman, 1992.

[38] *Daily Telegraph (Australia),* 29 May 1998.

[39] In interview, 19 February 1998.

[40] Lesbian judges were not even raised as an issue by the Lord Chancellor's Department. Like Queen Victoria, the department seems to have operated from the premise that such relationships did not exist.

[41] *The Toronto Star,* 23 September 1997.

[42] Canon 2(C) 1990 Judicial Code of Conduct.

[43] In 1997, Lord Mackay, then Lord Chancellor, refused a request of the Home Affairs Select Committee to compile a list of those judges who were freemasons on the grounds that he was not able to make a request of the judges which was outside their duties as judges. He did agree to ask the judges to help the council by informing them on a voluntary basis. See *The Lawyer,* 28 January 1997.

7 Conclusion

Thirty years ago the judiciary was a largely self-selecting, self-regulating and self-taught body which operated within its own informal rules almost entirely free of external scrutiny. This degree of insulation was relatively uncontroversial at a time when judges enjoyed high status and exercised limited power. Today, the work of the judiciary directly or indirectly affects the lives of more people than ever before and as its influence has grown, so have the criticisms of its closed structures and working practices. The consequence of this pressure for change has been that the elitism, secrecy and amateurism which were traditionally the hallmarks of the judiciary are slowly being replaced by diversification, openness and professionalism.

The implications of these developments are long-term. They are part of a process of transformation which will ultimately reshape the judiciary in ways which are only just beginning to emerge. Identifying the effects of the changes is complicated by the fact that they do not affect all ranks of judges equally. The introduction of increased formalisation and mechanisms of accountability has not been evenly spread but is primarily directed at the expanding ranks below the High Court. As a consequence, the way that the lower ranks are appointed, trained and scrutinised is now significantly different from that of the higher judiciary. The present occupants of the High Court and above will probably be the last cohort who have little or no exposure to the requirements of judicial accountability. The next generation, weaned on the new processes, may bring with them a different judicial culture to the upper ranks.

In addition, the demographic profile of the upper and lower ranks is more distinct than it has ever been. The increasing heterogeneity in the make-up of the judiciary has almost all occurred at the lower ranks while the profile of the senior judges still conforms much more closely to that of a traditional judge. Although the judiciary as a whole is still highly unrepresentative of society at large, the upper ranks are themselves unrepresentative of the rest of the judiciary. A Law Lord and an Assistant Recorder on the first step of the judicial ladder can no longer be assumed to share essentially the same characteristics, separated only by seniority. They are more likely than ever to be of a different sex and social background, to come from different branches of the legal profession and to be fulfilling different judicial functions; with the lower ranks providing a social service role in day to day dispute resolution and the upper ranks increasingly engaging in policy-orientated decision-making.

In terms of demographic make-up this gap is likely to narrow to some degree as some younger judges move up to the senior ranks. The speed and extent of the change depends largely on the nature of reforms to the appointments process. If a more heterogeneous bench is left to evolve spontaneously through the 'trickle-up' of more representative candidates and the structural and cultural bars to appointment are not addressed, the change is likely to be very slow. Nevertheless, the general trend is clearly towards greater consistency in the make-up between the different ranks.

In contrast, the difference in the functions which the judges fulfil looks set to widen as the policy-making and constitutional role of the senior judges increases in the years after the implementation of the provisions of the Human Rights Act. Although there are no plans to create a separate court designated to hear human rights cases with law-making and policy-making implications, in practice, Law Lords, Lords Justices and High Court judges will be acting in the capacity of a supreme court or constitutional court in the US, Canadian or South African sense. The difference is that senior judges in England and Wales will continue to be appointed from those candidates who have followed the traditional judicial career pattern. By contrast, most constitutional courts include judges with more diverse backgrounds, such as academics, former politicians and lawyers with little judicial experience in order to provide a breadth of experience appropriate for the court's policy-making role. But although the structural arrangements of the courts and the appointments process of the English judiciary may not reflect the extent of the senior judges' new role, the distinction between their daily work and that of the rank and file judiciary will inevitably grow sharper as their function moves closer to that of supreme court justices.

Despite these differences within the judiciary, some of the effects of increasing accountability are being experienced by all judges. In particular, the loss of their unique status which once distinguished them from other public servants. The introduction of greater scrutiny and the demands for more open procedures challenges the interpretation of judicial independence as requiring that judges occupy a place apart in public life. The erosion of this elevated insulation limits the scope of judicial independence but secures its long-term future by reinforcing the legitimacy of the judiciary. As its power increases the temptation for the executive, the legislature and powerful non-governmental bodies to circumvent and negate its decisions will increase. Ultimately, the only protection which judges have against this abuse is the existence of public opinion which values the rule of law and recognises that judicial independence is a prerequisite for its continued survival.

To guard its independence the judiciary must not make over-inflated claims for the principle. Judges have often argued that the public fails to appreciate the nature of judicial independence. This is hardly surprising if the principle is defined as a fluid and boundariless concept which protects the judges from almost all forms of accountability. If the scope of judicial independence is limited to the need to ensure impartiality between parties in court, its requirements become clearer. It does not allow judges to claim immunity from all external or internal influences, but it provides them with the basis to insist upon freedom from any improper interference in their decision-making which endangers their impartiality. If judicial independence is redefined not as a right to be enjoyed by the judiciary but a standard which they have a duty to uphold in order to protect the parties to an action from oppression and injustice, it will command universal support since it cannot be mistaken for judicial self-interest. Properly defined, judicial independence is a principle which can, and should, be vigorously promoted by the judiciary without sacrificing the requirements of good judicial administration and greater accountability.

The new judiciary is a body in transition. It faces a challenging period of change in which the price of expanding power must be paid for. The job of judging is unquestionably a more demanding one than it has ever been. The judiciary is required to demonstrate not only that it is competent and incorruptible, but also that it fulfils the requirements of soft accountability by demonstrating greater representativeness and openness. Moreover these changes must be adopted by almost three thousand judges, all of whom are being required to rethink some of the assumptions which they brought with them to the bench. Many of them would agree that a more representative and responsive judiciary which employs greater transparency in its processes is a change for the better which will address the criticisms of elitism and isolation and will help to further the demystification process. Being displaced from a pedestal may bruise judges' dignity, but it also relieves them of the myth of infallibility and allows them to demand the necessary support and assistance to do their jobs well. They are losing the security of an exclusive club but in return they are gaining the support mechanisms which come with the structures of an open professional body. The consequence is that whilst they are less free to make mistakes with impunity they do not have to fear that they will be left in isolation to commit the same errors time and again.

The reward for accepting a narrower definition of judicial independence, which allows for the development of more effective mechanisms of accountability, will be the chance for the judiciary to regain the public confidence which it once took for granted. It will never again enjoy unquestioning authority, and nor should it do so in a modern liberal democracy. But by continuing to reshape itself in response to its new roles and changing public expectations, it has the opportunity to regain the high level of public confidence which in so many respects it deserves.

Bibliography

Abel-Smith, B. and Stevens. R. (1967), *Lawyers and the Courts: A Sociological Study of the English Legal System, 1750-1965*, Heinemann, London.

Abel-Smith, B. and Stevens. R. (1968), *In Search of Justice*, Penguin, London.

Ackner, Lord (1996), 'The Erosion of Judicial Independence', *New Law Journal*, p. 1789.

Addison, N. (1996), 'Model of Independence', *The Lawyer*, vol. 10, p. 16.

Alozie, N. (1990), 'Distribution of Women and Minority Judges: The Effects of Judicial Selection Methods', *Social Science Quarterly*, vol. 71, p. 315.

American Bar Association, (1995), *A Society without Judicial Independence*, Chicago.

American Judicature Society, (1994), *Model Judicial Selection Provisions*, Chicago.

American Judicature Society, (1995), *Judicial Merit Selection: Current Status*, Chicago.

Armytage, L. (1995), 'Judicial Education on Equality', *Modern Law Review*, p. 58.

Armytage, L. (1997), *Educating Judges*, Kluwer Law International, The Hague.

Ashenfelter, O. et al., (1995), 'Politics and the Judiciary: The influence of Judicial Background on Case Outcomes', *Journal of Legal Studies,* vol. XXIV, p. 257.

Ashman, A. and Alfini, J. (1974), *Judicial Nominating Commissions: The Key to Judicial Merit Selection*, American Judicature Society, Chicago.

Ashworth, A. (1995), *Sentencing and Penal Policy*, Butterworths, London.

Baar, C. (1991), 'Judicial Activism in Canada' in K. Holland, (ed) *Judicial Activism in Comparative Perspective,* Macmillan, London.

Barr, J. and Willing, T. (1993), 'Disciplining the Federal Judiciary', *University of Pennsylvania Law Review*, vol. 25, p. 142.

Beatty, D. (1997), 'The Canadian Charter of Rights: Lessons and Laments', *Modern Law Review*, vol. 60, p. 481.

Beckman, M. (1992), 'Removing Errant Judges', *New Law Journal*, p. 1382.

Bell, J. (1985), 'The Models of the Judicial Function', in Dhavan R. et al. (ed.) *Judges and the Judicial Power*, Sweet & Maxwell, London.

Bingham, Lord (1996), *Judicial Independence*, Judicial Studies Board, London.

Bradley, A.W. (1988), 'Constitutional Change and the Lord Chancellor', *Public Law*, p. 165.

Bridge, Lord Justice (1978), *Report of the Working Party on Judicial Studies and Information*, HMSO, London.

Brown, D. (1986), 'Judicial Independence - An examination', *Australian Quarterly*, vol. 58, no. 4, p. 348.

Browne-Wilkinson, N. (1988), 'The Independence of the Judiciary in the 1980s', *Public Law*, p. 44.

Centre for the Independence of Judges and Lawyers, (1990), *The Independence of Judges and lawyers: A Compilation of International Standards*, Bulletin number 25-26.

Champagne, A. and Haydel, J. (eds) (1993), *Judicial Reform in the States*, New York: University Press of America.

Cockrell, A. (1997), 'The South African Bill of Rights and the "Duck/Rabbit"', *Modern Law Review*, vol. 60, p. 513.

Cornish, W. (1997), 'Judicial Legislation' in R. Rawlings (ed) *Law, Society and Economy*, Clarendon, Oxford.

Cunningham, H. (1996) (ed.), *Fragile Bastion: Judicial Independence in the Nineties and Beyond*, Judicial Commission of New South Wales, Sydney.

Denning, Lord (1955), *The Road to Justice*, Stevens and Sons, London.

Department of Justice, (1992), *Judicial Independence and the Administration of the Courts*, New Zealand Policy and Research Division, Auckland.

Devlin, P. (1976), 'Judges and Lawmakers', *Modern Law Review*, vol. 39 p1.

Devlin, P. (1978), 'Judges, Government and Politics', *Modern Law Review*, vol. 41, p. 501.

Devlin, P. (1979), *The Judge*, Oxford University Press, Oxford.

Dhavan, R. et al. (eds) (1985), *Judges and the Judicial Power*, Sweet & Maxwell, London.

Dhavan, R. (1985), 'Judges and Accountability', in R. Dhavan et al. (eds) *Judges and the Judicial Power*, Sweet & Maxwell, London.

Dhavan, R. (1985), 'Judging the Judges', in R Dhavan et al. (eds) *Judging and the Judicial Power*, Sweet & Maxwell, London.

Downey, G. (1987), *Public Accountability: Fact or Myth?*, London, National Audit Office.

Doyle, J. (1997), 'The Well-Tuned Cymbal', in H. Cunningham. (ed) *Fragile Bastion*, Judicial Commission of New South Wales, Sydney.

Drewry, G. (1992), 'Judicial Politics in Britain: Patrolling the Boundaries', *West European Politics*, vol. 15, p. 9.

East, P. (1995), *Attorney General's Speech to the New Zealand Bar Association*, Department of Justice, Auckland.

Easton, D. (1953), *The Political System*, Knopf, New York.

Fitz-James, M. (1993), 'Free Expression and the Judges', *New Law Journal*, p. 22.

Frank, J. (1949), *Courts on Trial*, Princeton University Press, Princeton.

Friedland, M. (1995), *A Place Apart: Judicial Independence and Accountability in Canada*, Canadian Judicial Council, Toronto.

Galligan, B. (1991), 'Judicial Activism in Australia', K. Holland (ed) *Judicial Activism in Comparative Perspective*, Macmillan, London.

Gearty, C. (1996), 'The Judicialisation of Democracy', Paper to the Administrative Bar Association, 7 July.

Ghai, Y. (1997), 'Sentinels of Liberty or Sheep in Woolf's Clothing? Judicial Politics and the Hong Kong Bill of Rights', *Modern Law Review*, 60: p. 459.

Gleeson, A. (1997), 'Foreword', in H. Cunningham (ed) *Fragile Bastion: Judicial Independence in the Nineties and Beyond*, Judicial Commission of New South Wales, Sydney.

Glick, H. R. (1978), 'The Promise and the Performance of the Missouri Plan: Judicial Selection in the Fifty States', *University of Miami Law Review*, vol. 32, p. 509.

Goldfinch, S. (1993), 'Judicial Independence and the Administration of the Courts in New Zealand', *Political Science*, vol. 45 no. 2, p. 153.

Greene, I. (1990), *Judges and Judging: Inside the Canadian Judicial System*, Toronto: Lorimer.

Greene, I. (1995), 'Preface', in D. Marshall (ed) *Judicial Conduct and Accountability*, Carswell, Scarborough.

Griffith, J.A.G. (1991), *The Politics of the Judiciary*, Fontana Press, London.

Griffith, J.A.G. (1997), 'Judges and the Constitution', in R. Rawlings (ed) *Law, Society and Economy*, Clarendon, Oxford.

Griffith, J.A.G. (1997), *The Politics of the Judiciary*, Fontana Press, London.

Hailsham, Lord (1983), *Hamlyn Revisited: The British Legal System Today*, Hamlyn Lecture.

Hamilton. (1788), *The Federalist Papers No. 78*, Penguin, Harmondsworth.

Harlow, C. (1986), 'Refurbishing the Judicial Service', in C. Harlow (ed) *Public Law and Politics*, Sweet and Maxwell, London.

Henschen, B. et al. (1990), 'Judicial Nominating Commissions: A National Profile', *Judicature*, vol. 73.

Hodder, J. (1974), 'Judicial Appointments in New Zealand', *New Zealand Law Journal*, p. 80.

Hodder-Williams, R. (1996), *Judges and Politics in the Contemporary Age*, Bowerdean, London.

Holland, T. and Stevens, R. (1997), 'Lord Ackner and Judicial Independence', *New Law Journal*, p. 699.

House of Commons Home Affairs Select Committee, (Session 1995-96), *Judicial Appointments Procedures*, vols. I. and II, HMSO, London.

Institute for Public Policy Research, (1991), *The Constitution of the United Kingdom*, London.

Irvine, Lord, (1996), Interview in *The New Statesman*, 6 December, p. 18.

Irvine, Lord, (1996a), 'Judges and Decision-Makers: The Theory and Practice of
    Wednesdbury Review', *Public Law,* Spring, p. 69.
Ison, T. (1997), 'A Constitutional Bill of Rights - The Canadian Experience',
    Modern Law Review, vol. 60, p. 499.
Judicial Appointments Advisory Committee, (1992), *Report*, Toronto.
JUSTICE (1992), *The Judiciary in England and Wales*, JUSTICE, London.
Kaufman, I.R. (1981), 'Fair Pay and Judicial Independence', *Judicature*, vol. 64
    no. 10, p. 134.
Kentridge, S. (1996), 'Bills of Rights - The South African Experiment', *Law
    Quarterly Review*, p. 237.
Kentridge, S. (1997), 'Parliamentary Supremacy and the Judiciary under a Bill of
    Rights: Some Lessons from the Commonwealth', *Public Law,* p. 96.
Krivosha, N. (1990), 'In Celebration of the 50th Anniversary of Merit Selection',
    Judicature, p. 74.
Labour Party, (1995), *Access to Justice*, London.
Lawrence, T. (1993), 'Judicial Appointments - A System Fit for Change?',
    Medicine, Science and Law, vol. 33, p. 279.
Lee, S. (1988), *Judging Judges*, Faber, London.
Mackay, Lord, (1991), 'The Chancellor in the 1990s', *Current Legal Problems*,
    p. 241.
Mackay, Lord, (1994), *The Administration of Justice*, Sweet & Maxwell, London.
Mackay, Lord, (1996), *Parliament and the Judges - A Constitutional Challenge?*,
    Speech to the Citizenship Foundation, 8 July, Sadlers Hall, London.
McLelland, M. (1990), 'Disciplining Australian Judges', *Australian Law Journal*,
    vol. 64 p. 388.
Malleson, K. (1993), *Review of the Appeal Process*, London, HMSO.
Malleson, K. (1997), *The Use of Judicial Appointments Commissions: A Review of
    the US and Canadian Models*, Lord Chancellor's Department, Research
    Paper no. 6.
Marshall, D. (1995), *Judicial Conduct and Accountability*, Carswell,
    Scarborough.
Martin, J. (1993), *Merit Selection Commissions: What do they do? How Effective
    are they?*, American Bar Association, Chicago.
Mason, A. (1997), 'The Appointment and Removal of Judges', in H. Cunningham.
    (ed.) *Fragile Bastion: Judicial Independence in the Nineties and Beyond*,
    Judicial Commission of New South Wales, Sydney.
Mayhew, P. and Percy, A. (1996), *The British Crime Survey,* Home Office
    Statistical Bulletin 19/96.
McCormick, P. and I. Greene. (1990), *Inside the Canadian Judicial System*,
    Toronto.
McGarvie, R. (1991), 'The Foundation of Judicial Independence in a Modern
    Democracy', *Journal of Judicial Administration*, vol. 1.

McHugh, M. (1988), 'The Law-making Function of the Judicial Process', *Australian Law Journal*, vol. 62, p. 15.

McKillop, B. (1996), *The Judiciary In France*, Unpublished Research Paper, Faculty of Law, University of Sydney.

McKillop, B. (1997), 'The Judiciary in France', H. Cunningham. (ed.) *Fragile Bastion*, Judicial Commission of New South Wales, Sydney.

Melone, A. P. (1996), 'The Struggle for Judicial Independence and the Transition towards Democracy in Bulgaria', *Communist and Post-Communist Studies*, vol. 29, p. 231.

Miller, B. (1991), 'Assessing the Functions of Judicial Conduct Organisations', *Judicature*, vol. 75, p. 16.

Mohamed, I. (1997), *Welcoming Address*, First Orientation Course for New Judges, 20 July, Magaliesburg, South Africa.

Montequieu, (1961), *De L'esprit des lois,* vol. I, Garnier Freres, Paris.

Munday, R. (1996), 'The Bench Books: Can the Judiciary Keep a Secret?', *Criminal Law Review*, p. 296.

Munro, C. (1992), 'Judicial Independence and Judicial functions', in M. Wasik and C. Munro (eds) *Sentencing, Judicial Discretion and Judicial Training*, Sweet & Maxwell, London.

Nejelski, P. (1985), 'Canadian Conference Explores Judicial Independence and Expectations of Justice', *Judicature*, vol. 69, no. 1, p. 51.

Nicholson, R (1993), 'Judicial Independence and Accountability: Can they Co-exist?', *Australian Law Journal*, vol. 67, p. 404.

Nolan, Lord, (1997), 'The Judiciary', in Lord Nolan and S. Sedley (eds) *The Making and Remaking of the British Constitution*, Blackstone, London.

Okeeffe, L. H. (1986), 'Administrative Law Judges, Performance Evaluation and Production Standards: Judicial Independence versus Employee Accountability', *George Washington Law Review*, vol. 54 no. 4, p. 591.

Oliver, D. (1986), 'The Independence of the Judiciary', *Current Legal Problems*, p. 237.

Oliver, D. and Drewry, G. (1996), *Public Service Reforms: Issues of Accountability and Public Law*, Pinter, London.

Olowofoyeku, A. (1993), *Suing Judges, A Study of Judicial Immunity*, OUP, Oxford.

Palmer, G. (1993), 'Judicial Selection and Accountability: Can the New Zealand System Survive?', Paper prepared for the Legal Research Foundation Seminar - *Courts and Policy: Checking the Balance*, 5 August, Aotea Centre, Auckland.

Pannick, D. (1988), *Judges*, Oxford University Press, Oxford.

Partington, M. (1994), 'Training the Judiciary in England and Wales: The Work of the Judicial Studies Board', *Civil Justice Quarterly*, vol. 13, p. 319.

Paterson, A. (1981), *The Law Lords*, Macmillan, London.

Pitcher, C. (1998), 'The Future of Judicial Training', *Judicial Studies Board Journal*, p. 18.

Purchas, F. (1994), 'What is Happening to Judicial Independence?', *New Law Journal*, p. 1306.

Quirk, W. and Bridwell, R. (1997), *Judicial Dictatorship,* Transaction Publishers, New Brunswick.

Reid, Lord, (1972), 'The Judge as Law Maker', *Society of Public Teachers of Law*, vol. 12, p. 22.

Robertson, G. (1998), *The Justice Game*, Chatto and Windus, London.

Rock, A. (1996), *Federal Judicial Appointments Process*, Department of Justice, Ottawa.

Roll, J.M. (1990), 'Merit Selection: The Arizona Experience', *Arizona State Law Journal*, vol. 22, p. 837.

Rosenberg, G.N. (1992), 'Judicial Independence and the Reality of Political Power', *Review of Politics*, vol. 54, no. 3, p. 369.

Rozenberg, J. (1994), *The Search for Justice*, Hodder & Stoughton, London.

Rozenberg, J. (1997), *Trial of Strength*, Richard Cohen Books, London.

Russell, P. (1982), 'The Effects of the Charter of Rights on the Policy-Making Role of the Canadian Courts', *Canadian Public Administration*, vol. 25.

Russell, P. (1987), *The Judiciary in Canada: The Third Branch of Government*, McGraw-Hill Ryerson, Toronto.

Russell, P. and J. Ziegel. (1991), 'Federal Judicial Appointments: An Appraisal of the First Mulroney Government's Appointments and the New Judiciary Advisory Committees', University of Toronto Law Journal, vol. 41, p. 4.

Russell, P. (1995), 'Canadian Constraints on Judicialization from Without', in N. Tate and T. Vallinder (eds) *The Global Expansion of Judicial Power*, New York University Press, New York.

Russell, P. (1996), 'Judicial Free Speech: Justifiable Limits', *University of New Brunswick Law Journal*, vol. 45, p. 155.

Russell, P. (1996), *Towards an Accountable and Responsive South African Judicial System*, The Community Peace Foundation.

Russell, P. (1996a), 'Towards a Theory of Judicial Independence', Interim Meeting of the Research Committee on Comparative Judicial Studies of the International Political Science Association, Hebrew University, Jerusalem.

Rylaarsdam, W.F. (1993), 'Judicial Independence - A Value Worth Preserving', *Southern California Law Review*, vol. 66, no. 4, p. 1653.

Sedley, S. (1997), 'Autonomy and the Rule of Law', in R. Rawlings (ed) *Law, Society and Economy*, Clarendon Press, Oxford.

Septe, J. and Campbell, I. (1995), 'Performance Appraisal of the Judiciary?', Paper presented at seminar on *The Status of Judges in Europe*, ENM Paris.

Shapiro, M. (1995), 'The United States', in N. Tate and T. Vallinder (eds) *The Global Expansion of Judicial Power*, New York University Press, New York.

Shetreet, S. (1976), *Judges on Trial*, Amsterdam.

Shetreet, S. (1984), 'Judicial Independence and Accountability in Israel', *International and Comparative Law Quarterly*, p. 979.

Shetreet, S. and Deschênes, J. (1985) (eds), *Judicial Independence: The Contemporary Debate*, Dordrecht, the Netherlands.

Shetreet, S. (1987), 'Who will Judge: Reflections on the Process and Standards of Judicial Selection', *Australian Law Journal*, 766.

Skordaki, E. (1991), *Judicial Appointments: An International Review of Existing Models*, The Law Society, London.

Stevens, R. (1993), *The Independence of the Judiciary*, Clarendon Press, Oxford.

Stevens, R. (1993a), 'Unpacking the Judges', *Current Legal Problems*, 46, p. 1.

Stevens, R. (1996), *Judges, Politics, Politicians and the Confusing Role of the Judiciary*, Hardwicke Building Lecture, London.

Steyn, Lord (1997), 'The Weakest and Least Dangerous Department of Government', *Public Law*, p. 84.

Sunkin, M. (1995), 'The United Kingdom', in N. Tate and T. Vallinder (eds) *The Global Expansion of Judicial Power*, New York University Press, New York:

Tate, C. (1995), 'Why the Expansion of Judicial Power?', in N. Tate and T. Vallinder (eds) *The Global Expansion of Judicial Power*, New York University Press, New York.

Tate, C. and Vallinder, T. (1995), 'The Global Expansion of Judicial Power: The Judicialization of Politics', in C. Tate and T. Vallinder (eds) *The Global Expansion of Judicial Power*, New York University Press, New York.

Taylor, Lord (1992), *The Judiciary in the Nineties*, The Richard Dimbleby Lecture, London.

Thomas, C. (1997), *Judicial Appointments in Continental Europe*, Lord Chancellor's Department, London.

Thompson, R. S. (1986), 'Judicial Independence, Judicial Accountability, Judicial Elections and the California Supreme Court: Defining the Terms of the Debate', *Southern California Law Review*, vol. 59, no. 4, p. 809.

Volcansek, M. and Lafon, J. (1988), *Judicial Selection: The Cross-evaluation of French and American Practices*, Greenwood Press, New York.

Volcansek, M. (1982), 'The Effect of Judicial Selection Reform - What We Know and What We Do Not', in P. L. Dubois (ed) *The Analysis of Judicial Reform*, Lexington, Massachusetts.

Volcansez, M. (1992), 'Judges, Courts and Policy-Making in Western Europe', *West European Politics*, vol. 15, p. 1.

Waltman, J. (1991), 'Judicial Activism in England', in K. Holland (ed) *Judicial Activism in Comparative Perspective*, Macmillan, London.

Webster, P.D. (1995), 'Selection and Retention of Judges: Is there one "best" Method?', *Florida State University Law Review.*

Wilson, B. (1992), 'Will Women Judges Really Make a Difference?', in F. Morton (ed) *Law, Politics and the Judicial Process*, University of Calgary Press, Calgary.

Woolf, Lord (1995), *Access to Justice -Interim Report to the Lord Chancellor on the Civil Justice System of England and Wales*, London: HMSO.

Zander, M. (1989), 'The Judges and Solicitors' Rights of Audience', *Law Society's Gazette*, vol. 38.

Zander, M. (1989), *A Matter of Justice*, Oxford University Press, Oxford.

Zander, M. (1997), *A Bill of Rights,* Sweet & Maxwell, London.

Index